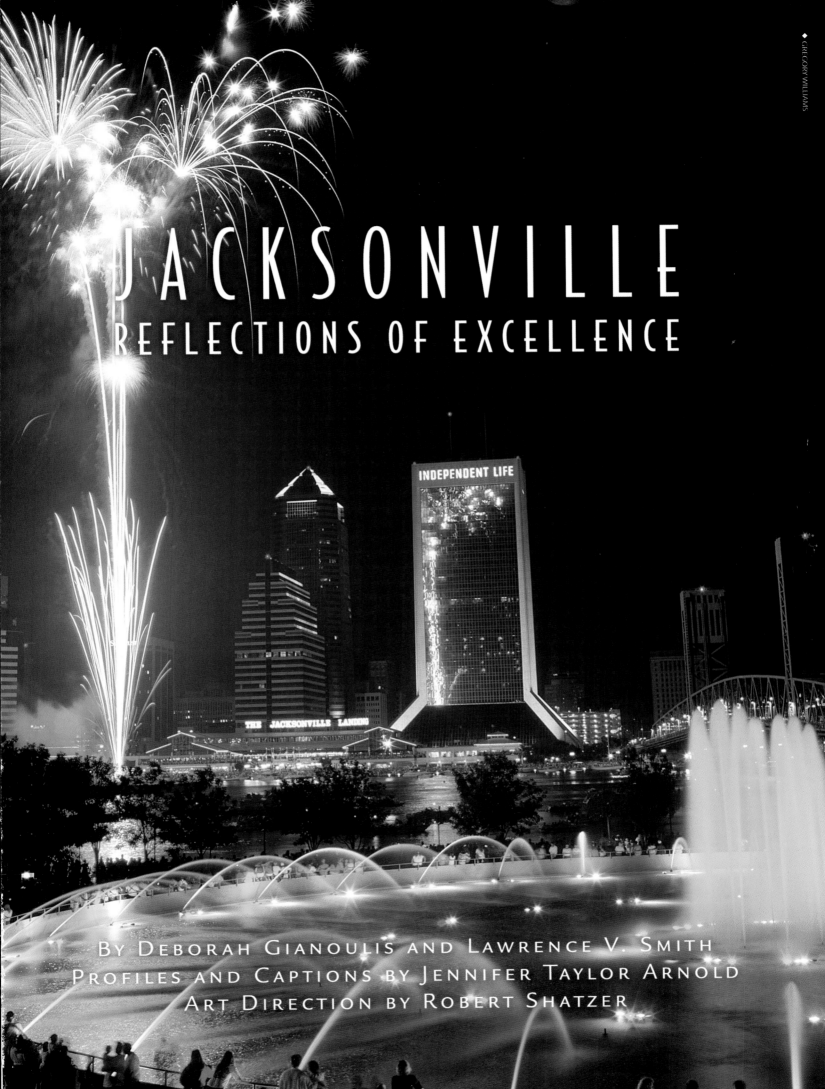

JACKSONVILLE
REFLECTIONS OF EXCELLENCE

INDEPENDENT LIFE

THE JACKSONVILLE LANDING

BY DEBORAH GIANOULIS AND LAWRENCE V. SMITH
PROFILES AND CAPTIONS BY JENNIFER TAYLOR ARNOLD
ART DIRECTION BY ROBERT SHATZER

▲ ANN S. FONTAINE

LIBRARY OF CONGRESS CATALOGING-IN-PUBLICATION DATA

Gianoulis, Deborah, 1954-
    Jacksonville, reflections of excellence / by Deborah Gianoulis and
Lawrence V. Smith ; profiles in excellence and captions by Jennifer
Taylor Arnold ; art direction by Bob Shatzer.
        p.   cm. — (Urban tapestry series)
    Includes index.
    ISBN 1-881096-54-8 (alk. paper)
    1. Jacksonville (Fla.)—Civilization. 2. Jacksonville (Fla.)-
-Pictorial works. 3. Business enterprises—Florida—Jacksonville.
4. Jacksonville (Fla.)—Economic conditions. I. Smith, Lawrence
V. (Lawrence Victor), 1931-   . II. Arnold, Jennifer Taylor, 1967-
. III.   Title.   IV.   Series.
F319.J1G53   1998
975.9' 12—dc21
                                                         97-32536
                                                          CIP

URBAN
TAPESTRY
SERIES
TOWERY
PUBLISHING, INC.

Towery Publishing, Inc., 1835 Union Avenue, Memphis, TN 38104

PUBLISHER:
J. Robert Towery
EXECUTIVE PUBLISHER:
Jenny McDowell
NATIONAL SALES MANAGER:
Stephen Hung
MARKETING DIRECTOR:
Carol Culpepper
PROJECT DIRECTORS:
John Lorenzo, Robert Philips
EXECUTIVE EDITOR:
David B. Dawson
MANAGING EDITOR:
Michael C. James
SENIOR EDITORS:
Lynn Conlee, Carlisle Hacker
EDITORS/PROJECT MANAGERS:
Mary Jane Adams, Lori Bond

STAFF EDITORS:
Jana Files, Susan Hesson, Brian Johnston
ASSISTANT EDITORS:
Pat McRaven, Jennifer C. Pyron, Allison Ring
CREATIVE DIRECTOR:
Brian Groppe
PROFILE DESIGNERS:
Laurie Beck, Kelley Pratt, Ann Ward
DIGITAL COLOR SUPERVISOR:
Brenda Pattat
DIGITAL COLOR TECHNICIANS:
Jack Griffith, Darin Ipema, Jason Moak
PRODUCTION RESOURCES MANAGER:
Dave Dunlap Jr.
PRODUCTION ASSISTANTS:
Geoffrey Ellis, Enrique Espinosa, Robin McGehee
PRINT COORDINATOR:
Beverly Thompson

NORTHEAST FLORIDA WAS ONCE HOME to several Native American tribes, most notably the Seminoles, who thrived on the bounty of the area's abundant waterways and woodlands (ABOVE). Today, it's jaguars that roam the land.

One of the league's newest franchises, Jacksonville's NFL team has brought a heightened level of prestige and pride to the city, and "Jaguars fever" shows no sign of cooling off anytime soon (OPPOSITE).

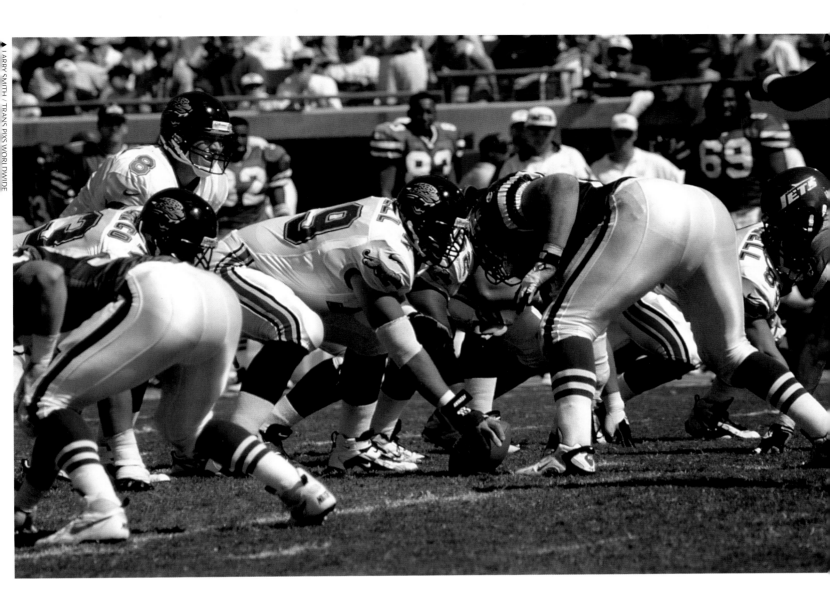

Contents

THE MAGNIFICENT ST. JOHNS RIVER IS
the heart and soul of Jacksonville,
playing an integral role in both the
business and recreational needs of area
residents.

INDEPENDENT LIFE

By Deborah Gianoulis

THE ONLY TIME IT'S GREAT TO BE AN UNDER-dog is when you pull off an upset. Until a few years ago, Jacksonville had a reputation as a fumbler on the gridiron of American cities. In fact, after all we'd been through trying to attract an NFL franchise, the term "underdog" seemed like an understatement. Until, that is, November 30, 1993, when Jacksonville pulled off an upset of major-league proportions.

Suddenly, we were the "Home of the Jaguars." Yet, it wasn't really sudden at all. What may have seemed like an overnight success to the rest of the country was really the result of more than two decades spent developing a game plan that would win us an NFL franchise and boost Jacksonville into the national spotlight.

Before this, the city had suffered from a bit of a bad image. Tourists who drove through Jacksonville knew the city as the place that smelled like rotten eggs (due to nearby pulp and chemical plants), or as the town where you had to pay to get in (we once had a toll on the Interstate).

Those who lived here had a more immediate problem: A 1979 public opinion poll found that Jacksonville's biggest problem was its own self-image, its own attitude. We were, the study suggested, the worst kind of underdog because we simply didn't believe in ourselves. We expected to be losers, and when it came to landing an NFL team, we were. That study confirmed what many of us already knew: Jacksonville had no vision, no dream.

LITTLE EVIDENCE REMAINS THAT modern-day Jacksonville was once called Cowford, meaning "the place where cows are forded across the river." Today, seven bridges span the St. Johns at various points, including the Alsop—or Main Street—Bridge (OPPOSITE).

Renamed in 1822 to honor Andrew Jackson, the city pays homage to its fearless namesake with a nine-foot bronze statue outside the Jacksonville Landing (RIGHT).

CHRIS VANHOUTEN

If you think it's a bit simplistic to lay so much of our image on the doorstep of the National Football League, think again. It was our decades-long courtship with the NFL that spurred a great many civic improvements—not the least of which was the recent renovation of the Gator Bowl, now ALLTEL Stadium. The NFL drive also gradually changed our attitude toward ourselves. It gave us the confidence we needed to compete against any other city in the country. It raised our expectations about the quality-of-life issues that define big-league cities. And in striving to meet those expectations, we became "big league" in every sense.

Over time, we began to value what we already had: the magnificent St. Johns River, our gorgeous beaches, our innovative form of metropolitan government, and our gracious Southern hospitality. And what we didn't have, we created. Our arts and cultural life blossomed. We built the University of North Florida, which has become a major state university in less than 30 years. We cleaned up the environment through a series of tough air and water protection laws. And we attracted world-class corporations and professional institutions like the Mayo Clinic and Merrill Lynch.

During this process, Jacksonville gradually became a city with not one dream, but hundreds of them. And by the time the NFL named the Jaguars as its 30th franchise, Jacksonville had the self-confidence of a Super Bowl contender.

AS AN OCEAN CITY AND A RIVER TOWN, Jacksonville naturally has a special relationship with the water. Locals and tourists are often drawn to the pristine beaches of Ponte Vedra Beach, one of the most upscale communities in the state (TOP), and no one can pass up a leisurely stroll along the old-fashioned, 1.2-mile river walk that lines the south bank of the St. Johns (BOTTOM). Featuring a man-made alternative to Mother Nature's aquatic handiwork is Friendship Park, site of one of the world's tallest fountains, which spouts water at heights of up to 120 feet (OPPOSITE).

LANS STOUT

GORDON JOHNSON

▲ ROBERT S. KANNER

A RE YOU READY FOR SOME FOOTBALL? Locals were more than ready when the NFL announced in 1993 that Jacksonville would receive one of the league's newest franchises. The news not only boosted morale throughout the community, but also brought national exposure to the River City. Local resident and Jaguars owner Wayne Weaver is given credit for being a major player in bringing the beloved team to town (OPPOSITE).

THERE HAS NEVER BEEN ANY DOUBT about Jacksonville's football pedigree. This is football country, where beginning in late August, gridiron diversions become the third religious event of the week (after Sunday morning and Wednesday night church). When the University of Florida Gators play at home in Gainesville, Jacksonville becomes a virtual ghost town. The two biggest events of the year are traditionally the Florida-Georgia game in ALLTEL Stadium (which most of us, out of habit, still call the Gator Bowl), and the Gator Bowl game itself at New Year's.

Yet, when we tried to move to the next level and attract an NFL franchise, we were spurned. Our first suitor was Robert Irsay, owner of the then Baltimore Colts, who put the word out that he would move his team if the city of Baltimore didn't build him a new stadium. Jacksonville, he

ROBERT S. KANNER

LONG BEFORE THE JAGUARS PROWLED local streets, the Gators ruled Jacksonville. Residents have always made the short pilgrimage to "the Swamp" in Gainesville to root for the University of Florida (OPPOSITE). Fortunately, the arrival of an NFL team did nothing to cool the city's ardor for college football's former national champions; it just created a new type of fan: the Jagator (LEFT).

assured us, was on his short list. We responded by turning out—50,000 strong—to greet Irsay when he came to check out the city. His arrival at the Gator Bowl via helicopter was such a spectacle of "Colt Fever" that it made the national news, and the spirit of the NFL drive pulled the city together like nothing had before. People from all neighborhoods, all age groups, all races, and all economic backgrounds believed our football passion would convince Irsay to move his Colts here. As fate would have it, he *did* move the team, but not to Jacksonville.

JAGUARS FANS COME IN all shapes and sizes. Games are a family event in Jacksonville, and no one is too small to don the teal and gold and sport a few paw prints.

A number of other suitors tried to use Jacksonville as a bargaining chip to up the ante back home. Wanting new (or improved) stadiums, they would inevitably threaten to move to Jacksonville if their demands weren't met. Each time, we responded with a civic display of enthusiasm. And each time, we learned something more about ourselves, coming away a little smarter. The result was that we upped the ante *here*, building a better city to attract that elusive NFL team.

There's obviously much more to life in Jacksonville than football. In our river city by the sea are world-class businesses and neighborhoods, arts and culture, year-round recreation, U.S. Navy bases, sunshine and salt air, and other qualities that make natives and newcomers alike feel at home.

But if you want to know about the character of the city, or the resolve of its citizens, just look for the nearest Jaguars jersey, which in a way says it all.

GREGORY WILLIAMS

BOB LIBBY

THE JACKSONVILLE LANDING IS A
favorite downtown gathering spot.
Its casual restaurants and unique shops
boast a breathtaking view of the St.
Johns River, and an open-air stage
features free concerts and other events
throughout the year. On warm summer
nights, "boat parking" is often at a
premium at the Landing's public dock.

Long an economic asset, Jacksonville's port spurred the city's growth
at the beginning of the 20th century,
as many people came to work at the
docks and enjoy the favorable climate
(PAGES 18 AND 19).

J ACKSONVILLE MAY BE A RELATIVE NEWCOMER to the national limelight, but our history predates Plymouth Rock. Jacksonville is one of Florida's oldest communities. (St. Augustine, America's oldest city, is just a half hour south.) Spanish, French, and English settlers all found and fought over this region of Florida centuries ago. And in recognition of that heritage, we refer to our area as the First Coast.

Newcomers are often surprised to learn that Jacksonville is every bit as much a river town as it is an ocean city. The St. Johns is the river that runs through it, literally dividing the city into north and south. The St. Johns is our signature.

Seven bridges span the St. Johns as it makes its way to the Atlantic. Many were dubbed "bridges to nowhere" by critics when they were built, but in time, each brought growth and prosperity. The bridges and the river they span are now a part of daily life—the commute, the commerce, and the beauty of the great river that defines us.

KELLY LADUKE

The St. Johns is not only the physical center of the city, but it also lies at the core of Jacksonville's history. The first European Protestant settlement in America, Fort Caroline, was established here by French Huguenots in 1564, two years after Jean Ribault "discovered" the river's mouth. A replica of that fort exists today at the Fort Caroline National Monument.

T HE CIVIL WAR IS REMEMBERED AT Fort Clinch State Park, a protected area featuring more than 1,000 acres of beaches and nature trails, not to mention a living history museum that re-creates life during the mid-1800s. Built over 20 years starting in 1847, the fortress was held by the Confederacy from the beginning of the war until March 3, 1862, when Yankee troops took it over. Today, rangers dressed in authentic Union uniforms reenact the daily chores of soldiers in 1864.

COURTESY FLORIDA STATE ARCHIVES

IT'S NO SECRET THAT SAND and sunshine have always been plentiful in Jacksonville. Although the area's beaches drew an abundance of tourists in the early 1900s, today they are less congested than those farther south in the Sunshine State.

Compared to that 16th-century date, Jacksonville is still a young city. First settled around 1820, it was known as Cowford—literally, a place where cattle were herded across the river at a narrow point. Bucolic, perhaps, but in 1822, the name was changed to honor Andrew Jackson, hero of the Seminole Wars and soon-to-be president.

In its early years, Jacksonville was a port city and a center

THOUGH THE AREA'S LIGHT-
houses have been re-
placed by more modern means
of navigation, they were once
the only guides for ships pass-
ing down the deep St. Johns
River. Recognized for their
historic significance, many
of the beacons have been
preserved, and some, like
the St. Johns Lighthouse at
Mayport Naval Station, are
listed on the National Register of Historic Places.

of commerce. In the late 1800s, Union soldiers who'd been
stationed in the area during the Civil War relocated their
families to the warm climate, while wealthy northerners
created a winter recreation playground here. Henry Flagler
brought the railroad to North Florida and built the first rail
bridge over the St. Johns. But soon, tourists were bypassing
Jacksonville for his fancy resorts in St. Augustine.

In 1901, the city was all but wiped out by a devastating fire. Throughout this century, the story has been, first, one of a slow rebuilding and then, by 1950, one of a more rapid and steady progress, aided by the presence of the military, paper mills, and chemical plants, and by the continued rise in Florida's popularity as a mecca for business, tourism, and retirement.

Consolidation of Jacksonville and Duval County in 1968—an idea that was finally brought about due to a corruption scandal in local government—created the largest "city" in America, with a metropolitan area of 844 square miles. One mayor. One council. One tax structure. One zoning department. Jacksonville's reputation as Florida's premier business city was enhanced by this one-stop shopping at City Hall. The result has been continued progress in what has become one of the nation's most vibrant metropolitan areas.

IN 1936, JACKSONVILLE WAS ON THE cutting edge of mass transit as its new bus line replaced electric trolleys. Today, the Jacksonville Transportation Authority manages an expansive fleet of buses, as well as the city's innovative monorail system, Skyway Express.

ODAY, JACKSONVILLE'S SKYLINE REFLECTS THE city's economic heritage as a commercial, financial, and transportation center. Here, industries such as banking, insurance, and railroads that played a prominent part in the formation of Florida's first metropolis remain leaders in its economy today.

With the longest heritage in the land, it's no wonder that the region is returning to its roots and its unique natural environment. Preservation of historic sites provides insight into what the early settlers found when they discovered Florida's First Coast. One of the most notable is the Buccaneer Trail, which runs from Fernandina Beach to St. Augustine. This pathway through history provides a leisurely visit to old Florida as well as a nice alternative to the packaged fantasy vacations of make-believe Florida.

BOB LIBBY

IPPING HIS HAT TO THE PROSPEROUS business center Jacksonville has become is the statue of Andrew Jackson, located outside the Jacksonville Landing (OPPOSITE). Offering a salute of their own are the tribesmen in Fred Dana Marsh's *The Legend of Tomokie* (LEFT). A depiction of Chief Tomokie, mythical leader of the Timucua tribe, the 40-foot-tall, art deco piece was erected in Tomoka State Park in the mid-1950s. Once occupied by a Timucuan village and an 18th-century British indigo plantation, the park is today an important archaeological site that features a museum, as well as camping and picnic grounds.

Historic Fernandina Beach, located north of Jacksonville on Amelia Island, is chock-full of restored Victorian homes and charming shops in an old-fashioned, Main Street atmosphere. Many of the distinctive houses have been converted into bed-and-breakfast inns and today welcome city-weary travelers with some good old southern hospitality.

On the north end of the trail is the charming fishing village of Fernandina Beach, with its Victorian-era homes and its attractive downtown. Centre Street runs to the docks, where the shrimp boats bring in the daily catch. The most famous Centre Street landmark is the Palace Saloon, where the Carnegies, Rockefellers, and DuPonts relaxed in the late 19th century—back when Miami was little more than a mangrove swamp and Northeast Florida was known as the winter playground for the rich. Fernandina Beach remains a popular side trip for the well-heeled travelers who frequent nearby resorts, including the famous Ritz-Carlton Hotel at historic Amelia Island (settled in 1566). And each

May, thousands of revelers descend upon this popular village for the much-loved Fernandina Beach Shrimp Festival.

Travelers along the Buccaneer Trail can also visit the oldest surviving plantation in the state. Called Kingsley Plantation, the site is part of Jacksonville's Timucuan Preserve (named for the native Indian tribe), where wildlife flourishes and the landscape inspires a sense of adventure amid the nation's largest freshwater park. The trail includes a ferry ride across the St. Johns to the sleepy fishing village of Mayport. At the end of the trail is St. Augustine, where trolleys, horse-drawn buggies, and walking tours tell a story of more than 400 years.

WHILE STILL A PART OF THE CITY OF Jacksonville, Mayport enjoys its own unique heritage as a historic fishing village. The community is also home to a U.S. Navy base, as well as a large commercial shrimping fleet.

THE PALACE SALOON IS FERNANDINA Beach's most famous landmark, dating back to the late 1800s when Northeast Florida was a favorite winter destination for the nation's wealthiest families. With its hinged half-doors, punched tin ceiling, and massive antique wooden bar, the Palace still looks like it could welcome everyone from a Carnegie to a cowboy.

THE SHEER SIZE OF METRO JACKSONVILLE MEANS that most residents identify as closely with their neighborhoods as they do with the city as a whole. Some of the first neighborhoods were built along the river in what is today the residential area closest to downtown. Among them are San Marco, Riverside, Avondale, and Ortega. Some of these neighborhoods have active preservation societies that seek to maintain communities in which homes are within walking distance of attractive squares and shopping boulevards.

The Southside is "new Jacksonville." Most of the jobs created in the past two decades are located south of the river. Once the site of orange groves, tree farms, pastures, and magnificent moss-draped oaks along the river, the Southside and Mandarin (even farther south) became the fastest-growing areas for new subdivisions. The Mayo Clinic's Jacksonville facility, Merrill Lynch, and the University of North Florida are all located here. Newcomers continue to flock to this area, and to such beach communities as Jacksonville's Atlantic Beach to the north and Ponte Vedra Beach to the south in St. Johns County.

HISTORIC NEIGHBORHOODS LIKE RIVER-side and Avondale, situated on the north banks of the St. Johns, feature lovingly restored homes in a variety of architectural styles. Proud residents enjoy celebrating the history of their homes and showing off the beauty of their courtyards and gardens.

BUD LEE

The Northside is "old Jacksonville." Its neighborhoods are generally blue-collar, which is not surprising considering the presence of Anheuser-Busch and a number of pulp and chemical plants. People who live north of the river have complained for years that they have felt neglected, as roads, subdivisions, shopping centers, and new jobs keep moving south. Today, most city leaders consider the Northside—

with its easy access to the seaport and the airport, and its reasonable land values—to be the next frontier.

The Westside (called the "best side" by those who live there) is home to country music and pickup trucks, nationally ranked Little League teams, and potluck suppers at area churches. Since two of Jacksonville's three military bases are on the Westside, the neighborhood is popular with navy

FROM CHARMING ABODES IN THE CITY'S older neighborhoods to modern, gated mansions, Jacksonville's homes are as diverse as its residents. Despite a local penchant for suburban growth and plenty of new construction, it's often the old-world details of the city's historic houses that attract many home owners.

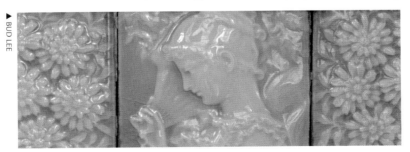

families and is home to a number of "double-dippers"—navy retirees who have chosen to make the city their home for their second career. In fact, Jacksonville is the favorite East Coast retirement destination of U.S. Navy personnel.

This is in large part due to Mayport Naval Station, which is home to more than 13,000 active-duty personnel, making it one of the largest bases in the eastern United States. Jacksonville has a long-standing love affair with the navy. For example, when Lieutenant Commander Scott Speicher, a Jacksonville-based pilot, became the first American casualty of the Gulf War, all of Jacksonville wept along with his widow and two small children.

Speicher had flown his final mission from the carrier USS *Saratoga*, which was based at the Mayport Naval Station from 1956 until its decommissioning in 1995. When the *Saratoga* returned home that spring after the Gulf War, civilians waited on the pier for hours, side by side with military spouses and children. They lined the streets of Mayport with "welcome home" signs. And the lingering image we will never forget—the first thing sailors saw as the *Saratoga* approached the Mayport jetties—was a lone man who had walked out as far as he could on the rocks, waving a giant American flag.

GREATER JACKSONVILLE IS THE PROUD home of the Mayport Naval Station and its more than 13,000 active-duty personnel. Thanks in part to a mild climate, the First Coast is also one of the most popular spots for retired naval personnel to put down roots after years of the nomadic military life.

F ISHING IS MORE THAN A SPORT IN
Jacksonville; it's a way of life. The
St. Johns, the Atlantic Ocean, and the
Intracoastal Waterway provide plenty
of opportunity for amateur and professional anglers. The First Coast also hosts
several world-class fishing tournaments
each year that draw contestants from
far and wide.

Mayport may be known for the navy, but it also has
a life of its own as a unique fishing village and home of
the Mayport Ferry. Many take the ferry to Little Talbot
Island State Park for five miles of unspoiled beaches,
where the seagulls share the skyline with ships' masts.
The Mayport and All That Jazz music festival became
so popular it had to move downtown to a riverfront
park where there was room to stage what has since
become the acclaimed Jacksonville Jazz Festival.

With a year-round average temperature of 63 degrees, Jacksonville is able to hold outdoor festivals and recreational events all year long. And citizens support them all. Jacksonville's River Run was primarily a local event, until 2,000 runners signed up the first year. Today, the River Run is a USA 15K Championship Race, and draws more than 10,000 competitors, with scores more joining in as spectators along the route—handing out drinks and cheering for the runners.

B LESSED WITH A TEMPERATE CLIMATE, Jacksonville is the perfect host for all types of outdoor events. The annual River Run has grown from a small, local contest into a USA 15K Championship Race that attracts more than 10,000 runners and countless spectators.

Spectator sports were popular in Jacksonville long before professional football came to town. The PGA TOUR is headquartered in nearby Ponte Vedra Beach. Since the late 1970s, THE PLAYERS Championship at Sawgrass has brought visitors from all over the world to Jacksonville. The course's famous 17th hole is among the area's most recognizable landmarks. (It has even been duplicated on a number of computer golf games.) Southwest of Ponte Vedra Beach, the PGA TOUR is building its World Golf Hall of Fame, which will complement the more than 50 golf courses in the area.

The Association of Tennis Professionals is also headquartered in Ponte Vedra Beach. While all of Florida is noted for its tennis facilities, Jacksonville is emerging as a favorite spot for this sunny-weather sport.

NOT SURPRISINGLY, GOLF IS A VIRTUAL obsession in Northeast Florida, a region that boasts some of the nation's finest courses and a climate that allows players to tee off year-round. Maintaining its headquarters in Ponte Vedra Beach, the PGA TOUR is committed to making the First Coast a mecca for golfers around the world, holding THE PLAYERS Championship here each spring. Payne Stewart is one of many professional golfers who have competed in the heated contest (OPPOSITE).

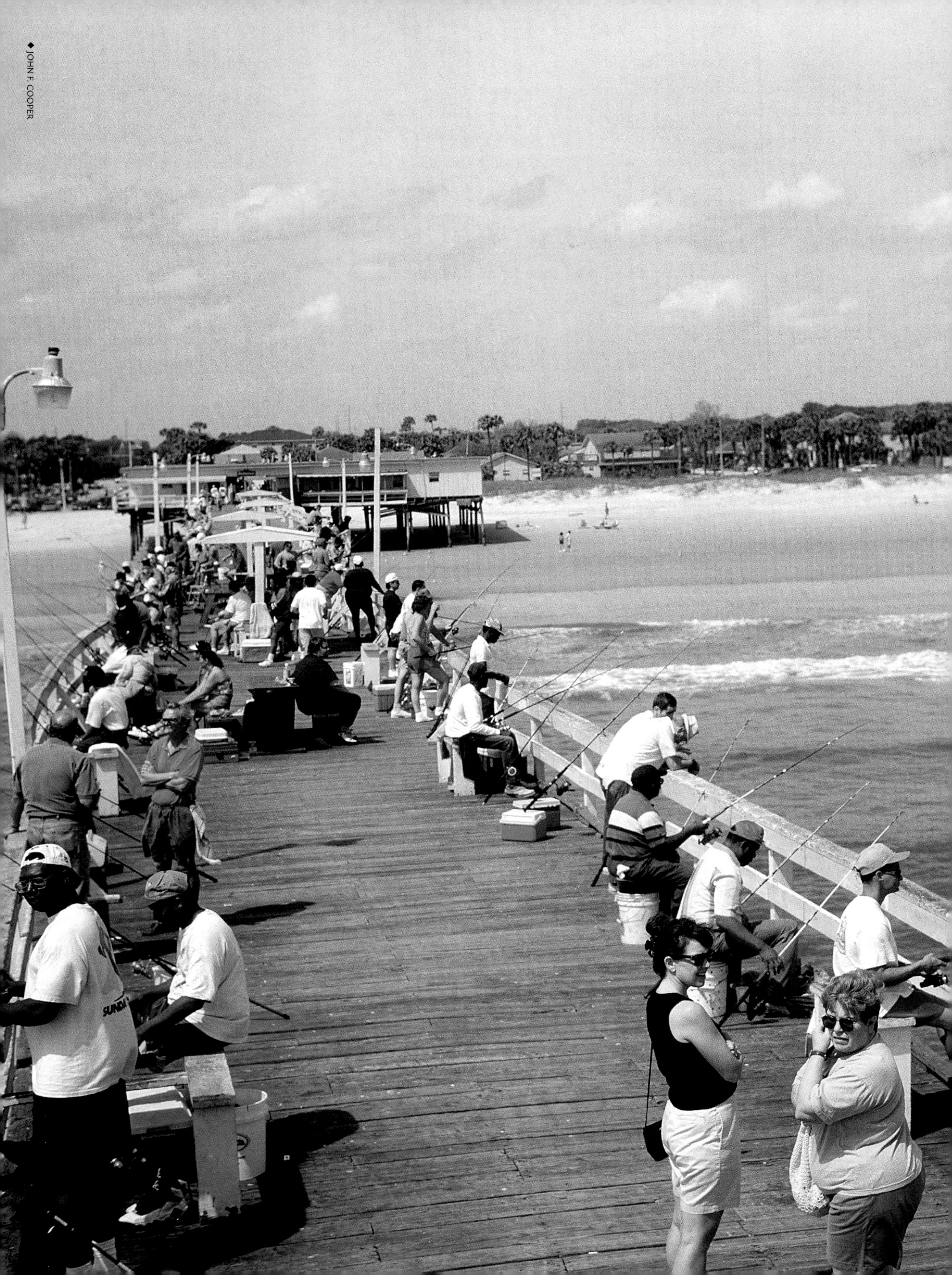

JOHN F. COOPER

But of all the sports available to athletes at all levels, fishing may be the most popular. The St. Johns River, the Atlantic Ocean, and the Intracoastal Waterway provide year-round enjoyment to anglers. The biggest offshore events are the summertime Kingfish tournaments, with the largest originating in Jacksonville in mid-July, when 1,000 boats take off at dawn to compete over a two-day period for more than $50,000 in cash and prizes. Just an hour south of Jacksonville, the St. Johns River communities claim to be the bass fishing capital of the world; the small city of Palatka holds the largest bass tournament east of the Mississippi the first week in May.

▶ BUD LEE

WHILE SOME ANGLERS ENJOY THE warm sunshine, sea air, and camaraderie at the Jacksonville Beach Pier (OPPOSITE), others opt for solitude and a breathtaking sunset (LEFT). Every fisherman, though, yearns for the coveted largemouth bass that swim in the St. Johns, considered by many to have the best bass fishing in the world (PAGES 46 AND 47). Each May, nearby Palatka hosts the largest bass fishing tournament east of the Mississippi River.

BUD LEE

On the occasional cloudy day, locals can venture indoors and still take in the beauty. The Cummer Gallery of Art in historic Riverside features Western and Asian masterwork paintings, as well as a world-famous collection of Meissen porcelain.

Our good fortune extends well beyond sporting activities. Jacksonville is home to a wealth of attractions and events, from outdoor concerts at Metropolitan Park to Broadway shows and symphony concerts at the Performing Arts Center on the St. Johns. Among the area's many exciting attractions are the Museum of Science and History, with numerous ocean-oriented exhibits; the Jacksonville Landing, an enter-

tainment complex of shops and restaurants on the river; Jacksonville Zoological Gardens, located on the river a short boat ride from downtown; the Cummer Gallery of Art, which is framed by beautiful gardens along the river; and the Jacksonville Museum of Contemporary Art, which is currently looking for a home along the river to be a part of the waterfront scene as downtown continues to develop.

A JACKSONVILLE ICON SINCE 1927, THE Florida Theatre was fully restored to its original splendor in 1983. The former vaudeville house remains one of the city's most treasured architectural and cultural landmarks, today hosting a variety of events from Broadway productions to ballet.

ST. JAMES

RECENTLY, JACKSONVILLE'S CITY HALL MOVED into the St. James Building, one of downtown's most historically significant structures. Located (appropriately) near the river, the St. James was designed in the Prairie Style by the city's most celebrated architect, Henry John Klutho. The building held its grand opening in 1912 as the ninth-largest department store in America, and attracted a huge crowd (for the time) of 28,000 people. It represented then what it represents now: a new era, a new attitude, a defiant determination—the same spirit that we have shown since the great fire at the turn of the century that threatened to wipe us off the map.

Fortunately, today's Jacksonville does not have to start over. The foundation is solid. The future has never looked brighter. There is new respect for the past.

If you need proof, just pay a visit to St. Andrews Episcopal Church, the only major downtown church to survive the historic blaze. No longer an active place of worship, St. Andrews has been restored with a new reverence for the past as the first permanent home of the Jacksonville Historical Society. Yet, as you step outside, you can see the future, just a block away: the imposing presence of Jacksonville's ALLTEL Stadium.

And on Sunday afternoons, there's not an underdog in sight. ✳

◀ VAN R. JONES / WJCT

JACKSONVILLE IS AN INTERESTING MIX OF old and new, with historically significant structures neighboring ultramodern newcomers. In recent years, the city has placed a renewed emphasis on restoring important buildings like the St. James, which recently became home to Jacksonville's City Hall. And in 1997, ALLTEL agreed to pay $6.2 million over 10 years for the right to put its name on the former Jacksonville Municipal Stadium, also known as the Gator Bowl.

PROVIDING REFUGE FROM THE HUSTLE and bustle of downtown, the beautiful marshes on Fort George Island support a delicate ecosystem of flora and fauna. Nature lovers can reach the island via ferry, departing from the historic fishing village of Mayport.

N ATURAL BEAUTY ABOUNDS ALONG
Florida's eastern coastline, where
the Atlantic Ocean and the Intracoastal
Waterway meld in an exquisite marsh-
land display.

ONLY AN HOUR'S DRIVE FROM THE city, wildlife flourishes in its natural habitat, oblivious to the world-class urban center that exists just a few miles away. Human compatriots often immerse themselves in this carefree environment, if only for an afternoon of fishing.

THE DIVERSE PARKS AND RECREATION areas of the First Coast feature many miles of nature trails that meander through woodlands, marshes, and swamps. The observant stroller can catch a glimpse of such indigenous animals as egrets, swamp deer, and the occasional alligator.

INDEPENDENT LIFE

THERE'S NO BETTER WAY TO SPEND a Sunday afternoon than sauntering along the boardwalk at the Jacksonville Landing. The city's temperate climate makes it ideal for such peaceful promenades.

If you're looking for a party, the place to go is the Jacksonville Landing, a festival marketplace that hosts a variety of special events throughout the year. Restaurants in the Landing are also a favorite gathering spot of Jaguars fans who want to watch the game when the team's on the road.

JACKSONVILLE KNOWS HOW TO MIX BUSIness with pleasure. The majority of downtown's tall towers make the most of their river views, and nearby marinas add a whole new twist to the concept of commuting.

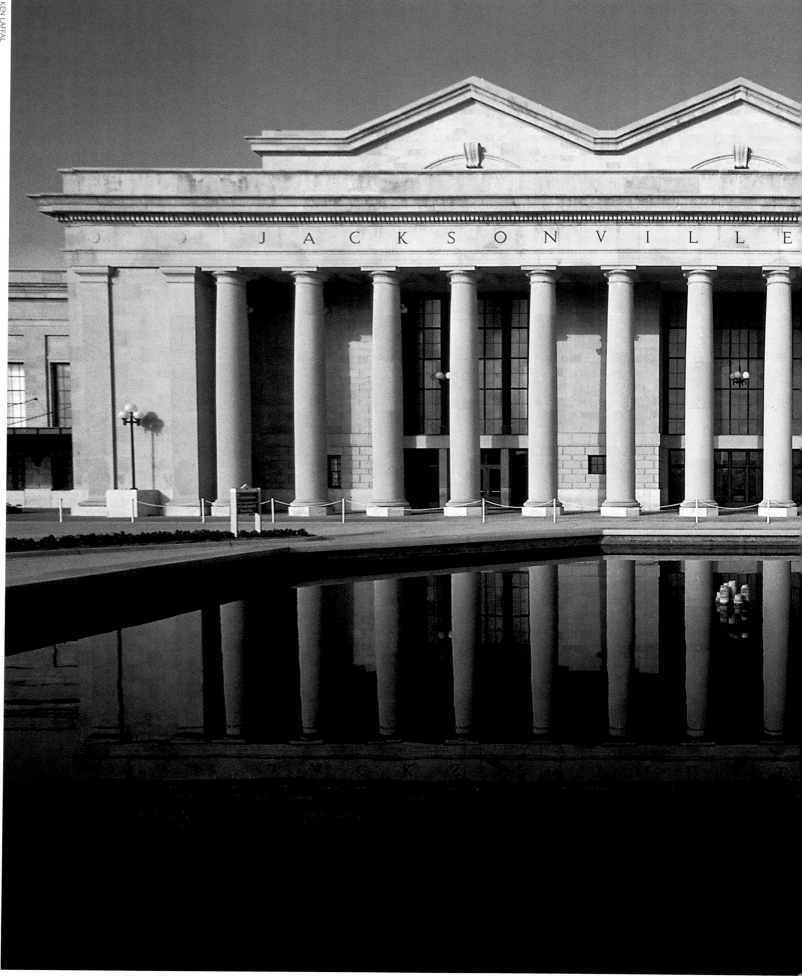

THE FORMER JACKSONVILLE TERMINAL depot has found new life as the Prime Osborn Convention Center. With a total of 118,000 square feet of meeting space, the historic facility has been a boon to the city's travel and tourism industry since it reopened in 1986.

A WALKING TOUR OF DOWNTOWN reveals a laundry list of landmarks, including the Prime Osborn Convention Center, originally opened in 1913 as the city's train station, and the statue of Andrew Jackson, for whom the River City was named.

ANDREW JACKSON
r Whom Jacksonville Was Named
1822

J ACKSONVILLE IS POISED TO LEAP INTO THE
next century, thanks to its forward-
thinking civic leaders. The city's ongoing resurgence is a reflection of the
communitywide development plan put
into action years ago.

THE SKY'S THE LIMIT IN JACKSONVILLE, where there's a wealth of opportunity for businesses and individuals. Time and again, newcomers cite the area's quality of life, low cost of living, and favorable climate as reasons to make the First Coast home.

DEDICATED IN 1910, THE IMMACULATE
Conception Catholic Church is a
true landmark in downtown Jacksonville. The beautiful cathedral, with
its twin spires and Gothic details, is
listed on the National Register of
Historic Places.

H ISTORIC ST. JOHNS EPISCOPAL
Cathedral has no trouble distinguishing itself among the modern buildings of downtown Jacksonville.

The church's imposing Gothic presence at Duval and Market streets is a symbol of the city's unique ability to blend old and new.

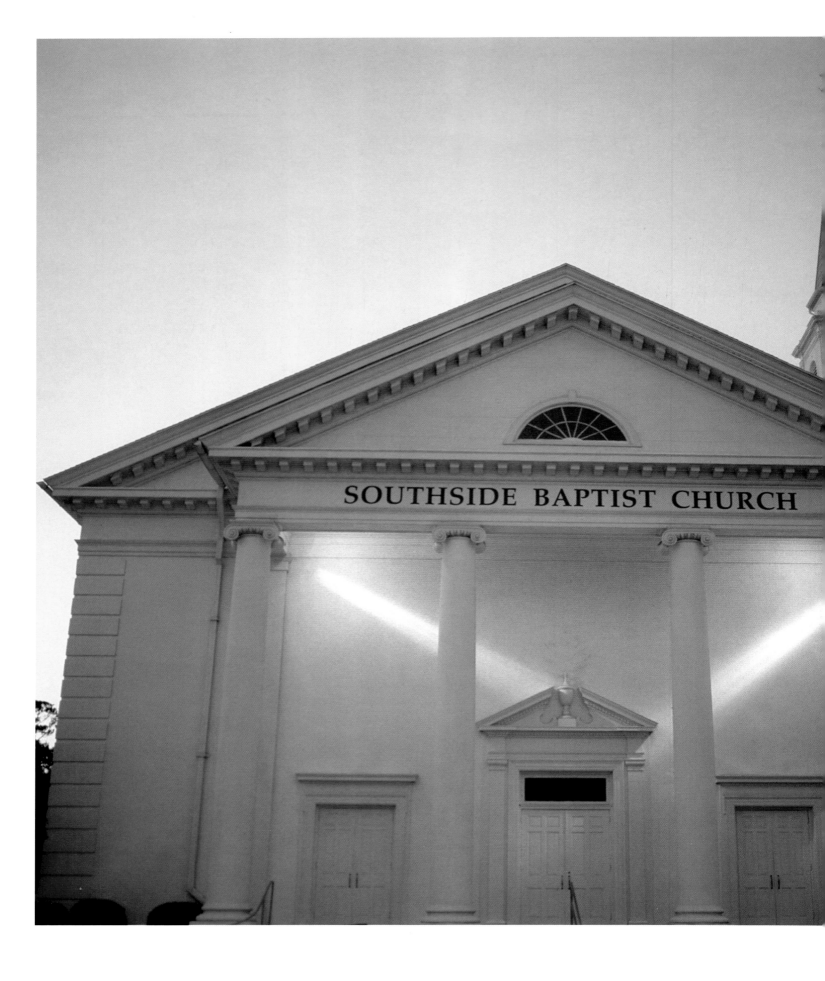

SYMBOLS OF SPIRITUALITY ABOUND IN Jacksonville, headquarters city for the Florida Baptist Convention. For many local residents, the church you attend is as much a part of your identity as the team you root for on game day.

Dedicated in 1838, historic Bethel Baptist Institutional Church was the first organized church of its denomination in Jacksonville. Its worship services still inspire parishioners to don their Sunday best.

TAKE A STEP BACK IN TIME AT THE farmers' market on West Beaver Street, a multiacre collection of tin-roofed produce stands where fresh, homegrown fruits and vegetables and plenty of homemade goodies are available seven days a week.

EVERYONE LOVES A PARTY, AND JACK-sonville is no exception. The pavilions on the Southbank Riverwalk are popular spots for outdoor events, with plenty of room for fun and entertainment for the whole family. And don't forget the food—there just wouldn't be a party without it.

ATCHING THE RIVER FLOW IS OFTEN the cure for what ails you in this city, where almost everything is referenced by its proximity to the St. Johns. The Riverplace Tower on the south bank features an exquisite, glassed-in atrium that overlooks the magnificent waterway (OPPOSITE), but nothing can beat a front-row seat in one of Jacksonville's riverfront pavilions (ABOVE).

LOCALS AREN'T THE ONLY ONES WHO are head over heels about Jacksonville. In 1995, *Money* magazine ranked the city third on its list of the best places to live in the United States. Since then, Jacksonville has consistently gained mention on the annual list.

IN JACKSONVILLE, IT'S NEARLY IMPOSSIBLE to avoid the teal and gold. Jaguars fans are everywhere, and they aren't at all shy about demonstrating their "cat-itude."

94

SINCE THEIR INAUGURAL GAME IN 1995, the Jaguars have become a force to be reckoned with. The team made it to the AFC Championship game in only its second year, ending the season just one win away from the Super Bowl.

THE JAGUARS' INFLUENCE CAN BE SEEN throughout the city, from street banners to the huge paw prints that adorn the roads leading to ALLTEL Stadium. Jim Draper's larger-than-life outdoor mural at Bay and Ocean streets is a constant reminder of the team's avid fan support.

LOCATED IN THE HEART OF DOWN-
town Jacksonville, the Greenleaf
& Crosby Building is an impressive

architectural masterpiece. Its gilded
door and high, arched entranceway
often give passersby pause.

W HETHER YOUR TASTE IS FOR A CUP of fresh-brewed java, a light lunch, or a fabulous antique, Jacksonville's host of quaint specialty shops and cafés are sure to satisfy any appetite.

MOM ALWAYS SAID THAT THE WAY to a man's heart is through his stomach. Ever testing that theory, Greater Jacksonville's restaurants and taverns—including (FROM OPPOSITE LEFT) European Street, As You Like It, the Sun Dog Diner, and the Palace Saloon—are taking hold of local affections and appetites by offering gourmet food and drink. In addition, new and innovative markets and dining spots continue to crop up all over town.

PARKVIEW

THE PARKVIEW CAFE IS ONE OF THE success stories of Springfield, a neighborhood near downtown that is undergoing a revitalization program to restore its historic properties to their former beauty. Opened in 1993, the restaurant is unique for its antique light fixtures, art deco interior, and beautiful view of Confederate Park.

Noted for its annual Ringhaver Leukemia Cup Regatta, which raises money for the National Leukemia Society, the Epping Forest Yacht Club combines exquisite landscaping with unique architecture.

LOCATION, LOCATION, LOCATION. In Jacksonville, the most coveted location is, of course, on the river. The city's most spectacular homes, both new and old, are most often found along the banks of the St. Johns and its offshoot waterways. In addition to the lovely view, home owners in many riverfront communities can take advantage of private boat access in their own backyards.

F ROM CHARMING BUNGALOWS TO traditional colonials and everything in between, Jacksonville's historic homes are graced with beauty and warmth.

Locals like to call Jacksonville "the biggest small town you'll ever live in." Despite the huge land mass, the River City is still a community of neighborhoods and small-town sentiment, where generations of families gather to celebrate summer holidays and courting on a park bench is not yet passé.

Nearly year-round, residents can delight in the sights and sounds of outdoor Jacksonville, where numerous parks, public sculptures, and manicured gardens complement Mother Nature's beauty. All creatures great and small enjoy a romp through the plaza on a warm fall day or a leisurely afternoon spent by the river.

EVERYTHING UNDER THE SUN: JACK-sonville relishes its diversity and always finds a reason to head out-doors and celebrate (PAGES 112 AND 113).

Everything under the sun: Jacksonville relishes its diversity and always finds a reason to head outdoors and celebrate (PAGES 112 AND 113).

WHEN IT COMES TO CULTURE, Jacksonville doesn't clown around. In recent years, the local arts scene has blossomed, and the city is now home to a number of talented artists, not to mention a nationally recognized symphony, several museums, and many colorful performance troupes.

116

OLD-FASHIONED FUN IS THE NAME OF the game during River City Kids' Day, an annual event sponsored by Wolfson Children's Hospital and other area organizations. Along with rides, games, and other carnival fun, volunteers take the opportunity to distribute children's health and safety literature.

THE UNOFFICIAL HEADQUARTERS OF Jacksonville's young, bohemian crowd, Five Points is a funky, offbeat part of town that presents a new perspective on the city's style. Adjacent to the gracious, old-style neighborhoods of Riverside and Avondale, Five Points is home to art galleries, innovative ethnic restaurants, and performance clubs.

ART IS NOT ALWAYS FOUND WITHIN THE walls of a museum. A uniquely American innovation, graffiti art portrays powerful messages and emotions on an unconventional canvas.

THE JACKSONVILLE MUSEUM OF Contemporary Art—the city's oldest museum—is one of the First Coast's greatest cultural treasures. The gallery's permanent collection includes works by such artists as Alex Katz, Juan Hamilton, Leon Berkowitz, and Richard Anuszkiewicz.

THE CUMMER GALLERY OF ART features classic masterwork paintings and sculpture, as well as a renowned porcelain collection. Located on the banks of the St. Johns in picturesque Riverside, the facility also boasts one of the finest sculpture gardens in the region.

OPENED IN 1997, THE TIMES-UNION Center for the Performing Arts has been a tremendous boon to Jacksonville. Carefully designed with flexibility in mind, its three halls can accommodate a variety of productions. The Jacksonville Ballet Theatre, which stages most of its performances at the Florida Theatre, was a part of the opening-day celebration at the state-of-the-art venue (BOTTOM LEFT).

◀ TERRY TAYLOR   ▲ SUPER STOCK, INC.

UNDER THE DIRECTION OF ROGER Nierenberg, the Jacksonville Symphony Orchestra, founded in 1949, is the oldest symphony orchestra in the state and one of the premier performing arts organizations in the Southeast. Its new home within the Times-Union Center, the Robert E. Jacoby Symphony Hall, features a classic European shoe box design and is the only acoustically perfect concert venue in Florida.

EVEN THOUGH THE CITY RARELY SUFFERS a cruel winter, locals still fervently celebrate the arrival of spring. The annual Spring Festival in Jacksonville Beach attracts countless revelers ready to enjoy warmer days.

ANY BEACH BUM KNOWS THAT VOLLEY-ball is *the* sport of the sand. But amateur players know it's time to step aside when the Professional Beach Volleyball tournament comes to Jacksonville Beach.

COME ON A SURFING SAFARI AT ONE of the First Coast's beautiful beaches. Local teenagers spend many a summer lifeguarding—a great way to earn some money and soak up the sun at the same time.

FOR GENERATIONS, JACKSONVILLE Beach has been a favorite leisure-time destination. While it may look a lot different today, the locale is still a great place to gather with friends, stroll with family members, and enjoy the sights and sounds of the sea.

AH, THE EXUBERANCE OF YOUTH. THE First Coast's beaches are popular with the younger set, who seem never to tire of sand and sea. The ocean's waves are a welcome cushion for ex-perimental gymnasts, and the smooth sand provides miles of inspiration for aspiring artists and sculptors. The area's more "mature" residents also find myriad ways to enjoy the water.

Fishing, boating, sailing, and surfing all provide much-needed respite from the hustle and bustle of everyday life (PAGES 136 AND 137).

U NDERSTANDABLY, SAILING IS A favorite pastime in Jacksonville. The St. Johns River, the Intracoastal Waterway, and the region's other creeks, rivers, and streams make the perfect avenues for every captain's vessel.

R E F L E C T I O N S   O F   E X C E L L E N C E

"CATCH A WAVE AND YOU'RE SITTIN' on top of the world," sang the Beach Boys. It's easy to forget your cares when you're riding high on the ocean's swell, but even the experts sometimes meet their match during the WaveMasters Society Surfing Contest at Jacksonville Beach.

S URFERS COME IN ALL SHAPES AND
sizes, and no one is too old or
too young to enjoy the rush of riding
the perfect wave.

GREATER JACKSONVILLE'S BEACHES welcome all kinds, whether they prefer a regular surfboard or a miniature version with wheels. Testing the law of gravity, this youngster triumphantly soars above Kona Skateboard Park.

SINCE THE EARLY 1900S, WHEN THE area was a major destination for wealthy families from the North, Jacksonville's beaches have been a tourist's paradise. Quaint seaside shops offer a dizzying array of T-shirts, conch shells, and other tempting treasures.

ALLIGATORS SEEM TO BE EVERYWHERE in Florida, including a 13-foot stuffed version that welcomes visitors to Jacksonville. It's an image that vacationers young and old can't help but take with them when they leave.

THE FIRST COAST IS KNOWN FOR ITS commercial shrimp fleets that harvest the succulent sea creatures each season, much to the delight of discriminating palates.

NAUTICAL INFLUENCES ARE HARD TO escape in Greater Jacksonville, and many locals depend on the fruits of the ocean for their livelihood. Forever in search of the best bait, area fishermen don't have to look far for reminders of their elusive prey (PAGES 154 AND 155).

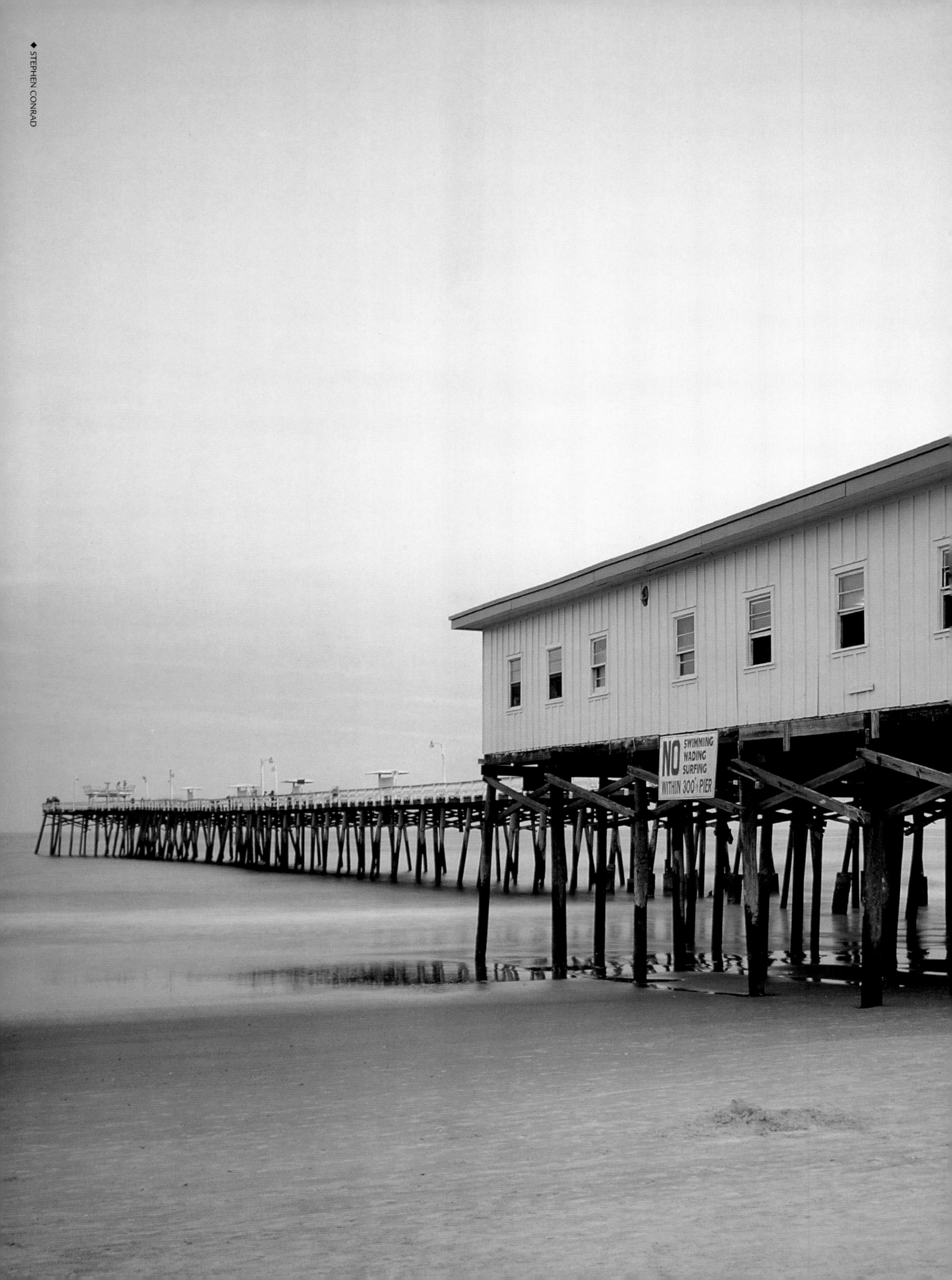
NO
SWIMMING
WADING
SURFING
WITHIN 300
PIER

◆ STEPHEN CONRAD

USK IS A PEACEFUL TIME AT THE
Jacksonville Beach Pier, where
sundown signals a brief respite before
serious fishermen return for another
long day of baiting their hooks
(PAGES 156 AND 157).

Fishing is a great way to enjoy the water, soak up some rays, and, if you're lucky, bring home some dinner. Anglers of all kinds eagerly cast their lines in the waterways of Northeast Florida, but some find the effort downright exhausting.

P ELICANS PURSUE A LOCAL FISHERMAN after a successful day of solitary crabbing. Both man and fowl admire the impressive catch.

EVEN WEEKEND FISHERMEN TAKE THEIR sport seriously on the First Coast. Fishing is a popular pastime and, as a side benefit, provides a great opportunity to work on your tan. On Northeast Florida's large commercial fishing boats, however, the goal is not sun and fun, but a net full of tasty sea critters.

B OATS HAVE LONG BEEN CHARACTER-
ized with feminine qualities and
names. *Miss Joann* and *Frances M*—two
wise old matrons of the sea—still exert
their womanly wiles on their captains.

NOTHING TASTES BETTER THAN THE
fresh catch of the day, enjoyed
outside in the warm sea air and
washed down with a cold beer (PAGES
166 AND 167).

J ACKSONVILLE'S ANNUAL KUUMBA
Festival, started in 1987, celebrates
African-American culture and heritage.
In addition to its vibrant artistic displays and educational workshops, the
event showcases traditional dress,
food, and music.

THE JACKSONVILLE ZOOLOGICAL Gardens is undergoing a massive, $50 million renovation and building campaign that will transform it into a premier facility by the turn of the century. With many of the improvements already completed, the 61-acre park features a railroad and a petting zoo, a newly renovated elephant barn, and a raised boardwalk that allows visitors to traverse the naturalistic wildlife settings.

MOST PEOPLE KNOW THAT THE FIRST Coast has its share of Native American heritage, but some folks are surprised to learn that there are also plenty of cowboys in these parts. Floridians can mosey with the best of 'em, as these bull riders and barrel racers amply demonstrate.

NORTHEAST FLORIDA IS PROUD OF ITS place in American history. Signs of that fact are abundant throughout the area, where history buffs of all ages don period costumes and participate in Civil War reenactments.

Each April, the Springing the Blues Festival brings some of the nation's most notable jazz and blues artists to town for a weekend of music and festivities. Started in 1990, the event has attracted such superstars as Little Jimmy King, Clarence "Gatemouth" Brown, and B'nois King.

▶ PAULA J. GRIFFIN

The Jacksonville Port Authority, better known as JAXPORT, operates three marine facilities that employ more than 10,000 people. The largest of the three is the Blount Island Marine Terminal, which encompasses 867 acres and is one of the most extensive automobile import/export facilities on the East Coast.

THE POMP AND CIRCUMSTANCE OF the military is inexorably woven into the fabric of Jacksonville, where generations of sailors have served at area bases. The Mayport Naval Station was home to the USS *Saratoga* aircraft carrier from 1956, when it was commissioned, until 1995, when it was consigned to the scrap yard (OPPOSITE). Captain William Kennedy presided over the vessel's decommissioning ceremonies in 1994 (THIS PAGE).

While a trio of sailors look shipshape aboard their vessel (PAGE 183), a group of civilians demonstrate their own interpretation of being "at ease" (PAGE 182).

MAYPORT HAS LONG BEEN HOME TO a bustling navy base. Covering more than 3,000 acres, the naval station is one of the largest in the continental United States and boasts more than 20 ships, including AEGIS guided missile cruisers, Spruance-class destroyers, and guided missile frigates.

J ACKSONVILLE SHOWED THAT SOUTHERN hospitality knows no bounds when the city welcomed a Russian navy ship and its crew to Mayport Naval Station in 1991.

COMMISSIONED IN 1940, NAVAL AIR Station Jacksonville employs more than 16,000 people and is the base of operations for both the P-3C Orion long-range maritime surveillance aircraft (ABOVE) and the SH-3 Sea King ASW helicopter. The historic facility also housed a German prisoner-of-war camp during World War II and was the first home of the navy's Blue Angels flight demonstration team (OPPOSITE).

As William Shakespeare once wrote, "The apparel oft proclaims the man." That timeless aphorism still applies in modern-day Jacksonville—from a couple of well-suited firefighters to these would-be baggage handlers.

WITH SOME 250 ARRIVALS AND departures daily and service from a dozen major airlines, Jacksonville International Airport is positioning itself as the new gateway to the Southeast. An impressive place inside and out, the modern, two-story terminal features restaurants and kiosks, a PGA TOUR golf shop, and a striking, 60-foot-high atrium.

On a clear day in Jacksonville, you can see for miles—truly one of the perks of being a window washer.

SEVEN BRIDGES SPAN THE ST. JOHNS as it makes its way to the Atlantic Ocean. Critics dubbed many of them "bridges to nowhere" when they were built, but in time, each brought growth and prosperity. Today, they are an integral part of daily life—the commute, the commerce, and the beauty of the great river that defines us.

REFLECTIONS OF EXCELLENCE

A S EVENING APPROACHES, SURFERS,
sailors, and other water lovers
know that another day of sun and fun
is just a few short hours away.

JACKSONVILLE'S NAVAL HERITAGE IS celebrated on the Southbank Riverwalk, where a life-size statue of a vigilant sailor gazes out over the St. Johns with a duffel bag at his feet.

Created by Stanley Bleifeld in the mid-1980s, the sculpture is dedicated to the men and women of the U.S. Navy who have lost their lives in service to their country.

WE MAY NOT BE THE CITY THAT never sleeps, but you won't catch us napping either. Shrewd decision making and innovative, long-range planning have brought Jacksonville to its present-day position as the bold new city of the South.

JACKSONVILLE

WHEN DOWNTOWN'S OFFICE BUILD-
ings shut down for the day, the
Jacksonville Landing still has hours to
go. Its restaurants are a favorite spot
for an after-work drink or a late dinner
with a river view.

One of Jacksonville's most prestigious neighborhoods, San Marco is known for its beautiful riverfront mansions, its historic homes in a variety of architectural styles, and the old-fashioned Main Street feel of San Marco Square. On warm summer nights, residents can stroll down to the San Marco Theater for a $3 movie, people-watch from the arched pavilion in Ballis Park, or visit the 850-pound bronze lions, recently added to the San Marco Fountain.

AERIAL

THE FLORIDA THEATRE IN DOWNTOWN Jacksonville is a popular place to be after dark. Listed on the National Register of Historic Places, this restored vaudeville theater is the city's only remaining example of 1920s fantasy architecture. The venue's lavish interior and updated accommodations make it the ideal setting for cultural events year-round.

THE ANNUAL JACKSONVILLE JAZZ Festival is one of the city's largest events, drawing a number of renowned performers and countless fans. Held outdoors in Metropolitan Park, the colorful, two-day celebration lights up the night with its lively music (PAGES 212 AND 213).

Throughout the year, Metropolitan Park hosts plenty of other well-known performers who exercise their musical muscles on a variety of instruments. Among the stars who have thrilled local crowds are Chuck Mangione (OPPOSITE TOP), Willie Nelson (TOP), and Lou Rawls (BOTTOM).

INDEPENDENT LIFE

BELLSOUTH

THE JACKSONVILLE LANDING

T HANKS TO ITS RICH HERITAGE, thriving cultural life, diverse population, healthy business community, and temperate climate, Jacksonville never runs out of reasons to celebrate.

Profiles in Excellence

A look at the corporations, businesses, professional groups, and community service organizations that have made this book possible. Their stories—offering an informal chronicle of the local business community—are arranged according to the date they were established in the Jacksonville area.

ABC25 WJXX ■ ALLTEL ■ ATP Tour ■ Baptist/St. Vincent's Health System ■ Barnett Banks, Inc. ■ Bessent, Hammack & Ruckman, Inc. ■ Pam Bingemann Realty, Inc. ■ Blue Cross and Blue Shield of Florida ■ CELL-TEL International, Inc. ■ William R. Cesery Co. ■ Champion HealthCare ■ Compass Bank ■ Coopers & Lybrand L.L.P. ■ Crazy Elliot's Aetna Office Furniture, Inc. ■ CSX Transportation ■ Cypress Village Retirement Community ■ Easton, Sanderson and Company ■ Episcopal High School of Jacksonville ■ FOX 30 WAWS-TV Clear Channel Television, Inc. ■ W.W. Gay Mechanical Contractor, Inc. ■ Genesis Rehabilitation Hospital and Centers ■ HomeSide Lending, Inc. ■ IMA Plus ■ Institutional Asset Management Inc. ■ City of Jacksonville ■ *Jacksonville Business Journal* ■ Jacksonville Hilton and Towers ■ Jacksonville Transportation Authority ■ Jefferson Smurfit Corporation ■ KPMG Peat Marwick LLP ■ Kuhn Flowers ■ Landcom Hospitality Management, Inc. ■ Marriott at Sawgrass Resort ■ Mayo Clinic Jacksonville ■ MediaOne ■ Memorial Hospital Jacksonville/Orange Park Medical Center/Specialty Hospital Jacksonville ■ Merrill Lynch ■ Methodist Medical Center ■ Miller Electric Company ■ The Monticello Companies, Inc. ■ M.D. Moody & Sons, Inc. ■ Omni Jacksonville Hotel ■ The PARC Group, Inc. ■ Perdue Office Interiors ■ PGA TOUR ■ PrimeCo Personal Communications ■ PSS/WorldMedical, Inc. ■ Radisson Riverwalk Hotel ■ Revlon, Inc. ■ St. Luke's Hospital ■ Scott-McRae Group ■ Seaboard Credit Union ■ Specialty Hospital Jacksonville ■ Stein Mart ■ The Stellar Group ■ Arthur Treacher's Seafood Grille ■ Underwood Jewelers Corp. ■ Unisource ■ UPN 47 WTEV-TV ■ Vicar's Landing ■ Vistakon ■ Wellspring Resources, LLC ■ WJXT ■ WAPE-FM, WFYV-FM, WKQL-FM, WMXQ-FM, WOKV-AM, and WBWL-AM

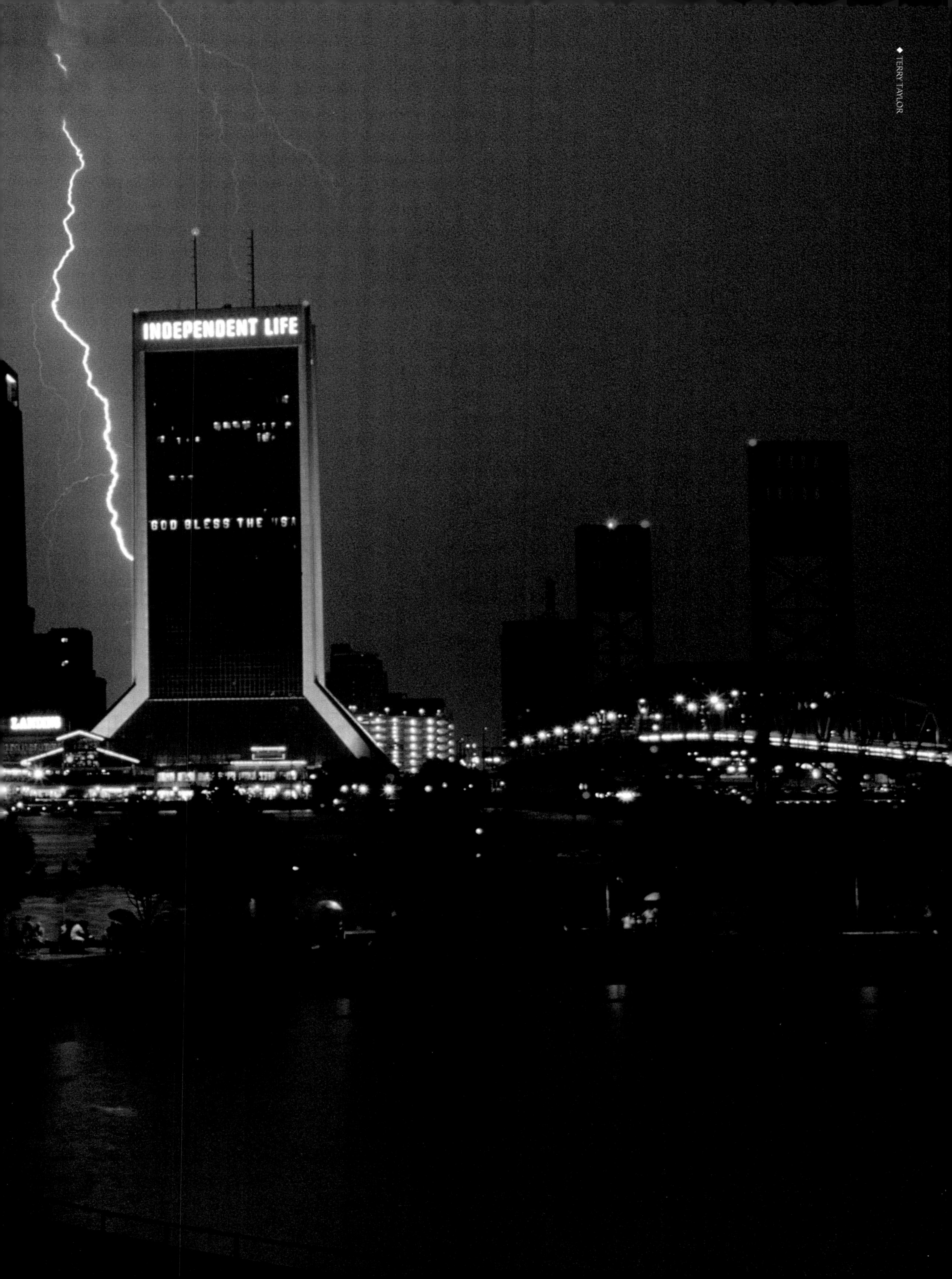

INDEPENDENT LIFE

GOD BLESS THE USA

1832-1959

1832	City of Jacksonville
1873	St. Luke's Hospital
1877	Barnett Banks, Inc.
1912	The Monticello Companies, Inc.
1913	M.D. Moody & Sons, Inc.
1916	Baptist/St. Vincent's Health System
1916	Perdue Office Interiors
1916	Scott-McRae Group
1919	Unisource
1928	Miller Electric Company
1928	Underwood Jewelers Corp.
1929	Seaboard Credit Union
1937	Jefferson Smurfit Corporation
1944	Blue Cross and Blue Shield of Florida
1947	Kuhn Flowers
1949	WJXT
1957	Crazy Elliot's Aetna Office Furniture, Inc.
1959	William R. Cesery Co.

THE CITY OF JACKSONVILLE

RENOWNED FOR ITS SOUTHERN GRACE, SCENIC BEAUTY, AND bustling, metropolitan atmosphere, Jacksonville is one of few cities in the United States that can boast the successful incorporation of all these charms. Born in 1562, the community experienced shifts in leadership several times over the

years, and by 1901, it had been destroyed, pillaged, deserted, and burned on various occasions. However, with true grace and determination, Jacksonville overcame these catastrophes, and, in this century, has become a city of exciting prosperity.

After World War II, Jacksonville established itself as a home base for the U.S. Navy. As a result, new commerce, residents, and visitors migrated to the city, and Jacksonville began to build upon its reputation as a healthy and successful metropolis.

In 1968, Jacksonville carried on its tradition of innovation, becoming the first consolidated city in the nation when its government was combined with Duval County's. The bold move served to further the City of Jacksonville's reputation as a national trendsetter.

BUILDING NEIGHBORHOODS

Today, Jacksonville is entering a new era of expansion. Led by Mayor John Delaney, Jacksonville has succeeded in initiating pro-

grams to fulfill the specific needs of its neighborhoods. A new Neighborhoods Department has been established to nurture and support the important foundations of the community.

One of the city's recently established programs—Clean It Up, Green It Up—encourages residents of all neighborhoods to join forces in improving the

appearance of the local community. In doing so, cooperation and communication between different groups and organizations in Jacksonville are enhanced, and residents work together to make their neighborhoods more beautiful.

According to Delaney, "Strong neighborhoods are the building blocks that create the foundation for a strong city." Based on this philosophy, four neighborhoods were targeted for the Intensive Care Neighborhoods Program. Increased attention has been devoted to demolishing condemned homes, lowering the crime rate, and improving the overall appearance of the communities. Education has assumed a significant role in the program as teams of mentors and tutors are assisting children in neighborhood schools. The benefits of this program are being realized with cleaner streets, decreased truancy, and increased citizen participation. Stronger neighborhoods are beginning to emerge.

And the world is taking notice of Jacksonville's increased prosperity. *Money* magazine has consistently

TODAY, JACKSONVILLE IS ENTERING A NEW ERA OF EXPANSION LED BY MAYOR JOHN DELANEY.

JACKSONVILLE HAS SUCCEEDED IN INITIATING PROGRAMS TO FULFILL THE SPECIFIC NEEDS OF ITS NEIGHBORHOODS.

placed the city near the top of its list of most livable cities, including ranking it second among large cities and first in terms of economy in 1997. The city is Florida's financial hub, a meld of heavy tourism, major port activity, and three U.S. Navy bases. It is also the home of the successful Jacksonville Jaguars football team, key medical centers, and more than 1 million residents.

A Truly Unique City

Jacksonville is more than a city of financial growth. It is an integrated community with traditions and cultures shaped by the many ethnic origins it hosts. Celebrations of these cultures have matured and expanded as the city grows and develops. "The communication and understanding among residents of various cultures is strong and allows all citizens to celebrate our differences in a way few cities can," says Delaney.

The heart of the City of Jacksonville is the same as it was in the early days. Southern charm is reflected in its gracious townspeople and their welcoming attitude toward visitors. Beauty is reflected in its natural waterways, scenic beaches, and gracious, stately homes. Yet, the city's future prosperity is reflected in its bustling, metropolitan expansion. Jacksonville epitomizes the South, blending all of its graces into one unique city of success, livability, and elegance.

▶ TOM SALLEY

THE HEART OF THE CITY OF JACKSONVILLE IS THE SAME AS IT WAS IN THE EARLY DAYS. SOUTHERN CHARM IS REFLECTED IN ITS GRACIOUS TOWNSPEOPLE AND THEIR WELCOMING ATTITUDE TOWARD VISITORS.

THE CITY'S MISSION IS TO MAKE JACKSONVILLE'S LOCAL GOVERNMENT THE MOST RESPOSIBLE AND EFFECTIVE GOVERNMENT IN AMERICA, AND JACKSONVILLE THE BEST PLACE TO LIVE, WORK, AND RAISE A FAMILY.

St. Luke's Hospital

S T. LUKE'S HOSPITAL CLAIMS MANY FIRSTS IN ITS HISTORY. IT WAS the first private hospital in the state of Florida. The state's first nursing school opened at St. Luke's in 1885. And throughout its colorful history, St. Luke's has been the site of several medical firsts, as well. But perhaps even more interesting is the story of the hospital's founding by three prominent local women with no medical training.

Anna Doggett, Susan Hartridge, and Myra Mitchell opened the hospital in 1873 to serve the homeless and destitute tourists who flocked to northern Florida in the winter months. The hospital was originally housed in a two-room cottage with only four beds and was only open during the tourist season. In 1882, the hospital became more formally organized and opened its doors year-round.

CLOCKWISE FROM TOP:
ST. LUKE'S HOSPITAL HAS EVOLVED FROM A TWO-ROOM, SEASONAL FACILITY TO A COMPLEX OF 289 PRIVATE PATIENT ROOMS, MORE THAN 16 OPERATING ROOMS, A SUBACUTE CARE UNIT, A NEW OBSTETRICAL UNIT, AND TWO PROFESSIONAL OFFICE BUILDINGS.

THE FAMILY BIRTH PLACE AT ST. LUKE'S FEATURES LABOR, DELIVERY, RECOVERY, AND POSTPARTUM (LDRP) ROOMS THAT WELCOME THE FAMILY IN A HOMELIKE ATMOSPHERE.

THE FAMILY BIRTH PLACE CARRIES THE PHILOSOPHY OF FAMILY-CENTERED CARE FURTHER, ALLOWING FAMILIES TO MAKE THEIR OWN CHOICES ABOUT CARE WHENEVER POSSIBLE.

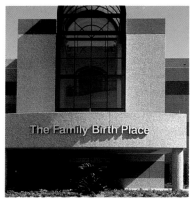

The Family Birth Place

FAMILY-CENTERED CARE

Over the years, St. Luke's has continued to grow and prosper in Jacksonville. The complex is now located on the city's Southside and consists of 289 private patient rooms, more than 16 operating rooms, a subacute care unit, a new obstetrical unit, and two professional office buildings. There are also five off-site primary care facilities, known as St. Luke's Healthcare Centers, throughout the city. St. Luke's employs more than 1,400 technical and support staff, including an all-RN nursing staff, and boasts more than 285 active physicians representing major medical specialties.

St. Luke's is very proud of its affiliation with the nearby Mayo Clinic Jacksonville, a branch of the world-renowned medical center founded in Rochester, Minnesota. As part of the Mayo Foundation, St. Luke's benefits from Mayo's videoconferencing network. This technology links all of the Mayo Clinic locations and their affiliated hospitals around the world. Located only nine miles east of St. Luke's, Mayo Clinic Jacksonville refers patients to the facility if their conditions require hospital admission.

In the spring of 1997, St. Luke's Hospital opened The Family Birth Place, an obstetrical unit that features labor, delivery, recovery, and postpartum (LDRP) rooms—a popular development in women's health care. Designed to handle the needs of a woman through each critical stage of childbirth, LDRP rooms welcome the family in a homelike atmosphere. The rooms feature a full private bath; a dining table and chairs; a television, VCR, and cassette player; and even a sleeper sofa for the father. "We believe we carry the philosophy of family-centered care one step further," says Sharon Hackney, public relations director at St. Luke's. Staff members focus on the needs and wishes of the family, allowing them to make their own choices about care whenever possible.

St. Luke's continues its involvement with Jacksonville's children through its support of the Challenger Learning Center at Kirby-Smith Middle School in the city. The hospital contributed generously to this project at the math, science, and technology magnet school as a "cosmic founder." Kirby-Smith was the first site in Florida for this special math and science educational program, founded by Dr. June Scobee Rodgers, the wife of the late astronaut Dick Scobee, commander of the space shuttle *Challenger*. There are now 28 Challenger Learning Centers throughout the country.

St. Luke's Hospital has come a long way since its founding in a two-room cottage. And today, the hospital serves many more residents than tourists. But the goals of providing quality health care to the community have not changed.

M.D. Moody & Sons, Inc.

MORE THAN 80 YEARS AGO, MAX MOODY STARTED A SMALL BUSINESS in Jacksonville for selling construction equipment to road builders. Today, that business is one of the top dealerships in the country for heavy construction equipment rental, sales, service, and parts. Now employing nearly 300, the company still bears its founder's name, and M.D. Moody & Sons is still a family business, with the third and fourth generations of Moodys now at the helm of this solid, American business.

Growing a Family Business

Max Moody founded his business in 1913, and for many years he played multiple roles in the day-to-day operations, including salesman, parts manager, and serviceman. Several decades later, the business was appointed as the Florida distributor for American Hoist & Derrick Company, now known as American Crane Corporation. The crane business proved to be Moody's niche, and the Jacksonville company quickly became the top distributor of American Crane's products in the United States.

In the 1940s, Max's sons, Max Jr. and Mueller, joined the business, and the company incorporated as M.D. Moody & Sons. The brothers took control after their father's death in 1949, and Max Jr. became president. Under his leadership, the company experienced a period of growth and expansion that included moving to its current headquarters on Phillips Highway in Jacksonville, as well as the establishment of branch offices in Tampa and Fort Lauderdale.

With the American Crane Corporation dealership as its main line of business, M.D. Moody & Sons has continued to excel. Today, the company is consistently ranked as the largest American Crane dealer in the world and the 10th-largest crane rental business globally for all crane manufacturers.

Diversification Ensures Success

The third generation of Moodys took the reins in 1987, when Max Moody III became president of M.D. Moody & Sons. The grandson of the founder diversified the family business by establishing MOBRO Marine, Inc. Operating a fleet of more than 100 barges and a fleet of tugboats, the company handles the rental of heavy marine construction equipment. MOBRO's barges and tugboats operate all over the world, including the Caribbean basin, Central America, and South America.

Another affiliated company is Moody Machinery Corp., which is based near Atlanta. With a branch office in Savannah, this division handles the sales and service of M.D. Moody's traditional lines in the Georgia region.

Recently, M.D. Moody & Sons entered a new line of business by offering remanufacturing services for cranes. Used equipment is remanufactured at Moody's Jacksonville facility in close cooperation with the manufacturer, American Crane Corporation. The refurbished machine is available at about half the cost of a new piece of equipment, though it is issued a new serial number and warranty. The success of this operation has encouraged Moody to begin offering this service in conjunction with other manufacturers it represents.

Moody equipment has been used on nearly every large-scale project on the First Coast, including the construction of the Buckman, Dames Point, and Acosta bridges, as well as the ALLTEL Stadium, home of the NFL's Jacksonville Jaguars. With a history of quality service, M.D. Moody & Sons is known and respected in its industry for its stability, integrity, and experience.

FOUNDED BY MAX MOODY IN 1913, M.D. MOODY & SONS, INC. IS NOW ONE OF THE TOP DEALERSHIPS IN THE COUNTRY FOR HEAVY CONSTRUCTION EQUIPMENT RENTAL, SALES, SERVICE, AND PARTS. IN THIS PHOTO, MOODY (ON RIGHT WITH TIE AND VEST) IS IN THE PROCESS OF DELIVERING AN ADAMS GRADER TO ST. JOHNS COUNTY IN THE MID-1920S.

Barnett Banks, Inc.

J ACKSONVILLE HAS BEEN CHARACTERIZED AS A BOOMTOWN IN RECENT years, as the city has grown into national prominence through its exceptional quality of life, a business-friendly environment, and a new National Football League franchise. The city's current trend as a strong growth market echoes a pattern similar to

when Jacksonville was still in its infancy. In 1877, William B. Barnett and his son Bion recognized that Jacksonville held a wealth of opportunity, and decided to open a new bank called the Bank of Jacksonville.

A Family Tradition

The small, upstart bank—which originally opened its office with only William, Bion, and one clerk on staff—survived many tragic and troubled times in Jacksonville. Over the years, the Barnett family established a reputation in Jack-

sonville as businessmen with hearts. The family's bank saw many of the city's citizens and businesses through hard times. When a yellow fever epidemic hit Jacksonville in 1888, many businesses went bankrupt, and residents fled. The Barnetts responded by suspending payments on installment loans and cashing checks for competing banks in distress. Just after the turn of the century, a citywide fire destroyed many homes, businesses, and all of the Barnetts' competing banks.

Through the restoration and rebuilding, the Barnetts provided space in their vault for the other businesses' cash and valuables. In spite of all the tragedy, the Bank of Jacksonville continued to grow and prosper.

After William died in 1903, Bion succeeded him as president and reorganized as Barnett National Bank of Jacksonville in his father's honor. Even after stepping down, it is said that Bion continued to have an impact on the bank's affairs well into the 1950s, when he died at the age of 101. Over the years, other Barnetts took the wheel, including Bion's brother William and later Bion's son, William R. Barnett. In fact, the younger William devoted his entire life to the bank, holding every executive position, including president and chairman, before his retirement in 1973. Today his son, William B. Barnett, carries on the family tradition as an officer of the bank.

Today, more than 120 years after its founding, the bank has grown into Barnett Banks, Inc., named after its forward-thinking founder. It has become the lead-

BARNETT CENTER IS LOCATED IN DOWN-TOWN JACKSONVILLE (LEFT).

ACCORDING TO CHARLES E. RICE, CHAIRMAN AND CEO OF BARNETT BANKS, INC., "WE'RE HELPING OUR CUSTOMERS SAVE TIME BY LETTING THEM BANK HOWEVER THEY CHOOSE, WHENEVER THEY'RE READY" (RIGHT).

ing bank in the state of Florida and one of the top 25 banks in the United States. The company employs nearly 20,000 workers throughout the region and holds more than $40 billion in assets. While continually recognized for its strong financial management and business acumen, Barnett is also known for its innovative programs in support of its employees.

Strong Financial Roots

Even in the early days, Barnett's bank was sound. In a mere 15 years, the Bank of Jacksonville grew from its original $10,000 in deposits to more than $1 million. The bank continues to post substantial gains today, as Barnett Banks, Inc. has reported record profits each year since 1978. Other financial indicators, including the company's earnings per share, revenue figures, and capital ratios, all reflect Barnett's strong, sound financial position.

Barnett has become what is known in banking circles as a superregional bank. Its traditional market includes Florida and southern Georgia, and in these areas, the bank commands the leading market share in virtually every major banking line of business. It is estimated that Barnett has a relationship with 40 percent of Florida's households, 25 percent of Florida's smaller businesses, and more than 40 percent of the state's larger companies. Barnett maintains this impressive market share by continually evaluating its product lines and striving to meet the needs of its diverse customers.

Choices for Customers

The bank is working to expand its investment offerings, create insurance products, and test innovative deposit accounts to attract and retain its retail customers. Barnett recognizes the growth trend in mutual funds

and other investment products, a market expected to grow five times as fast as the deposit market through the end of the decade. In response, it has become one of the few banks to offer both load and no-load mutual funds.

Advances in technology also allow Barnett to provide better services for its customers. In addition to personal computer, automatic teller machine, and telephone banking options, Barnett has opened in-store banking locations in Publix Super Markets throughout Florida. These full-service branches are open seven days a week, with nontraditional hours designed to meet the needs of today's busy consumer. State-of-the-art self-service technology is available, as well as experienced staff to assist customers who prefer a personal touch.

"Our customers want to choose when and where to do business with Barnett," explains Charles E. Rice, chairman and CEO of Barnett Banks, Inc. "With all of these options available, we're helping our customers save time by letting them bank however they choose, whenever they're ready." Keeping its hand on the pulse of new technology, Barnett is investigating new ways to provide better service in the future, such as interactive television and new, more sophisticated ATMs that cash checks and process bill payments.

In today's highly competitive financial services industry, banks have to expand traditional business lines as well as explore new areas for growth and development. Barnett has done that as

BARNETT HAS OPENED IN-STORE BANKING LOCATIONS IN PUBLIX SUPER MARKETS THROUGHOUT FLORIDA. THESE FULL-SERVICE BRANCHES ARE OPEN SEVEN DAYS A WEEK, WITH NONTRADITIONAL HOURS DESIGNED TO MEET THE NEEDS OF TODAY'S BUSY CONSUMER.

CLOCKWISE FROM TOP RIGHT:
ONE OF BARNETT'S CORE BUSINESSES IS
DEALER FINANCIAL SERVICES, AN INDIRECT
AUTO LOAN ORIGINATION DIVISION.

BARNETT'S CARE CENTERS, WHICH ARE
LOCATED THROUGHOUT FLORIDA, PRO-
VIDE CHILD CARE SERVICES FOR INFANT
THROUGH PRESCHOOL CHILDREN, AS WELL
AS A SATELLITE ELEMENTARY SCHOOL FOR
STUDENTS THROUGH THIRD GRADE.

BARNETT HAS BEEN PLACED ON *WORKING
MOTHER* MAGAZINE'S NATIONAL LIST OF
THE 10 BEST COMPANIES FOR WORKING
MOTHERS FOR FIVE CONSECUTIVE YEARS.

well, with recent expansion into mortgages, auto leasing, indirect lending, and other areas. Rather than just establishing these lines as divisions of the bank, Barnett has approached these opportunities innovatively. The bank significantly increased its penetration of the mortgage market by creating a partnership with BankBoston Corporation to form HomeSide, Inc., which has become the nation's seventh-largest servicer of residential mortgages. A service and marketing alliance was formed with Household Credit Services, Inc., one of the country's largest credit card issuers. Barnett also counts among its core businesses Dealer Financial Services, an indirect auto loan origination division, and EquiCredit, a consumer finance company.

All of these business lines are performing well, expanding Barnett's reach beyond its traditional geographic market of Florida and southern Georgia. Rice explains, "Building on core competencies in management, marketing, underwriting, and servicing, we're pioneering national franchises along several lines of strength. These expansion efforts are part of Barnett's goal to be nationally recognized as the top provider of financial services to individuals and businesses."

EMPLOYEE FRIENDLY

While expanding the bank's reach across the nation, Barnett has not forgotten to take care of the people at home. Continually recognized for its employee-friendly practices, even before such programs were popular, Barnett feels that these programs present a win-win opportunity for the company and its employees. The company has been placed on *Working Mother* magazine's national list of the 10 Best Companies for Working Mothers for five consecutive years. "We believe that creating an employee-friendly environment makes Barnett a better place to work, allowing our employees to be more productive," notes Rice. "We understand that our employees need to balance work and family/personal responsibilities."

The cornerstones of Barnett's employee-friendly environment are its care centers, located throughout Florida. The original location at Jacksonville's Barnett Office Park provides child care services for infant through preschool children, as well as a satellite elementary school for students through third grade. A second center opened in 1996 in the heart of Jacksonville's downtown. This $1.2 million family center provides not only child care, but parent education classes, a resource

library, and convenience services such as dry cleaning drop-off and snacks to help ease parents' busy schedules. While the Office Park location is open to Barnett employees only, the new downtown family center is also open to the community. A third center is in development at another Barnett location in Jacksonville. In addition, the company offers dependent care subsidies to its employees who are not able to use the company-sponsored day care centers.

Support of women in the workplace is another tenet of Barnett's philosophy. With women now making up 76 percent of the company's workforce, Barnett has recognized the need to reevaluate some of its management practices. In response, the bank supports several internal programs to aid women. One is the Executive Women Network and Mentorship Program, which provides assistance and encouragement to professional women at Barnett. Another is the Quality of Work Life Goal Team, which promotes progressive planning and development programs to ensure that women receive equal opportunity to compete for top management positions. These initiatives have paid off, as women at Barnett now account for 30 percent of its corporate senior executive staff and 47 percent of its vice presidents companywide. Barnett has been recognized on several occasions as the state's most woman-friendly company by the Florida Commission on the Status of Women. Many other organizations have recognized Barnett as a supportive environment for working parents and career women.

Barnett seeks to support and encourage all of its employees, regardless of their gender or family status. A companywide Workforce Diversity Initiative is in place to help management and staff recognize the inherent differences and commonalities in all people,

and learn how to use that knowledge to benefit their work teams. The bank has a YMCA on-site at several of its office locations, and reimburses employees for dues at other approved Wellness Fitness Centers throughout the state. And Barnett provides one of the most comprehensive benefit packages of any company in Florida, encompassing family, medical, and disability leave; stock purchase options; savings plans; and job sharing opportunities.

A COMMUNITY BANK

While the company strives to support the families of its employees, Barnett also generously supports broader initiatives throughout the state that benefit all of Florida's families and children. The bank is involved in several scholarship programs, including the Commissioner's Academic Challenge and the Florida Education Fund's Black Culture and History Brain Bowl, as well as educational assistance offered through local school boards and college assistance programs.

Barnett's commitment to youth education can also be seen through Take Stock in Children, a program founded by Barnett and supported by other corporate partners, local businesses, and individuals. At-risk youngsters are challenged to stay drug- and crime-free for a reward: a college scholarship. This program assures that all children have the opportunity to develop into productive adults.

Barnett regularly participates in INROADS, a national internship program for minority college students. The bank also contributes both dollars and hours to causes such as Habitat for Humanity, River City Kids' Day, the Boys & Girls Clubs, and Youth and Family Alternatives, Inc., in addition to many other charities and organizations.

Although the Barnett family is no longer at the helm, Barnett Banks, Inc. continues the legacy of William B. Barnett in many ways. The bank is sounder and stronger than ever, with an exceptional commitment to its employees and the communities it serves.

BARNETT'S COMMITMENT TO YOUTH EDUCATION CAN BE SEEN THROUGH TAKE STOCK IN CHILDREN, A PROGRAM THAT TARGETS AT-RISK YOUNGSTERS. THIS PROGRAM ASSURES THAT ALL CHILDREN HAVE THE OPPORTUNITY TO DEVELOP INTO PRODUCTIVE ADULTS.

The Monticello Companies, Inc.

AT ONE TIME, THE MONTICELLO COMPANIES HAD ONE OF THE best-known billboards in all of Jacksonville. The "666" Cold Formula billboard at the company's historic building in the city's downtown was a familiar sight for more than 80 years. Although the sign is gone—the Acosta Bridge is in its place—the company still manufactures the cold formula today, but it has kept pace with the industry, as well, broadening its interests considerably.

Monticello can trace its roots back as far as 1895, when T.S. Roberts developed the original cold medicine. Roberts owned a drugstore in Monticello, Florida, in the north central part of the state. He decided to name his business after his hometown when he created Monticello Drug Company in 1908. The 666 name came from the random number on the form first used to prescribe the cold formula, and it has been used ever since.

Roberts moved the business to Jacksonville in 1912 and occupied the historic building at the Broad Street Viaduct for more than 75 years. While best known for the trademark brand, Monticello Drug Company also was granted the original patent for quinine. In fact, the company supplied the drug to the U.S. government during the construction of the Panama Canal to help fight the spread of malaria. Over the years, the company's product line grew to include nasal spray, cold tablets, and other variations of the original formula.

A Family Tradition

Today, descendants of T.S. Roberts are still in control of the business, though it is now known as The Monticello Companies, Inc. Henry Dean III, Monticello's president and CEO, is the great-grandson of Roberts, and other family members work at the business and sit on its board. Recent generations have expanded the company's reach to include other over-the-counter pharmaceuticals, as well as real estate and banking.

Through a series of acquisitions, the Monticello product line now includes the Black-Draught laxative line, as well as products associated with DeWitt USA, Inc. In 1990, Monticello acquired DeWitt and its wide range of products, which include Otix ear wax removal aid, Clinomyn stain-removing dentifrice, and DeWitt's Pills.

Another of DeWitt's products is Nullo, a deodorant tablet typically used by colostomy and ileostomy patients to neutralize body odors. Interestingly, Monticello found that hunters were using Nullo to help them get closer to game. In response, the company designed Ghost Scent, a variation on the Nullo formula packaged specifically

THE MONTICELLO COMPANIES BEGAN IN 1895 AS A DRUGSTORE IN MONTICELLO, FLORIDA. IN 1912, THE COMPANY'S FOUNDER, T.S. ROBERTS, MOVED THE OPERATION TO JACKSONVILLE, WHERE ITS HEADQUARTERS REMAINS TODAY.

for game hunters. Ghost Scent is now one of the most successful products the company offers.

DIVERSIFIED INTERESTS

While expanding the pharmaceutical lines, Monticello's principals have worked to diversify the company's interests. The company has substantial real estate holdings, including a 5,600-acre tree farm on the city's Westside. In 1995, the company ventured into banking with the purchase of First Trust Savings. Now called Monticello Bank, this small community bank has two offices: one in Jacksonville's Mandarin section and another in Ponte Vedra Beach. "We focus on customer service with a small-town touch," Dean explains, "and also concentrate on small-business lending." The bank was ranked as one of the top 10 Small Business Administration lenders in the region for the first quarter of 1997.

Monticello has recently begun to revamp each of its product lines through new packaging and marketing efforts. As part of this modernization, the company has computerized its entire operation and developed a site on the World Wide Web at http://MonticelloCompanies.com.

Dean, who became president and CEO in 1996, points proudly to the efforts he has made to "move the business into the 21st century." In the future, Dean expects to continue to consolidate and build infrastructure at Monticello Bank, while expanding in the drug business by acquiring more lines. Monticello also plans to strengthen its position in the international market with its over-the-counter products.

The company also has changed its focus in regard to charitable gifts and donations. Monticello now focuses almost exclusively on organizations that provide direct services to children and the homeless, with a particular emphasis on local charities. "This is our home," explains Dean.

"We want our contributions to make our community a better place in which to be a child." Nearly 80 percent of Monticello's contributions go to such local organizations as Episcopal Children's Services and Volunteer Jacksonville. Monticello is also an active member of the Jacksonville Chamber of Commerce and other community and civic groups.

TODAY, DESCENDANTS OF T.S. ROBERTS, FOUNDER OF MONTICELLO COMPANIES, AND OTHER FAMILY MEMBERS AND LOYAL STAFF WORK AT THE BUSINESS AND SIT ON ITS BOARD (TOP LEFT AND RIGHT).

THE MONTICELLO COMPANIES FIRST SOLD ITS COLD MEDICINE AROUND THE TURN OF THE CENTURY AT THIS PHARMACY IN MONTICELLO, FLORIDA. PICTURED HERE IS WILLIE FRED ROBERTS AND HIS WIFE VIVIAN (BOTTOM RIGHT).

MUCH LIKE A PATCHWORK QUILT, BAPTIST/ST. VINCENT'S HEALTH System was built piece by piece over many years, as separate hospitals and health care organizations joined forces to better serve the needs of the community. Today, this integrated system includes five hospitals, a nursing home, home health service,

an occupational health division, and a network of primary care centers, to name a few of its services. The system spans both sides of the St. Johns River in downtown Jacksonville and extends into Jacksonville Beach, Nassau, Clay, and St. Johns counties, and Fernandina Beach as well.

Although many important steps were taken to create Baptist/St. Vincent's Health System, the most significant was the historic agreement reached in 1995, which joined Baptist Health System with St. Vincent's Health System. Separately, these two organiza-

tions were the largest health care groups in the region, and their merger created a faith-based, not-for-profit health care system of unheard-of proportions on the First Coast. Both organizations brought years of experience to the table, as well as a wide array of programs and specialties that contributed to the unique system that makes up Baptist/St. Vincent's today.

A HISTORY OF DEDICATED SERVICE

St. Vincent's traces its roots in Jacksonville back to 1916, when the bishop of St. Augustine asked

the Daughters of Charity to found a hospital in Jacksonville. The original facility moved to its present location on the west bank of the St. Johns in the Riverside section of the city in 1927. With the additions of new units, such as pediatrics and intensive care, the hospital continued to grow over the next several decades. In the 1970s, the hospital took on the name St. Vincent's Medical Center to reflect the creation of a number of subsidiaries, such as St. Catherine Labouré Manor, Inc., a nursing home. Another opportunity for expansion came in the 1990s, when St. Vincent's Medical Center purchased the old Riverside Hospital. This slow but steady growth resulted in a sprawling medical complex staffed by more than 3,000 physicians.

Baptist Medical Center followed a similar path of growth and expansion, but with a much later start. The charter for the original Baptist Memorial Hospital was filed in 1947, and the facility opened in 1955 with 125 beds, 35 of which were reserved for Wolfson's Children's Hospital, the only pediatric hospital in

CLOCKWISE FROM TOP:

TODAY, BAPTIST MEDICAL CENTER OCCUPIES A 16.5-ACRE MAIN CAMPUS THAT INCLUDES THE 190-BED WOLFSON'S CHILDREN'S HOSPITAL; THE NINE-STORY WOLFSON TOWER FOR MEDICAL AND SURGICAL PATIENTS; THE 17-STORY BAPTIST MEDICAL PAVILION, WHICH HOUSES THE WOLFSON CENTER FOR MOTHERS AND INFANTS; A HEALTH AND FITNESS CENTER; AND A HOTEL.

BAPTIST WOMEN'S PAVILION PROVIDES A NEONATAL INTENSIVE CARE UNIT.

MORE THAN 7,000 BABIES ARE BORN EVERY YEAR THROUGHOUT THE BAPTIST/ST. VINCENT'S HEALTH SYSTEM.

WOLFSON'S CHILDREN'S HOSPITAL IS THE ONLY HOSPITAL IN JACKSONVILLE DESIGNED SPECIFICALLY TO TREAT CHILDREN.

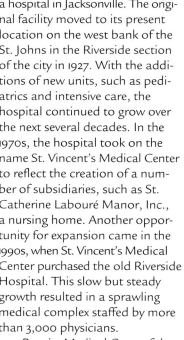

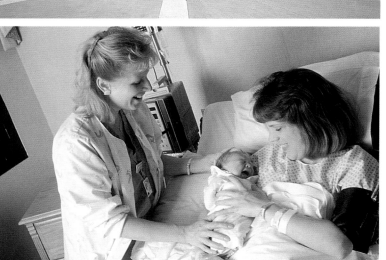

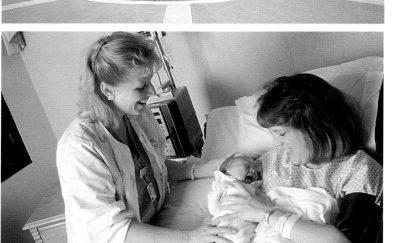

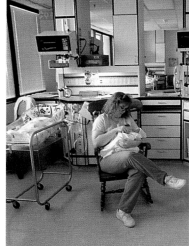

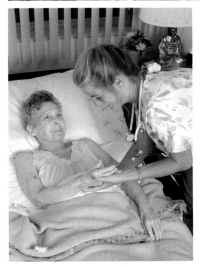

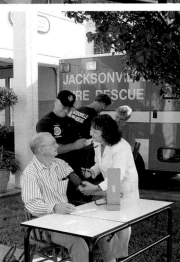

Jacksonville. The hospital grew quickly, establishing a reputation for bringing the latest in medical technology to Jacksonville. Baptist installed the city's first artificial kidney machine, as well as the first hypothermia unit, and was the first to place a battery-powered artificial pacemaker in a patient's heart. In 1977, the hospital became known as Baptist Medical Center, reinforcing its new status as a regional health care powerhouse.

Today, Baptist Medical Center occupies a 16.5-acre main campus that includes the 190-bed Wolfson's Children's Hospital; the nine-story Wolfson Tower for medical and surgical patients; the 17-story Baptist Medical Pavilion, which houses the Wolfson Center for Mothers and Infants; a health and fitness center; and a hotel. In addition, the complex includes the Total Energy Center, a generating facility opened in 1982, which made Baptist the first hospital in the United States to be completely energy independent. The outpatient campus includes the Baptist Regional Cancer Institute, Baptist Eye Institute, Diagnostic Services, and Reid Medical Building, which houses the Jacksonville Orthopaedic Institute.

Other members of the Baptist family include Baptist Medical Center-*Nassau*, which became part of Baptist Health System in 1994,

and Baptist Medical Center-*Beaches*, which joined in 1990. The Nassau facility, located north of Jacksonville in historic Fernandina Beach, was originally founded in 1939 as Nassau General Hospital.

Baptist Medical Center-*Beaches* opened its doors in 1961 under the name Beaches Hospital. It evolved into First Coast Medical Center, eventually reaching a lease agreement with Baptist in 1990. The hospital was renamed and later purchased along with Nassau General. Both acquisitions were followed by extensive renovation projects, which refurbished existing facilities and expanded available services.

Baptist/St. Vincent's Health System also includes many nonhospital divisions that have benefited from the union of the two health systems. The Baptist/St. Vincent's Primary Care network offers 42 locations throughout the First Coast region and includes more than 90 affiliated physicians representing a variety of specialties. Consolidated Health Services, Inc., another subsidiary of Baptist/St. Vincent's Health System, supplies durable medical supplies and equipment, offers pharmacies in a number of locations, and provides outpatient laboratory services, a not-for-profit home health agency, and many more services.

Despite the rapid pace of change at Baptist/St. Vincent's Health System, many things have

remained the same. The new organization still holds firmly to its foundation as a faith-based, not-for-profit health care provider—the principle on which both organizations were founded.

As the new organization continues to grow, it remains involved in a number of outreach programs that make health care more accessible, such as the Parish Nurse Program, the Mobile Health Unit, and the health clinic at the I.M. Sulzbacher Center for the Homeless. These efforts demonstrate the commitment of Baptist/St. Vincent's Health System to its mission: To continue the healing ministry of Christ by providing accessible, quality health care services at a reasonable cost in an atmosphere that fosters respect and compassion.

CLOCKWISE FROM TOP LEFT:
THE SLOW BUT STEADY GROWTH OF ST. VINCENT'S IN THE 1990S RESULTED IN A SPRAWLING MEDICAL COMPLEX STAFFED BY MORE THAN 3,000 PHYSICIANS.

BAPTIST/ST. VINCENT'S HEALTH SYSTEM REMAINS COMMITTED TO ITS MISSION: TO CONTINUE THE HEALING MINISTRY OF CHRIST BY PROVIDING ACCESSIBLE, QUALITY HEALTH CARE SERVICES AT A REASONABLE COST IN AN ATMOSPHERE THAT FOSTERS RESPECT AND COMPASSION.

AS THE NEW ORGANIZATION CONTINUES TO GROW, IT REMAINS INVOLVED IN A NUMBER OF OUTREACH PROGRAMS THAT MAKE HEALTH CARE MORE ACCESSIBLE, SUCH AS FREE BLOOD PRESSURE SCREENING.

BAPTIST/ST. VINCENT'S HEALTH SYSTEM OFFERS HOME HEALTH SERVICE.

PERDUE OFFICE INTERIORS

THE STUDY OF WORK ENVIRONMENTS HAS GOTTEN MORE ATTENTION in recent years, as researchers note that people are more effective, more satisfied, and healthier in certain types of work spaces. Corporate giants took note when they realized that constructively planned office environments raised employee morale and productivity. None of this was news to Perdue Office Interiors. With more than 80 years in the office furnishings business, the company knows that comfort and functionality go a long way toward making workers—and customers—happy.

DESKS, CHAIRS, AND BEYOND

Founded by R.W. Perdue in Jacksonville in 1916, the business rose to distinction by offering furniture made by Steelcase, one of the original manufacturers of metal office furniture, which included filing cabinets and desks.

Today, Perdue provides a wide range of design, facility planning, project management, and refurbishing services to some of the region's largest companies, and deals with more than 200 manufacturers of business furnishings, including Steelcase, Brayton, Vecta, and Details. In 1987, the company became part of Office Environments, Inc. of Charlotte, North Carolina, but the Perdue name and tradition live on in Northeast Florida.

Perdue's business is not just office furnishings. The company employs a professional sales team, as well as a staff of design and planning experts, who use high-tech graphics programs to plan the most efficient and effective use of work spaces. Perdue designers work to combine the aesthetic and practical elements of a project, considering such aspects as furnishings, lighting, and interior finishes. The design team also assists clients in the selection of artwork that will complement their work spaces.

In a recent move, Perdue Office Interiors deployed a full-service floor-covering division. Perdue Floorcovering is a Re:Source Americas partner, featuring Interface, Bentley, and Prince Street commercial floor coverings, as well as various manufacturers of broadloom, vinyl and ceramic tiles, and hardwood flooring.

Perdue is proud of its ability to meet the needs of any customer. It has served clients, large and small, in a variety of fields, including insurance, financial, health care, retail, and automotive dealerships. In the Jacksonville area, Perdue partners with Anheuser-Busch, Blue Cross & Blue Shield, Barnett Banks, CSX, First Union National Bank, Prudential Insurance, and AT&T, as well as federal and local governments. With its extensive product line, Perdue can satisfy any business, regardless of its size or budget.

A FACE-LIFT FOR EXISTING SURROUNDINGS

As a recognized leader in providing services, Perdue is able to offer an attractive option to buying new furniture by reconditioning and improving the appearance and useful life of existing office furnishings. These services include electrostatic

PERDUE OFFICE INTERIORS HAS SERVED THE JACKSONVILLE BUSINESS COMMUNITY SINCE 1916.

NEIL RASHBA

and "baked-on" enamel painting, refinishing, refurbishing, repairs, carpet and upholstery cleaning, and reupholstery. Perdue also offers a full range of maintenance services, which include ceiling tile restoration, air duct cleaning, and ultrasonic cleaning, as well as leather dyeing and repair. When compared to the cost of comparable new furniture, these services can save Perdue's clients up to 60 percent.

Office furniture and equipment are a sizable investment for any business. Perdue helps its clients manage their investment more effectively with its asset management program. Customers' furniture and equipment are warehoused in Perdue's Facility Services Center, which offers more than 95,000 square feet of horizontal and vertical storage, and saves the customer valuable space and money. A computerized inventory system creates an audit trail, which tracks the customer's product and allows for timely retrieval and delivery of product. Customers can even arrange to have their products reconditioned while in storage.

One of Perdue's newest businesses is its retail outlet, Workspace Anyplace. Opened in June 1996, the 16,000-square-foot showroom deals in furnishings for small businesses and home offices. The concept was developed to serve the growing niche market of home-based businesses, a nationwide trend that is increasing rapidly.

Perdue's success has not gone unrecognized. It is consistently listed in the First Coast 50, a local ranking of the region's largest privately owned companies. In addition, in 1996, Perdue received the Steelcase Founders Award in recognition of its overall excellence, as well as its practice of hosting other Steelcase dealers to share best practices. As part of the honor, Steelcase awarded a $5,000 scholarship in Perdue's name to a local university.

NEIL RASHBA

PERDUE OFFICE INTERIOR'S EXECUTIVE MANAGEMENT TEAM INCLUDES (CLOCKWISE FROM FOREGROUND) VIC SUMMERS, PRESIDENT; DORRIE FELDER, VICE PRESIDENT, SALES AND MARKETING; CARL TITUS, VICE PRESIDENT, CORPORATE ACCOUNTS; CHUCK LOWE, VICE PRESIDENT, OPERATIONS; CHARLIE KAMPFE, VICE PRESIDENT, FACILITY SERVICES; AND GAYE HANLEY, EXECUTIVE VICE PRESIDENT.

IN THE MAIN CONFERENCE ROOM, BRAYTON SEATING COMPLEMENTS A CUSTOM-MADE TABLE.

While Perdue takes care of the needs of many of the businesses in the area, the company feels strong commitments to the community. Perdue is a sponsor of such organizations as United Way, Two-gether for Life, American Cancer Society, and Otis F. Smith Foundation.

As business dynamics change and evolve into the next century, Perdue Office Interiors will be leading the challenge. The company is constantly looking ahead, noting emerging trends in work styles and business philosophies, and adapting its services to meet the changing needs of its customers.

SCOTT-McRAE GROUP

THOUGH THE SCOTT-McRAE GROUP HAS BEEN IN JACKSONVILLE for more than 80 years, few residents would recognize the name. That's because the group is better known by the names of its components: Duval Ford, Duval Acura, and Duval Honda. These dealerships, combined with dealerships in Tampa and a variety of dealer support services, make Scott-McRae a long-running success story.

FOUNDED IN 1916 AS THE DUVAL MOTOR COMPANY, THE ENTERPRISE KNOWN TODAY AS SCOTT-McRAE GROUP HAS DEEP ROOTS IN JACKSONVILLE. THE COMPANY'S LOCAL DEALERSHIPS—DUVAL FORD, DUVAL ACURA, AND DUVAL HONDA—AND DEALERSHIPS IN TAMPA HAVE MADE SCOTT-McRAE A LONG-RUNNING SUCCESS STORY.

A LONG HISTORY

Scott-McRae's roots in Jacksonville run deep. Soon after the 1916 founding of the original business, Duval Motor Company, people were flocking to it to purchase Model Ts for $360 each. In 1922, Walter McRae Sr. came on board as an employee, and within a few years he owned the business. McRae is credited with keeping the company together through the tough times of the depression and World War II.

During the war, civilian car production came to a halt. In order to survive, the company dealt in any product it could buy and sell, including pots, pans, and fertilizer. Ernie Kopp Sr., who joined the company in 1923, became "the buyer for everything and anything." Ernie Kopp Jr. joined the business in 1949, and today, Ernie Kopp III is president and COO of one of Scott-McRae's dealerships. The McRae family grew at Duval Motor Company when Walter McRae Jr. joined the business in 1946. He then persuaded his college classmate Jack Scott to come aboard the following year.

Thus began the McRae-Scott partnership that would lead Duval Motor Company into the future. Scott and McRae took a visionary step in 1968 when they decided to move their dealership to Cassat Avenue in west Jacksonville. At that time, Cassat was a little two-lane road in the wilderness. Today, Cassat Avenue is a bustling highway lined with automobile dealerships.

In 1977, Henry "Tip" Graham, a former attorney in Jacksonville, joined the partnership. Scott, McRae, and Graham formed the Scott-McRae Group holding company in 1982, and named Graham president and CEO. Together with Walter McRae Jr., chairman of the board, and Scott, vice chairman, the group continued to grow, establishing dealerships in other cities and with other automakers.

SERVICE AND SALES EXCELLENCE

All of the Scott-McRae dealerships are continually recognized for service and sales excellence. Duval Ford is the oldest continuously owned Ford dealership in Florida, and is a Ford Hall of Fame dealer, counted among the 50 largest dealers in the nation.

Duval Honda, acquired in 1972, was only the second Honda dealership in Florida. It is now rated second in its district for sales and first in customer service satisfaction in the Jacksonville metro area.

Duval Acura, added in 1986, was one of the first 24 Acura dealerships in the country. There are now more than 300 Acura dealers nationwide, with Duval ranked fifth overall and number one in the Southeast. The dealership is also a two-time winner of Acura's Precision Team Award for sales.

Though Scott-McRae may be a somewhat anonymous presence in the Jacksonville community, its companies have contributed greatly to the city. And with its dedication to service and sales excellence, the Scott-McRae Group will continue its long success story for many years to come.

UNDERWOOD JEWELERS CORP.

REATHTAKING JEWELRY, GORGEOUS CRYSTAL, AN AMAZING SELEC-
tion of fine china and silver—all the accessories of the good
life can be found at any shop of Underwood Jewelers.
Underwood's three locations are in San Marco, Avondale, and
Ponte Vedra, in charming shopping districts that encourage

tourists and locals alike to window-shop for perfect pieces.

Underwood Jewelers was established in 1928, and its position as the premier jeweler in Jacksonville has been solidly in place for more than half a century. In recent years, the store's owners have made significant efforts to expand Underwood's outstanding collection to meet the changing needs of its clientele. "Underwood Jewelers was always an upscale store," says Clayton Bromberg, president of Underwood Jewelers Corp. "But as the market has shifted in recent years and demonstrated that it would support an even more sophisticated approach, we repositioned ourselves."

The jewelry business is part of a long family tradition for Bromberg, who served as international president of the American Gem Society from 1995 through 1997. Bromberg Jewelers is the oldest business in the state of Alabama, and one of the 10 oldest continuously family-owned businesses in the country. When the Bromberg family bought

Underwood Jewelers in 1974, it recognized an opportunity to expand into the growing First Coast region.

Herbert F. Underwood, who founded the business, continued to manage Underwood Jewelers' locations in Jacksonville until his retirement in 1980. Underwood is a legend in the jewelry industry in his own right as one of only 25 people to receive the American Gem Society's prestigious Robert Shipley Award. He built Underwood Jewelers from a small jewelry and watch shop in Palatka to a successful, multiple-site business. In the 1960s and 1970s, Underwood expanded the business into nearly all of the region's malls and was a pioneer in television advertising, becoming a recognizable face and name throughout Jacksonville.

But the market began to shift in the 1980s and 1990s, with malls declining and shoppers becoming more conservative. Underwood Jewelers' new management took note, and began to consolidate its locations, eliminating the mall outlets and scouting for more

unique locations in the city's best areas. The company's headquarters is now in its largest shop, in the San Marco district, with additional locations in the landmark building formerly occupied by Richard's Florist in historic Avondale, as well as in the newer Shoppes of Ponte Vedra.

Bromberg says the strategy has worked very well. "Customers are looking for more value," he says. "We have a reputation of integrity and honesty, and we develop a relationship with our customers." Underwood Jewelers' clientele reciprocate with repeat business and with referrals. Bromberg says both are major sources of business for all of his locations.

As a member of the Jacksonville Symphony board of directors, and the Boy Scouts of America board, Bromberg is an active participant in the Jacksonville community. The business-customer relationship is also strengthened through Underwood Jewelers' participation in Jacksonville charitable events. Many customers are involved in local causes, which Underwood helps to support. "There are few businesses this size that do more in Jacksonville than Underwood Jewelers," notes Bromberg.

CLOCKWISE FROM TOP RIGHT:
THE EXTERIOR OF UNDERWOOD JEWELERS'
HISTORIC AVONDALE LOCATION FEATURES
DISTINCTIVE TOPIARIES THAT ARE AN AREA
LANDMARK.

UNDERWOOD JEWELERS OFFERS A
PLETHORA OF CHOICES IN THE SAN
MARCO LOCATION BRIDAL REGISTRY.

UNDERWOOD JEWELERS NOW HAS A
LOCATION IN THE SHOPPES OF PONTE
VEDRA.

UNISOURCE

NISOURCE'S 1996 ANNUAL REPORT BOASTS THAT "VIRTUALLY EVERY business in North America is a potential Unisource customer." And with locations in all 50 states, nine Canadian provinces, and Mexico, as well as the company's diversity of products, there is much evidence to support this statement. The

company distributes a wide range of papers for printing, imaging, and other business needs, as well as a variety of packaging materials for many industries.

Unisource also offers comprehensive products and such support services as material handling, equipment installation and repair, storeroom maintenance, and technical support. Thus, the company is a market leader in the printing, imaging, maintenance supply, manufacturing, and food processing industries it serves. Major clients include UPS, DuPont, and magazine and book printer World of Color.

ROOTS IN PAPER
Jacksonville figures prominently in Unisource's success, with some 800 employees in the city and more than 150,000 square feet of warehouse space. Unisource's Jacksonville operations trace their roots to 1919, when the Jacksonville Paper Company was founded. Over the years, through a series of acquisitions and name changes, the company came to be known

as Unijax, and established itself as a well-known business on the First Coast. In 1986, Unijax was purchased by Paper Corporation of America (PCA), the nation's largest independent wholesale paper distributor and converter, thereby completing PCA's national network of paper distributors. Unijax and its counterparts in the wholesale distribution of paper and office products formed the largest business segment for PCA's parent company, Alco Standard Corporation.

After changing the name to Unisource Worldwide in 1994, Alco Standard decided to spin off the paper distributing division as an independent public company. In 1997, Unisource Worldwide began to be traded on the New York Stock Exchange. Today, Unisource Worldwide is based in Wayne, Pennsylvania, and operates under the leadership of Chairman and Chief Executive Officer Ray B. Mundt and President and Chief Operating Officer Charles F. White. Through the decades of growth, Jacksonville has been a vital part of each company, and remains so today for Unisource.

AT HOME IN JACKSONVILLE
Today, Jacksonville is the site of Unisource's headquarters for the Southeast region, one of five domestic areas designated by the company. Under the leadership of Region President Paul Stewart, the Southeast region consists of 53 locations in 10 states with 2,400 employees. The region includes 2.24 million square feet of warehouse space, and a fleet of 306 of Unisource's signature red trucks, which travel more than 10 million miles each year. The Southeast division of Unisource, which had

JACKSONVILLE IS HOME TO ONE OF UNISOURCE'S TWO SOUTHEAST REGIONAL CUSTOMER SERVICE CENTERS.

UNISOURCE IS A LEADER IN IMAGING TECHNOLOGY SYSTEMS.

sales exceeding $1 billion in 1996, primarily targets general manufacturing, packaging, maintenance supply industries, printing paper, and graphic arts.

Beyond its role as regional headquarters, Jacksonville is the site of Unisource's Converting Division, which makes envelopes, straws, and cutlery kits (prepackaged sets of plastic silverware and napkins). These products are distributed to a variety of customers, such as UPS, CSX, Delta Air Lines, Wal-Mart, and Walt Disney World. This division achieved $40 million in sales in 1996.

Several other consolidated Unisource divisions operate out of Jacksonville as well, making the city an even more important part of the company's future. One of Unisource's two regional customer service centers is located in the city, with more than 200 local employees handling customer service, purchasing, and merchandising functions. Unisource Worldwide's Financial Processing department is also based in Jacksonville, employing an additional 200 Northeast Florida residents.

Unisource is an active member of the Jacksonville community, lending its support to many organizations and causes on the First Coast. The company is a United Way corporate sponsor; a booster of the city's NFL team, the Jacksonville Jaguars; and a contributor to the Jacksonville Zoological Gardens' mandrill exhibit. Unisource and its employees also support many other organizations and events throughout the year in the area.

"One Source. Many Solutions."

Unisource continues to look for new ways to improve its products and services, often through the use of new technologies. For example, the Jacksonville offices are in the process of installing a state-of-the-art, onboard tracking system called XATA in the entire truck fleet. This system will

assist Unisource in compliance with all Department of Transportation regulations, and allow the company to monitor activity, route and track stops and delivery time, and record fuel usage and mileage. Because information will interface with systems at the customer service center, customer service representatives will be able to assist customers more effectively.

At first glance, it may appear that the company's name has nothing to do with its business,

and that is not surprising. Unisource provides such an array of products and services that it is difficult to summarize its business lines. But the company explains its name and its mission in a few simple words: "One source. Many solutions." In its quest to reach virtually every business in North America, Unisource will continue to develop new products and services for the ever changing marketplace, and will work to remain the source for its customers' solutions.

UNISOURCE HAS A FLEET OF 306 SIGNATURE RED TRUCKS SERVING THE SOUTHEAST REGION (TOP).

THE SOUTHEAST REGION HAS MORE THAN 2,400 EMPLOYEES TO MEET THE NEEDS OF ITS CUSTOMERS (BOTTOM).

Miller Electric Company

T'S HARD TO BE COMPLETELY CERTAIN OF WHAT HENRY G. MILLER HAD in mind when he founded Miller Electric in 1928. But it's doubtful that he could have envisioned the business as it exists today. Miller Electric has grown from a fledgling residential and small-business electrical company into one of the largest electrical contractors in

the nation. The company also provides construction, management, engineering, and design services, and has contributed to hundreds of projects in Jacksonville, throughout the country, and even around the world. Through the years, the company has worked hard to preserve its founder's philosophies while expanding the company's reach.

Riding the Wave
Miller established himself in Jacksonville at an opportune time. When the first waves of the growth boom came to the Southeast, Miller Electric was well positioned to contribute to the trend. As industry developed, so did Miller Electric's range of experience and specialization. Many of the industries originally served by the company are still clients today, including pulp and paper, chemical processing and storage, and petroleum handling.

During World War II, Miller Electric worked in defense plants, constructing Liberty Ships at dry docks throughout the Southeast. For its contributions, the company was awarded the Army Navy Production Award, signed by President Franklin D. Roosevelt. The award honors Miller "for outstanding service in the greatest production force in the world today—a united and free army of American workers."

As the region grew, so did the demands for utility systems. Miller worked for many municipal power companies in Florida, including Jacksonville Electric Authority, Seminole Electric Cooperative, and the City of Tallahassee. Over time, a new source of power was discovered: nuclear energy. In 1951, Miller Electric became involved in the construction of one of the first nuclear plants in the country: the Savannah River Nuclear Facility in Aiken, South Carolina. Miller

continued to work at the Savannah River Plant for nearly 40 years, supporting the plant's continuous expansion and providing maintenance functions. While working at Savannah River, Miller set an industry safety record that still stands today—nearly 7 million person hours worked without a lost-time injury.

Seeing the Lights
Miller Electric and Jacksonville grew up together. Many of the buildings in the Jacksonville skyline contain the work of Miller electricians and engineers, including Blue Cross and Blue Shield, Barnett Bank, First Union, Prudential Insurance, and the Florida Theatre, to name a few. Miller has also worked on projects at the University of North Florida and Florida Community College, as well as many area hospitals, hotels, schools, and residential complexes.

BARNETT OFFICE PARK, ONE OF MILLER ELECTRIC'S PROJECTS, HAS UNDERGONE CONTINUAL MODERNIZATION AND EXPANSION SINCE ITS COMPLETION IN 1989.

Today, the pulp and paper industry provides the majority of Miller Electric's business. "We got heavily involved in the pulp and paper industry in the 1970s throughout Florida and the Southeast," says Henry E. "Buck" Autrey, president and general manager of Miller. Since that time, the company has contributed to more than 75 major projects in this industry.

Not all of Miller's contracts involve standard electrical contracting. Through the years, Miller has worked on some cutting-edge projects, including overhead and underground cable installations at Epcot Center in Disney World and the construction of launch complexes at Cape Canaveral. Miller also contributed to an endeavor close to every Jacksonville native's heart: the transformation of the Gator Bowl into the state-of-the-art ALLTEL Stadium. The home of the National Football League's Jacksonville Jaguars, ALLTEL Stadium is now considered one of the prototypes of the modern sports arena.

Miller's Service Group is a 24-hour-a-day, 7-day-a-week resource, providing electrical and telecommunications services, and is one of the largest in the southeastern United States. With more than 60 service trucks equipped with the latest in tools and technology, the company continues to support its slogan: Quality Service Since 1928. The performance of the Service Group's Business Continuity and Disaster Recovery Team throughout the Southeast exemplifies the dedication and skill of Miller's service personnel.

With revenues of $84 million in 1997, Miller Electric is showing no signs of slowing down. The company currently has 800 employees at locations in Jacksonville, Gainesville, and Miami, and at field offices in Virginia, South Carolina, North Carolina, Georgia, Alabama, and Arizona.

Autrey attributes Miller's success and growth to the company's commitment to pleasing the customer. "Customer satisfaction comes first in every phase of our business. The most important lesson we've learned is that repeat business is the key to our continuing success." Autrey also credits the staff of "dedicated, skilled employees." Typically, managers at Miller began as electricians, which ensures understanding between management and line employees. Autrey himself was an electrician with the company for 15 years before becoming president in 1966. Today, he and Jane Miller Wynn, who is Henry Miller's daughter and who serves as executive vice president and secretary/treasurer, are the controlling stockholders in the corporation.

GIVING BACK

Giving back to the industry and to the community is another philosophy that is highly prized at Miller. Autrey served as national president of the National Electrical Contractors Association from 1980 to 1986, and he continues to volunteer at the local and national levels. The company maintains a close relationship with the International Brotherhood of Electrical Workers (IBEW) as well. Miller employees are active in local organizations such as the Boy Scouts, United Service Organization (USO), Young Men's Christian Association (YMCA), and Rotary, as well as many other charitable and civic associations.

Chances are, if Henry Miller could see his company today, he'd be intrigued by the new business lines and wonder at the emerging developments in the industry. And it's a safe bet that he'd appreciate his successors' commitment to the customers and to their employees. Some things never change.

MILLER ELECTRIC HAS MAINTAINED A CONSTANT PRESENCE AT BLUE CROSS AND BLUE SHIELD SINCE ITS BUILDING WAS COMPLETED IN 1971 (TOP).

MILLER ELECTRIC CONTRIBUTED TO THE MODERNIZATION OF ANHEUSER-BUSCH'S BREWERY OPERATIONS (BOTTOM).

▶ AERO-PIC

▶ AERO-PIC

SEABOARD CREDIT UNION

EABOARD CREDIT UNION'S LITERATURE OFTEN STATES THAT IT IS "not too big, not too small, but just right." Its members and regulators all seem to agree. The Jacksonville-based credit union has been growing steadily and presenting solid numbers for more than 65 years, while being rated highly by both government authorities and independent firms.

Seaboard holds fast to the credit union philosophy of people helping people. For this reason, the credit union has chosen to serve the employees of a few key companies in the Jacksonville area—among them CSX Corporation, America Online, and Alco Standard Corporation—even though it is not restricted by its state charter and bylaws from serving other companies and individuals as well. "Seaboard cares for its members by focusing on their individual needs," says Neil S. Maddux, chairman of the board.

This approach has been successful for Seaboard, which holds nearly $86 million in assets and has more than 16,000 members. Additionally, the credit union has a strong capital position, which is a testament to its sound financial management. "We remain one of the most financially sound institutions in the United States," notes Nancy G. Mattox, Seaboard's president and CEO.

THE HIGHEST POSSIBLE RATING

Seaboard has received the highest possible rating from state and federal regulators, based on its capital adequacy, asset quality, management, earnings, and liquidity management. IDC Financial Publishing, Inc.—an independent publishing company that rates credit unions, thrifts, and banks nationally—gave Seaboard a superior rating, based on its calculations of more than 35 key financial ratios. In addition, all member deposits are insured up to $100,000 by the National Credit Union Administration (NCUA), an agency of the federal government.

Seaboard offers its members a wide range of financial services, from basic checking and savings accounts to home mortgages and lines of credit. Seaboard members also enjoy access to an automatic teller machine network that links them with some of the country's largest networks, such as CIRRUS and HONOR. Members also enjoy access to services such as direct deposit and payroll deduction, and they can receive account information 24 hours a day over the telephone.

Seaboard also provides financial planning services, such as annuities and mutual funds, and offers PC Banking service and VISA debit card products. The credit union has an Internet E-mail address, as well.

Seaboard's plans include a move to a new main office location in Southpoint Business Park in Jacksonville in early 1998. The new, 16,000-square-foot, state-of-the-art facility will include 24-hour lobby banking and several drive-through lines, as well as expanded office space to accommodate growing staff and training needs. In addition, children of patrons will have access to several entertainment booths designed especially for them.

Seaboard's history of steady growth, its sound financial footing, and its wide range of member services guarantee that the credit union will be serving the Jacksonville area for many years to come.

SEABOARD CREDIT UNION'S NEW MAIN OFFICE LOCATION IN JACKSONVILLE'S SOUTHPOINT BUSINESS PARK WILL OPEN IN 1998. THE NEW, 16,000-SQUARE-FOOT, STATE-OF-THE-ART FACILITY WILL INCLUDE 24-HOUR LOBBY BANKING AND SEVERAL DRIVE-THROUGH LINES.

CRAZY ELLIOT'S AETNA OFFICE FURNITURE, INC.

MANY RESIDENTS OF JACKSONVILLE KNOW A PARTICULAR STORE on Atlantic Boulevard by its famous sign: A wide-eyed man with a clownlike grin and hair that stands on end, smiling down on the busy city highway. This sign depicts Elliot Starr, who is better known as Crazy Elliot. His office furniture store has been located in Jacksonville since 1957, and today, it continues to provide customers with friendly service and quality products more than 40 years later.

Originally established as Aetna Office Furniture, the business moved to its present location in 1978, and has since expanded to 30,000 square feet of showroom and warehouse space. The closely held family business employs nine people, including an experienced, professional sales staff. Crazy Elliot's wide selection of new and used office furniture and accessories includes top brand names and modular panel systems. Fast delivery and installation add to the value of the store's inventory. Also, customers always appreciate the store's motto—Nobody, but nobody, undersells Crazy Elliot's!

INNOVATIVE MARKETING, EXCELLENT SERVICE

The original photo of Crazy Elliot in his eccentric glory is treasured by his family members, who have continued to manage the business since his death in 1986. His wife, Renee Starr, is still the owner, while son Scott Starr manages day-to-day operations as president. Another son, Howard, is vice president.

The store's off-the-wall marketing approach has been further developed through its commercials, which originally featured Elliot himself. Over the years, ads have depicted many far-fetched scenes, such as a desk being dropped in the Jaguars' football stadium from a helicopter and furniture being smashed with sledgehammers. Though far from typical, these commercials command the consumer's attention, and they have made Crazy Elliot a permanent icon in the memory of many Jacksonville residents. The company received a Silver Addy—a second-place award recognizing local advertising campaigns—for one of its commercials.

Innovative commercials, an attention-grabbing sign, and competitive pricing are the most obvious ways that Crazy Elliot's competes with the increasing number of large-scale chain superstores currently being developed on the First Coast. Scott Starr explains, "Many of our regular customers appreciate that we are still locally owned and operated, and that keeps their money in the city." In addition, Starr recognizes the importance of the company's smaller size and more personalized approach. "We're not order takers; we're experienced salespeople," he notes.

The business also offers leasing programs, which are popular for many start-up customers. Other clients take advantage of the store's special services, such as outside sales consultations and office planning, layout, and design. As with any product or service offered by Crazy Elliot's, the customer's satisfaction is always guaranteed.

Crazy Elliot's continues to compete and succeed against many other office furniture dealers in the area. In fact, the company was named one of the top 15 office furniture dealers on the First Coast in the *Jacksonville Business Journal*'s annual *Book of Lists*. Crazy Elliot's Aetna Office Furniture proves that small-town service can still make it in the big city.

CLOCKWISE FROM TOP: GUIDING CRAZY ELLIOT'S AETNA OFFICE FURNITURE, INC. TODAY ARE (FROM LEFT) HOWARD STARR, VICE PRESIDENT; RENEE STARR, OWNER; AND SCOTT STARR, PRESIDENT/COO.

CRAZY ELLIOT'S WIDE SELECTION OF NEW AND USED OFFICE FURNITURE AND ACCESSORIES INCLUDES TOP BRAND NAMES AND MODULAR PANEL SYSTEMS.

SERVING THE SOUTHEAST FOR MORE THAN 40 YEARS, CRAZY ELLIOT'S IS LOCATED ON ONE OF THE BUSIEST STREETS IN JACKSONVILLE.

▲ JOEY GLASS

▲▼ JOEY GLASS

JEFFERSON SMURFIT CORPORATION

PULP AND PAPER PRODUCTION IS ONE OF THE INDUSTRIES THAT PUT the First Coast on the map, and today, this industry remains strong in the region. For this reason, Jefferson Smurfit Corporation (JSC), a worldwide leader in the production of paper and packaging products, has established an impressive

local presence. Several of JSC's many divisions and subsidiaries have plants and mills in Jacksonville, nearby Fernandina Beach, and Nassau County, making Northeast Florida an important part of this international company's success.

Headquartered in St. Louis, Jefferson Smurfit Corporation manufactures a wide array of paper, paperboard, and packaging products made from recycled paper and renewable forest products. Through strategic acquisitions and an entrepreneurial management style, the company has grown substantially, tripling in size by 1986. In 1996, JSC posted nearly $3.5 billion in sales to more than 10,000 customers throughout North America.

ARRIVING IN FLORIDA

The acquisition of several companies in the First Coast region brought the Jefferson Smurfit name to Northeast Florida. The company entered the local market in 1979 with the purchase of the Alton Box pulp and paper operations in Jacksonville. Jefferson Smurfit later

expanded its local presence with the acquisition of Container Corporation of America's Fernandina Beach mill in 1986. Both mills have been in continuous operation since 1937.

The Containerboard Mill Division of JSC has the greatest presence in the region, including the mills in Jacksonville and Fernandina Beach. Also, the division is based in Jacksonville, making it the only JSC division not headquartered in St. Louis. The Containerboard group produces 1.4 million tons of unbleached kraft linerboard at its mills on the First Coast. This product is used by the group's diverse customers, who typically convert the material into corrugated containers and specialty products for marketing and distribution.

Another related department under the Containerboard Mill Division umbrella is Woodlands Operations. Products include wood chips, pulpwood, logs, and poles. This group handles forestry management and harvesting on JSC's 1 million acres of forestry land in Georgia, Florida, and Alabama.

Through the Woodlands department, JSC spends more than $6 million annually on tree research and advanced forestry practices. The ultimate renewable resource, JSC forestlands are replenished each year with close to 45 million seedlings nurtured in the corporation's own nurseries. While the woodlands are maturing, the lands provide natural habitat for wildlife and a foundation for native flora.

VERTICAL INTEGRATION

One of the ways JSC has remained competitive in its industry is by adopting the practice of vertical integration. Through its involvement in nearly every aspect of the pulp and paper industry—including forestry management, labeling, and paper recycling—JSC has been able to realize substantial cost savings and production efficiency. For example, virtually all of JSC's paper products are made with recycled materials, all of which come from the company's own recycling plants.

Jacksonville is also home to one of JSC's recycling plants, which operate under the name Smurfit

JEFFERSON SMURFIT CORPORATION'S MILL IN FERNANDINA BEACH IS PART OF THE COMPANY'S CONTAINERBOARD MILL DIVISION (LEFT).

THE CONTAINERBOARD MILL DIVISION OF JSC HAS THE GREATEST PRESENCE IN THE FIRST COAST REGION, INCLUDING THIS STATE-OF-THE-ART CONTROL ROOM AT THE JACKSONVILLE MILL (RIGHT).

Recycling Company. The company has three other Florida locations in Fort Lauderdale, Fort Myers, and Tampa. Jefferson Smurfit is the United States' top paper recycler, with nearly 50 plants across the country reclaiming huge amounts of newspaper, cardboard, and other paper products each year. In conjunction with JSC's other recycling arm, Pacific Recycling, the group markets more than 4 million tons of paper each year, and more than half is used in JSC mills and plants across the country. The remainder is sold to domestic and foreign companies, making the recycling division the largest U.S. exporter of wastepaper.

JSC's Container Division manufactures corrugated shipping containers in its 56 plants in the United States, Mexico, and Puerto Rico. Two of the division's plants are located in Jacksonville and Fernandina Beach. JSC maintains its commitment to environmental responsibility by significantly exceeding industry averages in recycled content. In addition, the division offers a full range of quality materials and services, such as graphic and structural design, and mechanical and custom packaging. These features combine to make the Container Division the second-largest producer of corrugated containers in the country.

Another JSC division with locations in Jacksonville is the

Industrial Packaging Division, which manufactures high-quality paperboard and packaging products, such as paper tubes and cores, furniture forms, storage bins, and paperboard pallets. The group is ranked third in the nation in paper tube and core production, making it an integral part of the JSC family.

Jefferson Smurfit's Consumer Packaging Division provides a variety of labels, contract packaging, laminations, and other specialty products. The division's facilities in Jacksonville specializes in the manufacture of heat-transfer labels featuring rotogravure printing. JSC's proprietary labeling system, Di-Na-Cal™, provides effective, high-speed heat-transfer labeling onto plastic containers, and makes the Jacksonville operation an

important component of JSC's overall success.

Environmental responsibility is taken very seriously at Jefferson Smurfit, and the corporation supports many efforts to preserve nature. JSC has also teamed up with the Okefenokee National Wildlife Refuge to establish a conservation easement for the protection of wildlife in southeastern Georgia.

Jefferson Smurfit Corporation believes that its success, and that of future generations as well, depends on the preservation and conservation of the environment. This commitment, as well as a determination to remain competitive in the pulp and paper industry, will help Jefferson Smurfit maintain its leadership position in the international marketplace.

CLOCKWISE FROM TOP LEFT: THE CONTAINERBOARD MILL DIVISION PRODUCES 1.4 MILLION TONS OF UNBLEACHED KRAFT LINERBOARD AT ITS MILLS ON THE FIRST COAST.

JEFFERSON SMURFIT IS THE UNITED STATES' TOP PAPER RECYCLER, WITH NEARLY 50 PLANTS ACROSS THE COUNTRY RECLAIMING HUGE AMOUNTS OF NEWSPAPER, CARDBOARD, AND OTHER PAPER PRODUCTS EACH YEAR.

VIRTUALLY ALL OF JSC'S PAPER PRODUCTS ARE MADE WITH RECYCLED MATERIALS, ALL OF WHICH COME FROM THE COMPANY'S OWN RECYCLING PLANTS.

Blue Cross and Blue Shield of Florida (BCBSF)

LUE CROSS AND BLUE SHIELD OF FLORIDA (BCBSF) IS PROUD to be Florida's health care leader and to provide more than 2 million Floridians with access to quality, affordable health care. ✳ By offering an array of health care options, including health maintenance organizations (HMOs), preferred

provider organizations (PPOs), and traditional fee-for-service plans, BCBSF has continued to meet the changing needs of its customers for more than 50 years. The company was created when the Florida Hospital Service Corporation, the forerunner of Blue Cross of Florida, began its operations in Jacksonville with a staff of four in 1944. Two years later, the Florida Medical Services Corporation was formed, eventually becoming Blue Shield of Florida. The two companies later consolidated in 1980 to form today's Blue Cross and Blue Shield of Florida.

From those first few employees, BCBSF has grown to become one of Jacksonville's largest private employers and a major force in the Florida economy. And while much has changed in the last five decades, one thing has not: BCBSF's commitment to provide Floridians with quality health care at reasonable cost with excellent service.

Employees at BCBSF share the company's strong sense of commitment, and actively reach out to help communities and neighborhoods in Jacksonville and across the state. Each year,

employees donate food to the Second Harvest Food Bank of Florida; raise money for the March of Dimes, American Heart Association, and Toys for Tots; help build houses with Habitat for Humanity; and make generous donations to the United Way.

Continuous quality improvement is another important component of BCBSF's commitment to provide customers with high-quality health care. BCBSF's Health Options—one of the fastest-growing HMOs in the country and the largest in enrollment of any HMO in Florida—has received full accreditation from the National Committee for Quality Assurance (NCQA), an independent, non-profit organization that accredits network-based health care plans.

This accreditation demonstrates that Health Options meets or exceeds NCQA's national standards for quality management and improvement, physician credentialing, preventive health services, and medical record management.

BCBSF provides its customers with health care that not only meets their needs when they're sick, but goes one step further to help prevent serious illnesses from occurring.

Customers benefit from advantages that include prenatal education and early intervention in high-risk pregnancies; preventive health care benefits that encourage and cover immunizations for children and health screenings for adults; programs designed to improve the quality of life for customers who suffer from chronic conditions such as asthma and diabetes; access to a 24-hour, toll-free number that makes getting answers to health care questions easy; and a range of affordable

BY OFFERING AN ARRAY OF HEALTH CARE OPTIONS, BLUE CROSS AND BLUE SHIELD OF FLORIDA HAS CONTINUED TO MEET THE CHANGING NEEDS OF ITS CUSTOMERS FOR MORE THAN 50 YEARS.

AMY CALFEE

options for seniors. In real terms, these and other programs make a significant difference in the health and well-being of more than 2 million Floridians.

As Florida's health care industry leader, BCBSF also works to keep its customers and other Florida consumers informed about health care issues under consideration in the state legislature or Congress.

Through a coordinated grass-roots program, Floridians who share BCBSF's commitment to make sure America's health care system evolves in a positive direction can get involved. They relate personal experiences and provide information to their representatives in Tallahassee or Washington, D.C., on the impact proposed legislation would have on their businesses, their employees, or their families. Together, BCBSF and concerned Floridians are working to ensure that nothing harms the quality, or raises the cost, of health care.

The health industry is dynamic. As a company, BCBSF is excited about the opportunities ahead to increase the value it provides its customers. BCBSF is expanding existing programs that emphasize wellness and prevention through early disease detection and childhood immunizations, as well as disease management programs that improve the quality of life for Floridians who suffer from such diseases as diabetes, asthma, or congestive heart failure.

Throughout a history that encompasses more than 50 years, BCBSF has delivered on its commitment to provide Floridians with quality, affordable health care. As BCBSF looks to the future, Floridians can rest assured the company will continue to provide the health care products and services that will meet—and exceed—their needs for the next 50 years.

BLUE CROSS AND BLUE SHIELD OF FLORIDA EMPLOYEES HAVE BEEN PARTICIPANTS IN THE AMERICAN HEART ASSOCIATION HEART WALK IN JACKSONVILLE.

BLUE CROSS AND BLUE SHIELD OF FLORIDA HAS GROWN TO BECOME ONE OF JACKSONVILLE'S LARGEST PRIVATE EMPLOYERS AND A MAJOR FORCE IN THE FLORIDA ECONOMY.

Kuhn Flowers

KUHN FLOWERS IS A FIXTURE IN JACKSONVILLE, AS MUCH AS THE ST. Johns River and the Jaguars. This homegrown business has been in Jacksonville for more than 50 years, and has established itself as a leader in the city and in its industry as well. While Kuhn Flowers is a huge operation by floral industry standards, its

management has not forgotten the personal and enjoyable nature of the work.

"We're only as good as the last order we sent out" is a favorite saying of Kuhn's president, Bill Cutting. Even by this standard, Kuhn Flowers does very well. The business employs more than 100 people in its four locations in the First Coast region and is consistently ranked in the top 10 nationally for flower sales, with more than $10 million in sales annually. Yet despite all the success, Cutting realizes that the measure of the business's success comes down to beautiful flowers arranged creatively and delivered on time, every time.

"Our business is built on the daily business," explains Cutting. This statement is supported by Cutting's sales statistics, which show that only about 28 percent of the company's business is attributable to major flower holidays, such as Mother's Day, Valentine's Day, and Christmas. Kuhn Flowers does an average of 400 deliveries a day, utilizing its own fleet of 22 trucks. On its busiest day,

Valentine's Day, this number can jump to more than 4,000 deliveries. But day in and day out, Kuhn employees work to make each arrangement special.

Kuhn Flowers is perhaps best known in the Jacksonville area for its elaborate holiday displays—particularly the Christmas extravaganza—at its headquarters location on Beach Boulevard. Since 1972, the company has created the 75-foot holiday display, which features up to 45 animated Santas, elves, and bears, as well

as seven themed Christmas trees and huge hanging wreaths. Each year, five people work for nearly a week to create the display, unveiling it a week before Thanksgiving and dismantling it after New Year's Day. Visiting the Beach Boulevard shop is now a First Coast holiday tradition, with admirers traveling from as far away as Georgia.

Yesterday and Today

Bob Kuhn started the business in 1947 on West Duval Street in

WITH FOUR LOCATIONS IN THE FIRST COAST REGION, KUHN FLOWERS IS CONSISTENTLY RANKED IN THE TOP 10 NATIONALLY FOR FLOWER SALES.

downtown Jacksonville. He met his future wife and business partner, Nancy, at a florist convention in Miami, and the two of them worked together for more than 30 years building their business. Cutting wasn't their only long-term employee; the company today has many staff members who have been with Kuhn Flowers for many years. Through strategic acquisitions, a commitment to excellence, and a lot of hard work, the Kuhns led their flower business to national prominence, reaching the $1 million mark in sales by 1972.

Cutting has been president of Kuhn Flowers since 1984, when the business was acquired by Miami-based Exotic Gardens. But this is not his first experience with the company. Cutting originally worked for the Kuhns from 1958 to 1973, when he left for a position with Florists Transworld Delivery, better known as FTD. When the founders retired in 1984, Cutting returned to the business as president.

Since his return to the company, Cutting has instituted a fully computerized, on-line order entry system. Kuhn Flowers was one of the first in the industry to use technology to increase the speed and accuracy of telephone orders. Today, approximately 85 percent of Kuhn's business comes from telephone orders, and the

business supports 40 full-time incoming telephone lines to handle the volume, which averages about 1,200 calls per day. Cutting himself frequently answers incoming calls that are routed to his telephone when all telemarketing representatives are busy. The on-line system allows each order to be routed automatically to the Kuhn location that will handle that order; the system also automatically prints out the card and envelope that will accompany each order.

Cutting has also led the expansion of Kuhn Flowers by opening new locations and acquiring competitors and related businesses. In the 1990s, Kuhn has opened stores in Jacksonville's Westside, Ponte

Vedra Beach, and St. Augustine. Plans call for continued growth, with a number of sites in the region currently under consideration.

Aside from its holiday decorations, Kuhn Flowers has also established a reputation in Jacksonville for its caring and generosity to those less fortunate. "We include a large budget for charities each year," says Cutting. The company strives to help people who are in circumstances beyond their control by giving to organizations such as the Ronald McDonald House, the Children's Miracle Network, and the Hubbard House, a local shelter for battered women. For Kuhn Flowers, it's all part of being a contributing member of the Jacksonville community.

KUHN MAKES AN AVERAGE OF 400 DELIVERIES A DAY, UTILIZING ITS OWN FLEET OF 22 TRUCKS. DAY IN AND DAY OUT, KUHN EMPLOYEES WORK TO MAKE EACH ARRANGEMENT SPECIAL.

WJXT

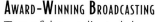

N JACKSONVILLE, WJXT IS KNOWN AS "THE ONE AND ONLY Channel 4." While it is certainly true that WJXT is the only television station to hold this position on the dial, it is also true that WJXT offers the city unique programming that has grown out of a rich history in Jacksonville and a long-standing tradition in the broadcast industry. In 1949, WJXT—then known under the call letters WMBR—aired its first broadcast in Jacksonville from its original location on Main Street. Now broadcasting from a state-of-the-art facility on the city's Southbank, the station is Florida's oldest CBS affiliate, with consistently higher ratings than the network receives nationwide. Serving 13 counties in Northeast Florida and Southern Georgia, WJXT is also constantly one of the highest-rated CBS affiliates in the country. WJXT is part of the Post-Newsweek group, the broadcast subsidiary of the *Washington Post.* Post-Newsweek owns six television stations nationwide.

WJXT'S NEW, STATE-OF-THE-ART FACILITY IS LOCATED DIRECTLY BESIDE THE STATION'S ORIGINAL LOCATION.

AWARD-WINNING BROADCASTING

Two of the syndicated shows on Channel 4's current roster have received the highest ratings among all national affiliates, namely, *The Oprah Winfrey Show* and *Inside Edition.* But local programming also does quite well. WJXT's *Eyewitness News at 6:00 PM* is watched by more people each day than all the other local newscasts combined. The station credits this to the excellence of its reporting and the stability of its news team.

Indeed, WJXT's news team has been recognized many times by its peers. *Eyewitness News* recently received the 1997 National Edward R. Murrow Award for Overall Excellence. This award was presented to News Director Mike Stutz by Walter Cronkite. The news team has also been honored three times with the prestigious Dupont-Columbia award for journalistic excellence and twice with the Chris McGill Award for Overall Coverage (1996 and 1997) by the Florida Associated Press. The station is a repeat recipient of many other awards from the broadcast news industry, including the Suncoast Regional Emmys, the Florida Associated Press Awards, the RTNDA Awards, and the Investigative Reporters and Editors Awards.

The tradition of excellence at the station breeds loyalty and stability among the staff. For

THE NATION'S LONGEST-RUNNING FOUR-PERSON ANCHOR TEAM INCLUDES (FROM LEFT) TOM WILLS, SAM KOUVARIS, DEBORAH GIANOULIS, AND GEORGE WINTERLING.

ROB SWEETING ANCHORS THE HIGHLY RATED *EYEWITNESS NEWS AT NOON*.

example, the lead news team—composed of Anchors Tom Wills and Deborah Gianoulis, Chief Meteorologist George Winterling, and Sports Director Sam Kouvaris—have been together for 17 years. This makes them the longest-running four-person anchor team in the United States. Winterling himself recently celebrated his 35th anniversary with the station. Many other journalists have moved on from Channel 4 to national positions over the years, including Steve Kroft of *60 Minutes*.

COMMUNITY INTEREST

With such a long and successful history in Jacksonville, it is no surprise that WJXT also has deep ties to the community and its causes. Over the years, the station has become involved in some unique

projects beyond the usual corporate campaigns and contributions. One example is a telethon the station organized to aid the victims of Hurricane Andrew in South Florida. WJXT produced a special four-hour broadcast four days after the hurricane left thousands of South Floridians homeless and destitute. More than $300,000 was raised in this effort.

In November 1997, Channel 4 proved that charity really does begin at home—by building one. WJXT's employees built a house for Habitat for Humanities in just five days. The project was showcased with live reports and a special "4 on the Road" broadcast.

WJXT is also the home of the annual Children's Miracle Network Champions telethon in Jacksonville, which has become one of the organ-

ization's most successful fund-raisers. In 1996, the telethon broke all previous records by raising more than $1 million. Funds raised in this effort remain in Jacksonville, benefiting the city's University Medical Center and Wolfson Children's Hospital.

Other community service projects include sponsorship of the Northeast Florida March of Dimes Walk-America and the Multiple Sclerosis Society's MS150 Bike Tour. The station also has participated in the Klothes 4 Kids drive and the Voter Van voter registration program.

It's easy to see why they call WJXT "The One and Only Channel 4." Deep roots in the city, journalistic excellence, and a tradition of serving the community add up to a unique and special station.

William R. Cesery Co.

EW SMALL BUSINESSES OPERATE ON A STREET THAT BEARS THEIR own name. But the real estate business of William R. Cesery Co. is among them and can be found easily on Cesery Boulevard, a major thoroughfare in Jacksonville's Arlington section. The Cesery family settled in the Jacksonville area in the early 1900s and became involved in the construction industry. Angelo Cesery, William R. "Bill" Ceserey's father, founded a plaster and tile company that did ornamental plaster work on some of Jacksonville's major buildings, including the St. James Building—now the newly renovated Jacksonville City Hall—and the mosaics in the downtown Morocco Temple.

Out of the Woods

Arlington was almost entirely an area of woods when Bill Cesery

WILLIAM R. "BILL" CESERY, FOUNDER OF WILLIAM R. CESERY CO., WAS DEVOTED TO THE DEVELOPMENT OF ARLINGTON, AS WELL AS NUMEROUS CIVIC AND COMMUNITY ORGANIZATIONS IN THE JACKSONVILLE AREA (TOP).

ANGELO JOHN CESERY (THIRD FROM RIGHT) IS PICTURED HERE WITH THE OFFICE STAFF AND CREW OF HIS COMPANY CIRCA 1910 (BOTTOM).

first examined it in 1950. Born and raised in Jacksonville, Cesery had just returned home after putting himself through the University of Florida. After World War II, he began a construction business. With some help from his brother Carl, Bill Cesery built small apartment houses in the city's San Marco district, on the south side of the St. Johns River. Looking for a new area for expansion, he found a rural area east of downtown— across the river—that was isolated from other parts of the city. Seeing an opportunity, Cesery purchased land in Arlington and developed the first subdivision there, called Lake Lucina, in 1951. As part of that development, he named a small road after his family.

Shortly thereafter, the city constructed the Matthews Bridge, which connects Arlington with downtown Jacksonville. Arlington began to grow, as did the William R. Cesery Co. Through the late 1960s, the company built more than 2,000 homes and hundreds of apartments in Arlington. Cesery was actually one of the first contractors to build garden apartments in Jacksonville. He convinced banks to support him by building the projects in phases of 30 units, and then proving that the idea worked. During the following decades, Cesery continued to build apartments, as well as homes and commercial projects.

William Cesery and the Growth of Arlington

The name of Cesery became almost synonymous with Arlington, and Bill became widely respected for his quality workmanship, his business acumen, and his active leadership in civic and community organizations. The elder Cesery served as a director on the Florida National Bank city and state boards, an elder of the South Jacksonville Presbyterian Church, and a director of the Bolles School, and was a member of the South Jacksonville Rotary.

Bill Cesery Jr., a licensed general contractor and real estate broker, joined the company in 1976 and today is acting president. Other family members involved in the company include Bill Sr.'s daughters Barbara Cesery, a broker who manages the commercial real estate and who is also a well-known artist in the community, and Martha Taylor, a broker and architect who works with the undeveloped property.

Today, Arlington is a fully developed community, and many of its residents continue to live in Cesery-constructed homes and apartments. The company still owns and manages more than 700 apartment units, as well as commercial properties and several parcels of unimproved land earmarked for future development.

The William R. Cesery Co.'s support of community organizations includes the Arlington Rotary, University of Florida Scholarship Fund, Jacksonville Museum of Contemporary Art, Cultural Council, Bolles School, and Jacksonville University, among others. Although William R. Cesery died in 1994, his legacy lives on through the continuing work of his children in the business he built and in the community he loved.

1960-1985

1960	CSX Transportation
1962	W.W. Gay Mechanical Contractor, Inc.
1962	Vistakon
1966	Episcopal High School of Jacksonville
1967	Methodist Medical Center
1969	Bessent, Hammack & Ruckman, Inc.
1969	Coopers & Lybrand L.L.P.
1969	KPMG Peat Marwick LLP
1969	Memorial Hospital Jacksonville
	Orange Park Medical Center
	Specialty Hospital Jacksonville (1992)
1971	Easton, Sanderson and Company
1971	Jacksonville Transportation Authority
1977	MediaOne
1978	Revlon, Inc.
1979	PGA TOUR
1980	Landcom Hospitality Management, Inc.
	The PARC Group, Inc. (1989)
1982	Genesis Rehabilitation Hospital and Centers
1982	WAPE-FM, WFYV-FM, WKQL-FM, WMXQ-FM, WOKV-AM, and WBWL-AM
1983	PSS/WorldMedical, Inc.
1984	IMA Plus
1984	Stein Mart
1985	*Jacksonville Business Journal*
1985	The Stellar Group

CSX Transportation

SINCE THE EARLY DAYS OF COWFORD—WHEN COWS ACTUALLY FORDED the river at the center of today's downtown—Jacksonville has been an important transportation crossroads. For more than 140 years, railroads have played a vital role in the development of Jacksonville and the state of Florida. ✳ Through a series of mergers and consolidations, Jacksonville in recent years has been headquarters for one of America's largest railroads, CSX Transportation. The city's role as a major railroad center promises to grow even more in the future as CSX moves to acquire nearly half of Consolidated Rail Corporation, better known as Conrail.

History in Jacksonville

The history of CSX in Jacksonville began in 1960, when Atlantic Coast Line Railroad moved its headquarters from Wilmington, North Carolina, to Jacksonville. Seven years later, Atlantic Coast Line merged with Seaboard Air Line Railroad of Richmond, Virginia, and the new railroad—renamed Seaboard Coast Line (SCL)—retained the Jacksonville headquarters. Then, in 1980, SCL united with the Chessie System to create a new holding company, CSX Corporation.

Through subsequent consolidations, SCL and Chessie united all of their railroad operations to form CSX Transportation, under the holding company umbrella. Through all of these years of change, Jacksonville remains the headquarters for this industry leader, which now employs nearly 6,000 people in the city and close to 29,000 across the country. With the pending Conrail acquisition, this number will balloon to nearly 37,000 nationwide.

Serving the Nation

CSX Transportation provides rail service to more than 20 states, the District of Columbia, and Ontario, Canada, via 18,000-plus route miles of track. Its trains serve many industries, with concentration in automobiles, chemicals, forest products, coal, and phosphates. Major customers in Jacksonville include Anheuser-Busch, Maxwell House, Owens Corning, Jefferson-Smurfit, Jacksonville Electric Authority, and Jacksonville Port Authority, among others.

Jacksonville is more than just the executive headquarters for CSX Transportation's staff. The city is also home to the company's Transportation Center, which contains all of the dispatching and locomotive management operations for the entire railroad. On average, 1,300 trains are dispatched daily from this center. The Customer Service Center is also located in the city, handling up to 12,000 calls a day for railroad car orders, and shipping and billing information. The Advanced Information Technology Center also makes its home in Jacksonville, maintaining the railroad's computer operations, a vital link in today's fast-paced business world.

The CSX-Conrail merger is expected to significantly improve service quality while reducing costs for the railroad's customers. Benefits such as single-line routes, coordinated terminals and interchanges, and improved equipment utilization will provide greater financial stability for the company and allow the railroad to compete more aggressively with other transportation alternatives, such as trucking. CSX Transportation is confident that the new alliance positions the company for greater growth and expansion in the future.

A CSX Transportation coal train rounds a mountain in West Virginia. The company moves more coal than any other carrier.

EPISCOPAL HIGH SCHOOL OF JACKSONVILLE

TWO EMBLEMS ARE USED AT EPISCOPAL HIGH SCHOOL TO REPRESENT the school's challenging, yet nurturing environment: the roots of a great oak tree and an eagle in flight. School literature explains that these two symbols represent Episcopal's driving principle: that young people should be given a firm foundation coupled with a soaring imagination.

Faculty and staff at Episcopal High School in Jacksonville have dedicated themselves to this goal for more than 30 years. The success of the school's alumni and the enthusiasm of the current student body testify that the school is succeeding.

BUILDING THE CHARACTER OF JACKSONVILLE'S FUTURE LEADERS

Episcopal High School was founded in Jacksonville in 1966 to "develop doers of good and leaders of men." In addition, the founders wanted to create a school where students would receive a well-balanced education, including exposure to athletics and the arts. Today, Episcopal offers all this and more through a roster of more than 100 courses in eight academic areas. Before graduation, an Episcopal senior will have received instruction in not only the core curriculum—English, science, mathematics, and social sciences—but also numerous foreign languages, religion, computer science, and the fine arts. Honors and advanced placement courses are also available in a wide range of disciplines for students who choose to challenge themselves further. A similar course of study is followed at Episcopal's middle school, which serves students in grades six through eight.

Extracurricular activities are not just extras at Episcopal. Every student is encouraged to become involved, whether in the school's extensive fine arts program, on an athletic team, or in one of many clubs. Episcopal students are regularly recognized throughout the state for their artistic talents. In the athletic arena, more than 70 percent of the student body participates at the middle school, junior varsity, and varsity levels in 14 different sports. In competition, the school has brought home numerous championship victories in many different sports. Episcopal's Outdoor Club offers regular excursions to the mountains, white-water rapids, and hiking trails.

But perhaps what sets Episcopal apart from other schools is its focus on character. The school describes the environment as one that "reinforces traditional values such as honor, compassion, care, and concern." Faculty members encourage students to get involved in community service opportunities, which are available for each grade level in both the middle and upper schools. The spiritual focus also supports this ideal through regular worship experiences and religious study. While Episcopal was founded in the Christian tradition, the school is open to students of all faiths, and respects the beliefs of others.

The essential link that makes all of this possible is the faculty. Episcopal's faculty is composed of men and women from all over the world, who are not only outstanding teachers, but also enthusiastic advisers, club sponsors, and coaches. More than 60 percent of the faculty hold advanced degrees, many from the nation's most prestigious universities. Faculty members have been named Rockefeller grant recipients, Tandy Scholars, and Woodrow Wilson Fellows in recognition of their outstanding work.

Episcopal High School recognizes that this exceptional educational experience may not be within every family's financial reach. Through the efforts of the Episcopal High School Foundation, students who demonstrate financial need and meet other acceptance criteria can be part of the Episcopal tradition. Close to 20 percent of Episcopal's students receive some form of financial aid from the Foundation, a fact that reflects the school's commitment to opportunity and diversity in its student body.

PAUL FIGURA

PAUL FIGURA

PAUL FIGURA

CLOCKWISE FROM TOP:
THROUGH REGULAR WORSHIP, PROBING CLASSES IN JUDEO-CHRISTIAN STUDIES, AND AN ACTIVE COMMUNITY SERVICE PROGRAM, EPISCOPAL TRIES TO INSTILL IN ITS STUDENTS A SET OF VALUES AND COMMITMENTS THAT WILL EQUIP THEM FOR USEFUL, SATISFYING, AND UNSELFISH LIVES.

THROUGH ATHLETICS, THE FINE ARTS, AND AN ARRAY OF EXTRACURRICULAR ACTIVITIES, EPISCOPAL STUDENTS ARE ENCOURAGED TO DEVELOP THEIR OWN UNIQUE TALENTS AND INTERESTS.

EPISCOPAL HIGH SCHOOL'S 58-ACRE CAMPUS, LOCATED NEAR DOWNTOWN ON THE BANKS OF THE ST. JOHNS RIVER, OFFERS AN INVITING AND WELCOMING ATMOSPHERE FOR STUDENTS.

W.W. Gay Mechanical Contractor, Inc.

SIGNS PROMINENTLY DISPLAYED THROUGHOUT THE HEADQUARTERS OF W.W. Gay Mechanical Contractor, Inc. proclaim: Our Employees Are the Best in the Business. The company's original founder, current President and CEO William "Bill" Gay, holds this tenet close to his heart. Founded in 1962, the company has always prided itself on being a great company with which to do business, as well as a great place to work, and it has established itself as one of the largest mechanical contracting firms in the country.

Servicing Jacksonville's Skyline

A native Floridian, Gay has lived in Jacksonville since 1939. After graduating from the University of Florida in 1949, he worked in the mechanical contracting field

until he decided to start his own business. W.W. Gay Mechanical Contractor, Inc. today provides a wide range of commercial and industrial mechanical services, from traditional plumbing, heating, and air-conditioning to state-of-the-art communications.

Through its Integrated Communications Systems Company, Gay designs, installs, and services card access systems, intrusion detection systems, and other telecommunications projects, as well as special technology such as air sampling and gas detection.

W.W. Gay also offers facility automation services, such as air quality monitoring and energy management devices. The company has offices in Gainesville, Tampa, and Orlando, as well as offshore sites in the Bahamas and at the U.S. Navy base in Cuba, and serves clients throughout Florida and the Southeast.

With such a wide range of experience, it's no wonder that W.W. Gay has worked in most of the buildings that make up Jacksonville's skyline. Local projects include The Jacksonville Landing, Prime Osborn Convention Center, BellSouth Tower, Independent Life Building, the new Blue Cross and Blue Shield of Florida campus, and Municipal Stadium, home of the NFL's Jacksonville Jaguars. With an extensive client portfolio, W.W. Gay has contributed significantly to the growth of the First Coast.

Those contributions have not gone unrewarded. In 1994, W.W. Gay was named Company of the Year at the First Coast 50 Awards Celebration. This program recognizes the top 50 privately owned companies in the region in terms of revenue. The company has also been recognized consistently as one of the top 10 mechanical contractors in the nation in terms of revenue. Other awards include the Northeast Florida Builders Association's Pillars of the Industry award and Jacksonville University's Colonel Harry L. Kinne Free Enterprise Award. In 1996 and 1997, Gay's colleagues showed their esteem by nominating him for Florida's Entrepreneur of the Year award.

An Eye for Safety

One important area that has brought W.W. Gay recognition is its comprehensive safety policy, which includes pre-job analysis to evaluate potential accident exposure and regular inspections at various levels during a project. According to Henry Beckwith Sr., senior president at W.W. Gay, the firm's safety record improved 25 to 30 percent with the imple-

WILLIAM W. "BILL" GAY IS FOUNDER AND CEO OF W.W. GAY MECHANICAL CONTRACTOR, INC. (TOP).

THIS QUALITY INSTALLATION AT MEMORIAL HOSPITAL JACKSONVILLE WAS COMPLETED BY W.W. GAY (BOTTOM).

mentation of the safety policy. As a result, the company is a three-time winner of Anheuser-Busch's prestigious Alabaster Eagle for Safety award. This national recognition is awarded to contractors with zero reportable accidents. W.W. Gay employees working at the Jacksonville brewery logged more than 320,000 hours in 1994, 1995, and 1996 without a single reportable accident, an amazing accomplishment in a sometimes dangerous business.

W.W. Gay carried its safety commitment a step farther by adopting a drug-free workplace policy. The program's mandatory random drug testing is applicable to all employees, from the CEO on down, both in the office and in the field. Gay was the first contractor in Florida to establish a drug-free workplace, and the program has been recognized since by the State of Florida as a model for other businesses.

Throughout the years, the company has developed a family-like atmosphere, establishing programs that benefit its employees. Through its employee stock own-ership plan (ESOP) and profit sharing programs, W.W. Gay is an employee-owned business. The company's educational assistance program offers financial help with the cost of continuing education. Traditions like the annual Recognition and Awards banquet, the companywide family picnic, and the employees' Christmas dinner contribute to the family environment. While programs like these certainly benefit the bottom line, this isn't the sole motivation. Management at W.W. Gay Mechanical sees these initiatives as win-win opportunities.

This generous spirit extends beyond the W.W. Gay "family" as well. The company has also made major contributions of money, materials, and labor to several community organizations. The Boy Scouts of America's Camp Echockotee in north Florida was completely renovated and made handicapped-accessible, thanks to the company's efforts. Another local camp, Camp Tracy, which serves troubled youth, was rebuilt and expanded after a fire, under

Gay's guidance. And the company regularly donates time and materials to HabiJax, Jacksonville's branch of Habitat for Humanity. W.W. Gay contributes to many other community groups as well, from local Little League teams to the USO and Vision Is Priceless of Jacksonville.

From being an outstanding partner of Florida businesses to being a true asset for the greater community, W.W. Gay Mechanical Contractor, Inc. will continue its quest of excellence well into the next century.

VISTAKON

SINCE THE DAYS OF MARCO POLO, PEOPLE HAVE BEEN USING convex lenses to improve their vision. Now, centuries later, researchers at Vistakon's headquarters in Jacksonville are still finding new ways to make vision correction better, safer, and more convenient. This major international manufacturer develops, produces, and distributes disposable soft contact lenses worldwide, and is credited with three of the most revolutionary product breakthroughs in the history of the contact lens industry.

A division of Johnson & Johnson Vision Products, Inc., Vistakon is one of a wide range of companies under the Johnson & Johnson umbrella that provides innovative consumer, pharmaceutical, diagnostic, and professional health care products. Vistakon originated as Frontier Contact Lenses, Inc., and was founded in Buffalo in 1959. Frontier moved to Jacksonville in 1962, and produced a line of hard contact lenses through 1970. The company's use of innovative technology, combined with the success of its products, attracted Johnson & Johnson, who acquired the company in 1981. In June 1982, the company's name was changed to Vistakon.

The Breakthroughs Begin

In 1987, Vistakon introduced ACUVUE®, the world's first disposable lens for overnight wear. This development has been widely noted as the single most important event in vision correction since the introduction of soft contact lenses in the 1970s. Instead of the time-consuming cleaning and care regimen for other lenses, ACUVUE allows users to wear the lenses continuously for up to one week and then dispose of them.

The new lenses utilized a multipatented process developed by Vistakon called Stabilized Soft Molding (SSM). SSM ensures production of identical lenses, each one meeting exact specifications. This provided the repeatability and reproducibility needed to proceed with a disposable soft contact lens product. In fewer than three years, ACUVUE became the best-selling disposable contact lens worldwide.

But Vistakon did not stop there. The company followed the extraordinary success of ACUVUE with the introduction of SUREVUE® in 1991. This lens, designed to be removed each night, provided the comfort and convenience of ACUVUE to daily-wear contact lens users. SUREVUE lenses are disposed of and replaced every

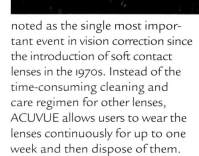

VISTAKON IS THE LARGEST MANUFACTURING EMPLOYER IN THE CITY AND HAS PRODUCTION FACILITIES IN DEERWOOD PARK.

VISTAKON INTRODUCED ACUVUE®, THE WORLD'S FIRST DISPOSABLE LENS FOR OVERNIGHT WEAR, IN 1987, AND SUREVUE® LENSES—WHICH CAN BE DISPOSED OF AND REPLACED EVERY TWO WEEKS—IN 1991. INTRODUCED IN 1993, 1-DAY ACUVUE® LENSES ARE DISPOSED OF AND REPLACED EACH DAY.

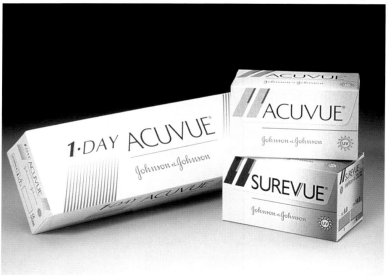

two weeks, with simple cleaning and disinfecting performed each day. This product has also been extremely successful, posting growth each year in the daily-wear contact lens segment.

Then, in 1993, Vistakon unveiled its newest development, 1-DAY ACUVUE®. In reality, this product became what many doctors only dreamed possible—a truly disposable lens. 1-DAY ACUVUE lenses are disposed of and replaced each day, providing the patient with the ultimate in convenience, comfort, and health benefits. To reach the staggering production volume that this product requires, Vistakon developed a totally automated manufacturing process. This new technology, referred to as Maximize, allows Vistakon to provide an estimated 730 lenses annually for each of the hundreds of millions of 1-DAY ACUVUE users.

In a six-year span, Vistakon completely transformed the contact lens market with the introduction of these three products, and experienced substantial growth in the process. Today, the company's international headquarters in Jacksonville employs more than 2,000 people. In fact, Vistakon is the largest manufacturing employer in the city.

Corporate Responsibility

But that is not the only measure of success for the company. Vistakon is a strong proponent of the Johnson & Johnson credo, which emphasizes the corporation's responsibility to the customer, but also to employees and the community as well. "Vistakon is a people-oriented company," says the company's president, Jim Callahan. "Our people are responsible for the success we've achieved."

Vistakon acts on this principle by providing employees with education benefits, diversity training, child care assistance, flexible benefits, and alternative work locations, as well as Johnson & Johnson's

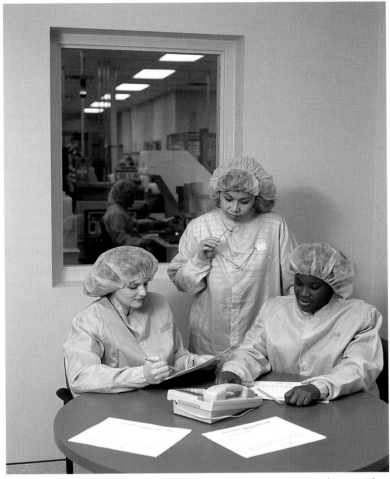

CROSS-FUNCTIONAL TEAMS OF EMPLOYEES PROMOTE A COMPANYWIDE COMMITMENT TO CONTINUOUS IMPROVEMENT AND QUALITY.

health and wellness program. Johnson & Johnson has been noted as a leader in progressive programs to help employees balance work and family issues, recognizing that personal and family concerns impact employee performance in the workplace.

The community aspect of the credo is well exercised in Jacksonville through a number of educational and charitable programs. Vistakon continually makes record-breaking contributions to the local United Way campaign, contributing $1.6 million in 1996, the largest contribution of any company in Northeast Florida by a large margin. The annual blood drive typically receives 100 percent participation from Vistakon employees, and in 1996, some 96 percent of employees participated in the U.S. Savings Bond program. Many other organizations benefit from more than 5,000 hours of community service

put in by Vistakon employees. The corporation demonstrates its support as well, by providing funding to more than 120 charitable groups on the First Coast.

Nationally, Vistakon's Professional Affairs Organization provides scholarships for optometry students and makes donations on a regular basis to the International Association of Contact Lens Educators and the American Optometric Association.

After such an innovative era, what does the future hold for contact lens wearers? "There is no place for complacency in today's marketplace. Customer focus and innovation are the ingredients of success," says Callahan. "That is what will allow Vistakon to move to the next level and continue to shape the future of vision correction." Whatever that future may hold, chances are Vistakon will be in the lead.

METHODIST MEDICAL CENTER

HEALTH CARE FACILITIES SEE THEIR SHARE OF MIRACLES ON A REGULAR basis, but Methodist Medical Center's miracle is unique. The marvel of Jacksonville's "Miracle on Eighth Street" is that Methodist has managed to survive, and in fact thrive, under circumstances that caused many to predict its failure.

DETERMINED TO SUCCEED

Methodist's roots in Jacksonville date back to 1901, when the George A. Brewster School of Nursing opened at the Boylan Missionary Home. The nursing school grew into a small hospital, serving mainly the minority residents of its downtown neighborhood. When the Women's Division of the United Methodist Board of Missions became involved with the facility, its name was changed to Brewster Methodist Hospital.

Under its new name, the hospital continued to provide health care services for the minority community in Jacksonville, growing into a comprehensive facility. When the Civil Rights Act of 1964 opened other area hospitals to its traditional patients, Brewster felt the need to modernize its facilities and reposition itself as a competitor. But costs were prohibitive, and the future

of Brewster Hospital did not look bright.

In 1966, Marcus E. Drewa, the newly appointed administrator, convinced the Women's Division of the Board of Missions not to close the hospital. The organization agreed to lease the facility to a group of local citizens for $1 per year. Drewa then spearheaded a campaign to raise money from local business and community leaders to renovate the dated hospital. Closed for one year, it reopened on October 1, 1967, as Methodist Hospital—the first in the state to feature only private rooms with baths.

Patients flocked to Methodist, and its leaders soon recognized the need to expand its services and facilities further. To that end, the board created a master development plan, which included the addition of two 10-story towers, or

"plazas," to the original hospital building. Plaza I opened in 1975, with the second following in 1980. The new complex houses a gift shop, cafeteria, educational theater, retail shops, and laboratories.

Plaza II also houses a hospice facility—the first of its kind in the state—designed to serve the needs of terminally ill patients and their families through a comprehensive home care program and dedicated inpatient unit.

In 1984, Methodist purchased the old St. Luke's Hospital property and renovated the adjoining buildings. This complex reopened in 1988 under the name Methodist Medical Center.

DEDICATED TO SERVICE

Methodist has developed a wide range of unique health care services to meet the special needs of its patients. Programs like the Diabetes Treatment Center, the Jacksonville Marrow Donor Registry, and the Laboratory for Transplantation and Cellular Immunology have established Methodist Medical Center as one of the most innovative health care facilities in the Southeast. Another groundbreaking initiative was the Jacksonville Transplant Center, the area's only solid organ transplant facility. And today, the building that housed the original Brewster Hospital is home to St. John's Horizon House, a casemanagement agency and residential center for people living with HIV/AIDS.

Through the dedication of a visionary administration, and a few miracles along the way, Methodist Medical Center now stands out as one of the First Coast's finest medical facilities.

METHODIST MEDICAL CENTER HAS SURVIVED CHANGES AND CHALLENGES SINCE 1901, AND NOW OFFERS A WIDE RANGE OF SERVICES TO ITS PATIENTS.

Coopers & Lybrand L.L.P.

THE ACCOUNTING FIRM COOPERS & LYBRAND L.L.P. CELEBRATES ITS 100th anniversary in 1998. Over this century, the firm has grown to include nearly 100 offices in cities across the country and employs almost 16,000 people. Jacksonville is one of the cities to benefit from a Coopers & Lybrand office, and many

of the region's top businesses look to this professional services firm for their accounting and consulting needs.

Service Offerings

The 75 professionals and four partners that make up Jacksonville's Coopers & Lybrand office work in six practice areas to meet the specialized needs of their clients: Business Assurance, Tax Service, Multistate Tax Services, Entrepreneurial Advisory Services, Consulting, and the Human Resource Advisory Group.

In addition to the traditional areas of financial audit, computer audit, and compliance services, the Business Assurance practice also covers health care reimbursement, environmental advisory, litigation support, and other related functions.

Client tax planning and cost-effectiveness strategies are handled by the Tax Service group. This knowledgeable team of consultants works with clients to analyze potential tax hazards and opportunities, and find favorable solutions. More specialized tax assistance can be found in the Multistate Tax Services practice. These professionals assist businesses who operate in several states to minimize their

tax burden, while identifying valuable incentives for establishing new sites.

Coopers & Lybrand's Entrepreneurial Advisory Services team provides guidance to closely held corporations in the middle market. Both start-up and established businesses look to this group for assistance on accounting, tax, and technology issues.

Proving that Coopers & Lybrand is not just an accounting firm, the Coopers & Lybrand Consulting (CLC) division provides a variety of technology, delivery, and management consulting services. Businesses look to this group to assist with complex issues such as performance evaluation and improvement, technology and business strategy development, and organization alignment. CLC also focuses on assisting organizations in developing strategies to address the year 2000 challenge.

The Human Resource Advisory Group provides companies with comprehensive human resources consulting services, including technology services, statistical analysis, and benefit and compensation plan management. Coopers & Lybrand Jacksonville has also developed a reputation

in the area as a strong SEC practice, with significant experience in handling initial public offerings.

Teamwork in Businesses and Communities

Many of Jacksonville's largest corporations utilize Coopers & Lybrand's experience and expertise, including AccuStaff, Inc.; Blue Cross and Blue Shield of Florida; AT&T Universal Card; AT&T American Transtech; Vistakon; PGA TOUR; and the new World Golf Village.

"At Coopers & Lybrand, we strive to foster a sense of teamwork among our people and with the communities in which we do business," notes John Strom, the Jacksonville office's managing partner. That sense of teamwork is strengthened by the firm's involvement in community and charitable organizations, such as the Chamber of Commerce, Cornerstone Economic Development, Junior Achievement, InRoads, and the United Way. The firm also works with the *Jacksonville Business Journal* to produce the "Dozen Done Deals," a special edition of the paper that focuses on the largest real estate transactions in Jacksonville, and the annual Economic Outlook Conference, a symposium for local community and business leaders.

SEVENTY-FIVE PROFESSIONALS AND FOUR PARTNERS MAKE UP JACKSONVILLE'S COOPERS & LYBRAND OFFICE. MANY OF JACKSONVILLE'S LARGEST CORPORATIONS UTILIZE COOPERS & LYBRAND'S EXPERIENCE AND EXPERTISE.

BESSENT, HAMMACK & RUCKMAN, INC.

THE GROWTH IN NORTHEAST FLORIDA HAS BEEN A BOON TO many businesses, but few have been involved in as many aspects of this expansion as Bessent, Hammack & Ruckman (BHR). BHR provides engineering, planning, landscape architecture, and surveying services, including highway design, utilities and land development engineering, and master planning. These skills have met a need in Jacksonville and the First Coast, as communities strive to expand while maintaining a vision for the future.

The founders of BHR had their own vision when they established the firm in 1969. At that time, the company focused solely on civil and environmental engineering at offices in Jacksonville and Lakeland. BHR became Jacksonville's largest purely civil engineering firm, but the founders recognized the need to diversify. Their plan called for balancing BHR's client base between governmental and private sector projects, while expanding the firm's areas of expertise. Land surveying, landscape architecture, and urban and military planning divisions were added, creating a firm that provided a full range of complementary services.

BUILDING JACKSONVILLE

Through its diversity, BHR has made many contributions to residential, commercial, and recreational projects in the Jacksonville area, as well as to the region's infrastructure. "We have engineered virtually everything east of the Intracoastal Waterway from J. Turner Butler Boulevard to the Plantation," notes BHR President Michael Saylor. Referring to the Ponte Vedra and Sawgrass area, surrounding golf's prestigious Players Club, Saylor is understandably proud of the firm's accomplishments.

BHR has been involved in the development of more than 40,000 acres of residential construction, including some of Jacksonville's most prestigious planned communities. The firm was engineer of record for both Regency Square Mall and Orange Park Mall, as well as Barnett Bank Office Park, Prudential Center, Marriott at Sawgrass Resort Hotel, and Jacksonville Landing festival marketplace. BHR has also performed professional services for hundreds of site development projects, such as Grand Haven at Palm Coast and Jacksonville's Westside Industrial Park.

Transportation is another major discipline at BHR. The firm's capabilities include improvements to existing highways, designing new interchanges, and improving drainage and driving safety conditions. The firm has worked on some unusual transportation projects, such as the shuttle bus route for ALLTEL Stadium and the Park Street Viaduct, bridging both a creek and a railway in downtown Jacksonville.

BHR's utility engineering team handles issues such as municipal water supply, sanitary sewer systems and treatment plants, fire protection systems, and industrial

THE ENGINEERING FIRM OF BESSENT, HAMMACK & RUCKMAN, INC. (BHR) HAS WORKED ON SEVERAL LARGE-SCALE PROJECTS IN NORTH FLORIDA, INCLUDING (CLOCKWISE FROM TOP) JACKSONVILLE'S SOUTHBANK RIVERWALK, THE I-10/I-295 INTERCHANGE, AND MEMORIAL PARK.

waste treatment. This division works with municipalities on a general consulting basis and with private utilities in a variety of capacities. The firm's environmental projects range from industrial waste management for Exact Inc., Portion Pac, Winn Dixie, and Seminole Kraft to the wastewater treatment plant expansion for Kings Bay Naval Submarine Base.

As the owner's construction representative, BHR has worked on several large-scale projects in North Florida, including Jacksonville's Southbank Riverwalk, a 1.2-mile pedestrian boardwalk on the bank of the St. Johns River. Another project of note is All Children's Playscape at Ringhaver Park, a five-acre playground on the city's Westside that accommodates physically challenged children. The design and implementation of the playground won BHR the Florida Planning and Zoning Association's (FPZA) Award of Excellence in 1991.

From Gators to Golf

Another well-known project in Jacksonville garnered top honors for Bessent, Hammack & Ruckman. The firm was the master planner and engineer of record in the transformation of the Gator Bowl into the state-of-the-art ALLTEL Stadium. This project involved more than just the stadium itself. BHR integrated the entire 150-acre site into a master plan, an area that includes the surrounding plaza, Jacksonville Veterans Memorial Coliseum, and the city's Metropolitan Park. The result earned BHR another design award.

The firm also has earned a reputation for its golf course and resort community projects. BHR has worked with the PGA TOUR engineering the Players Club at Sawgrass, and with Jack Nicklaus on two signature courses at Grand Haven and Hammock Dunes. The firm was involved in the design and development of the World

Golf Village, a showcase project that includes the World Golf Hall of Fame, the Slammer and Squire golf courses, a resort hotel and convention center, and other diverse amenities.

BHR has extended its reputation of excellence beyond the First Coast. The Florida Chapter of the American Society of Landscape Architects (ASLA) awarded BHR its Award of Merit for the firm's work on the Fort Bragg (North Carolina) Installation Design Guide (IDG). The IDG provides design recommendations that allow for future growth and expansion of Fort Bragg, home of the 18th Airborne and one of the nation's vitally important army installations. In addition to the traditional plan, BHR used today's technology to develop one of the first interactive

Web site design guides for the military.

The founders of BHR long ago established a tradition of public service through local civic clubs and community boards, such as the downtown Rotary, the Jacksonville Electric Authority, and the City's Environmental Protection Board. For five years Saylor has continued that tradition as a member of the Jacksonville Planning Commission, for which he served as chair in 1997.

It is nearly impossible for a resident or visitor to move through Jacksonville without noticing BHR's work. The firm has contributed to many of the landmarks of this bold city, as well as to the underpinnings that support its future growth and success.

THROUGH ITS DIVERSITY, BHR HAS MADE MANY CONTRIBUTIONS TO RESIDENTIAL, COMMERCIAL, AND RECREATIONAL PROJECTS IN THE JACKSONVILLE AREA, AS WELL AS TO THE REGION'S INFRASTRUCTURE. SOME OF THE FIRM'S LOCAL PROJECTS HAVE INCLUDED (CLOCKWISE FROM TOP LEFT) ALL CHILDREN'S PLAYSCAPE AT RINGHAVER PARK, THE JACKSONVILLE LANDING FESTIVAL MARKETPLACE, AND ALLTEL STADIUM SPORTS COMPLEX.

KPMG Peat Marwick LLP

ITH MORE THAN 1,000 OFFICES IN 140 COUNTRIES, KPMG Peat Marwick LLP is a presence in nearly every metropolitan area in the United States and around the world. One of these locations is in Jacksonville, where the Big Six accounting firm serves many of the First Coast's major corporations. ✳ KPMG Peat

Marwick works with 31 percent of the 1,000 largest companies in the world. The firm also services 38 percent of the world's 100 biggest insurance companies and 36 percent of the world's 500 largest banks. These impressive statistics demonstrate KPMG's global status as a business services leader.

A Full-Service Business Resource

The Jacksonville office of KPMG includes approximately 80 client service and support personnel. This experienced group provides a variety of business services to its clients, including personal financial planning, state and local tax advising, guidance for tax-exempt organizations, and business performance improvement services. Beyond the mechanics of taxes and accounting, KPMG strives to form relationships with its clients. "At KPMG, our goal is to be the single best resource for solving the business problems of our clients," says Larry Thoele, managing partner of the Jacksonville office. "To achieve this goal, we are absolutely committed to delivering unsurpassed customer service."

The firm works with a wide range of clients, including large, publicly held corporations; privately owned businesses; and entrepreneurs. Businesses are categorized into five major lines: Manufacturing; Retailing and Distribution; Financial Services, which includes banking, real estate, and insurance; Public Service, serving not-for-profit, educational, and government institutions; Health Care; and Information, Communications, and Entertainment. KPMG also provides tax advising on an individual basis.

Each year, KPMG sponsors a variety of seminars in the Jacksonville area on tax and personal financial planning issues. The firm also cosponsors the annual Excellence in Healthcare Awards, along with AvMed, a health insurance company, and the *Jacksonville Business Journal*. In 1997, KPMG began sponsorship of the Top Rank Florida luncheon, in conjunction with *Florida Trend* magazine. This program recognizes top public and private companies in the state and publishes an annual Top Rank booklet.

Proving that they are "more than just accountants," the staff at Jacksonville's KPMG office participate in a business partnership program with Matthew Gilbert Middle School in downtown Jacksonville. Through this partnership, KPMG managers and staff present monthly seminars to sixth graders at the school on topics such as bank account management, résumé writing, 1040 EZ federal tax form preparation, and business manners. At the end of each school year, the students are rewarded with a visit to the KPMG office, where they enjoy sending each other E-mail through the interoffice system and playing tax games.

KPMG staff have been recognized at Jacksonville's March of Dimes Walk-a-Thon as the top team among all participating accounting firms. Individual employees also volunteer at many local organizations, such as the American Cancer Society, the Boy Scouts of America, and the I.M. Sulzbacher Center for the Homeless. Recognized as a global leader, KPMG truly demonstrates the importance of supporting the local community as well.

REVLON, INC.

GLAMOUR, EXCITEMENT, INNOVATION—THAT IS THE REVLON Vision. For more than 60 years, these words have defined Revlon's image and guided its course to the top of the competitive cosmetics and personal care industry. Among the best-known names in cosmetics worldwide, Revlon stands for quality products at affordable prices.

Revlon was founded in 1932 by brothers Charles and Joseph Revson and chemist Charles Lachman (the *L* in Revlon). At a time when cosmetics were not common for the everyday woman, Revlon developed and manufactured the first opaque nail enamel in a variety of shades. Its overwhelming success sparked the company's forward momentum in the beauty industry with an expanding line that included matching lipsticks, another cosmetic first.

The innovative spirit that marked Revlon's first two product lines has continued to characterize the company throughout its history. Today, Revlon boasts one of the strongest brand franchises in the world, with sales in excess of $2 billion and a presence in more than 175 countries worldwide. Revlon includes some of the world's most popular brands, such as ColorStay, Age Defying, Almay, and Ultima II. It also offers a complete line of skin care products, fragrances, personal care items, and professional salon products. Salon brands include American Crew, Roux Fanciful, Arosci, Realistic, Creme of Nature, Fermodyl, and Voila.

Revlon is traded on the New York Stock Exchange under the symbol REV. The company's Web site can be found at www.revlon.com.

STRONG JACKSONVILLE PRESENCE

Revlon headquarters is located on Madison Avenue in New York City. The company has other important sites around the world including Jacksonville, where Revlon Professional bases its domestic manufacturing and distribution operations. Revlon Professional is one of the largest U.S. suppliers of professional products to beauty salons and is a market leader in professional ethnic hair care and treatment products. It employs more than 1,900 people worldwide, about 450 of whom are in Jacksonville.

Revlon first came to Jacksonville in 1978 when it acquired Roux Laboratories. At the time, Roux—a leader in the professional beauty business that focuses primarily on hair color products—had been in Jacksonville since 1969.

Growth of the business throughout the 1980s increased the size and focus of Revlon Professional and the Jacksonville operation. The facility, which now totals more than 500,000 square feet, produces more than 50 million pieces annually.

PEOPLE AND INITIATIVES

Revlon prides itself on a world-class workforce of trained, motivated, informed, and empowered employees who understand the value of teamwork in bringing winning products to market. Revlon is committed to employee development and offers excellent benefits and support programs competitive with those of other leading global organizations.

On a corporate level, Revlon is committed to supporting women's health issues. In 1990, a gift from the Revlon Foundation helped establish the Revlon/UCLA Women's Cancer Research Program, which conducts leading-edge research into new ways of diagnosing and treating breast and ovarian cancer. Collectively, Revlon has committed more than $20 million to women's health initiatives. Revlon is also committed to supporting the communities in which its employees are located. In Jacksonville, Revlon is a regular contributor to the Jacksonville Fraternal Order of Police, Jacksonville Firefighters, Junior Achievement, PACE for Girls, and River City Playhouse. The company is also a member of and supports the Jacksonville Chamber of Commerce, Florida Chamber of Commerce, First Coast Manufacturer's Association, Jacksonville Urban League, and Jacksonville Chamber Cornerstone.

REVLON BOASTS ONE OF THE STRONGEST BRAND FRANCHISES IN THE WORLD THROUGH SOME OF THE WORLD'S MOST POPULAR BRANDS, SUCH AS COLORSTAY, AGE DEFYING, ALMAY, AND ULTIMA II.

MEMORIAL HOSPITAL JACKSONVILLE/ORANGE PARK MEDICAL CENTER/SPECIALTY HOSPITAL JACKSONVILLE

MEMORIAL HOSPITAL JACKSONVILLE, ORANGE PARK MEDICAL CENTER, Specialty Hospital Jacksonville, and several outpatient centers throughout the area provide quality treatment, care, and service to the people of Northeast Florida. ✳ Memorial Hospital Jacksonville—a 353-bed, acute care facility—offers a full range

of medical and surgical services, as well as specialty areas such as oncology, cardiology, and orthopedics. The state-of-the-art Women's Center provides the latest in maternity care and medical services for women of all ages. The new, 7,200-square-foot Endoscopy Suite recently opened its doors at the hospital as the area's premier endoscopy lab, featuring seven procedure rooms and 12 holding/observation beds specific to gastroenterology and pulmonology. Memorial is also recognized as the only hospital in the region that performs positron-emission tomography scans, a noninvasive procedure used in the early detection of heart disease.

Orange Park Medical Center, opened in 1974, is a 224-bed, acute care hospital in Clay County. Services include cardiac catheterization, inpatient and outpatient psychiatric care, a skilled nursing unit, perinatology and neonatal intensive care, and a Level II emergency department.

Specialty Hospital Jacksonville opened in 1992 as the first long-term, acute care facility of its kind in North Florida. Assisting patients who require a longer stay than would be practical in an acute care hospital, Specialty Hospital features comprehensive wound management, ventilator weaning and pulmonary rehabilitation, treatment for infectious

processes, medically complex patient management, and rehabilitation therapies for ventilator and medically complex patients.

OUTPATIENT FACILITIES
The Memorial Healthcare Centers—located throughout Jacksonville, including Mandarin, Regency, and San Pablo—provide access to physicians and specialists, as well as

ORANGE PARK MEDICAL CENTER (OPMC) IS A 224-BED, ACUTE CARE HOSPITAL IN CLAY COUNTY. OPEN SINCE 1974, OPMC INCLUDES A LEVEL II EMERGENCY DEPARTMENT, AS WELL AS FULL-SERVICE ACUTE CARE AND SURGICAL SERVICES.

MEMORIAL HOSPITAL JACKSONVILLE—A 353-BED, ACUTE CARE FACILITY—OFFERS A FULL RANGE OF MEDICAL AND SURGICAL SERVICES, AS WELL AS SPECIALTY AREAS SUCH AS ONCOLOGY, CARDIOLOGY, AND ORTHOPEDICS.

X-ray, imaging, and other diagnostic services. The Northeast Florida Wound Care Centers, located in Regency and Orange Park, provide care to patients with nonhealing wounds, while five surgery centers, throughout the area, make outpatient surgery more convenient and accessible to patients than a trip to the hospital.

One Woman's Place Cancer Care Center, newly opened in the Memorial Healthcare Plaza, addresses the needs of women diagnosed with breast cancer, featuring the latest in treatment along with a full-service boutique and salon to serve the special needs of the breast cancer survivor. A team of physicians holds weekly breast cancer conferences to discuss current cases and determine the best possible treatment. This team approach helps reduce the time between the discovery of a breast lump and the diagnosis and/or treatment. The innovative inclusion of the salon and boutique helps support breast cancer patients as they recover from their treatment and/or surgery.

COMMITTED TO THE FIRST COAST COMMUNITY

Memorial Hospital Jacksonville, Orange Park Medical Center, Specialty Hospital Jacksonville,

and the outpatient facilities are very generous with time and resources in support of many causes because they know it takes more than medicine to keep a community healthy. They are involved with American Heart Association, American Cancer Society, March of Dimes, American Diabetes Association, United Way, Twogether for Life, Combined Health Appeal, YWCA, Jacksonville Symphony, Museum of Science and History, and many more. The employees participate in many local activities, such as the Juvenile Diabetes Foundation's Walk for the

Cure, the American Heart Association's Heart Walk, and the American Diabetes Association's Walk for Diabetes. The Employee Giving Campaign, a program that encourages employee involvement in the community, enhances the commitment to the First Coast area.

Whether it's improving the health or merely the well-being of First Coast residents, Memorial Hospital Jacksonville, Orange Park Medical Center, and Specialty Hospital Jacksonville are dedicated to the community and its individual residents.

W HEN MEMORIAL HOSPITAL FIRST BECAME INVOLVED WITH Specialty Hospital Jacksonville, its prognosis was not good. The small, community hospital, then known as Jacksonville Medical Center, had suffered years of decline, and had finally filed for bankruptcy in the spring of 1992. W. Raymond C.

Ford became aware of the hospital through his work with an out-of-town health care consulting firm that had been brought in to assist a local health care system, Health South Inc., in its evaluation of an affiliation with Jacksonville Medical Center.

The consultants and cooperating study team recommended that the hospital change its focus to long-term acute care, which would fill a void in the area's health care continuum while complementing the traditional hospital services provided by Health South's other Jacksonville facilities, Memorial Hospital and Memorial Rehabilitation Hospital. Jacksonville Medical Center was acquired by Health South, Inc., the facility's name was changed to Specialty Hospital Jacksonville, and Ford was recruited

PATIENTS AT SPECIALTY HOSPITAL JACKSONVILLE (SHJ) ARE EXPECTED TO TAKE AN ACTIVE ROLE IN THEIR RECOVERY. MORE THAN 85 PERCENT OF PATIENTS RECEIVE PHYSICAL THERAPY DURING THEIR STAY, AND A STAFF OF MORE THAN 150 PHYSICIANS ALLOWS ACCESS TO MULTIPLE SPECIALISTS.

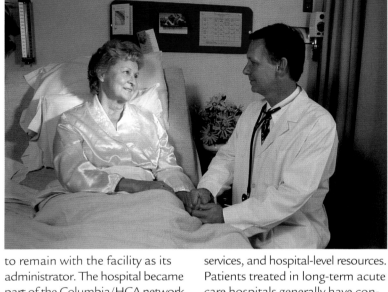

to remain with the facility as its administrator. The hospital became part of the Columbia/HCA network in 1995.

While those decisions pointed the hospital in a new direction, it was only the beginning of a long and arduous uphill climb to its present-day success and solvency. Today, Specialty Hospital Jacksonville (SHJ) is highly successful, with excellent physician and patient satisfaction ratings, rising utilization figures, excellent clinical outcomes, and growing employment. More important, the hospital has operated in the black for the past three years under Ford's conservative and careful leadership.

Serving Jacksonville's Long-Term Acute Care Needs

What is a long-term acute care facility? This relatively new health care term refers to patients who no longer require the intensive resources and critical care environment provided in a traditional hospital, but still have complex medical problems that necessitate aggressive clinical and therapeutic intervention 24 hours a day, extensive physician involvement and ancillary

services, and hospital-level resources. Patients treated in long-term acute care hospitals generally have conditions that require this level of service for an extended period of time. SHJ patients' average length of stay is 25 days, compared to five to six days in a regular hospital.

Facilities like SHJ present an option in which everyone involved benefits. The patient receives specialized treatment in a small, caring environment totally devoted to this type of care. Physicians appreciate that they can refer patients to these specialized facilities and still remain involved in their care, although they may be affiliated with another hospital. And operating costs are typically lower than traditional acute care hospitals, which is a benefit to all.

Long-term acute care hospitals are not traditional hospitals, but they should not be confused with nursing homes. Long-term acute care hospitals serve the sickest of patients. Patients in long-term acute care hospitals typically have multiple body system complications and failures, and are medically complex and severely debilitated. Patients at SHJ are expected to

improve their conditions while under the staff's care, not just receive comfort care. Typical conditions include respiratory complications requiring ventilator weaning and respiratory rehabilitation; spinal cord and brain injuries that result in ventilator dependency; complicated infectious processes requiring extended intravenous antibiotic treatment; and severe wounds and skin conditions. The hospital also specializes in nutritional strengthening for patients who need to become stronger before receiving more treatment, or who have been weakened by treatment they have already received elsewhere. Strengthening includes a full in-house program of physical, occupational, speech, and recreation therapies.

INNOVATIONS IN PATIENT CARE

Specialty Hospital Jacksonville has received recognition for its innovative program designed to help wean patients from ventilator use. Under new protocols developed at SHJ, 55 percent of ventilator-dependent patients are successfully weaned, which places the hospital in the upper echelon of health care programs in this field.

Patients suffering from the effects of spinal cord injuries are

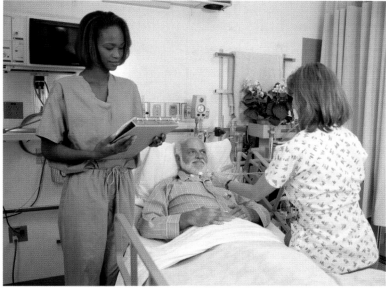

another group who are well served by SHJ. While many of these patients are also ventilator dependent, spinal cord injuries result in many other conditions that the long-term acute care facility is uniquely designed to handle. SHJ treats such patients with a team approach, which includes nurses, respiratory therapists, dietitians, physical therapists, occupational therapists, speech and recreational therapists, psychologists, and many other specialists.

The hospital had been operating in this niche for several years when Health South attracted the attention of Columbia/HCA, which had many other hospitals in the

state, but was looking for a presence in the growing Northeast Florida area.

Long-term acute care hospitals are still relatively rare and offer multiple patient benefits. SHJ is one of fewer than 200 such facilities in the country, and is the only free-standing long-term acute care facility in the Columbia/HCA family of hospitals. For this reason, SHJ receives patients from all over North Florida and south Georgia. In fact, SHJ patients are referred from a wide range of hospitals within a two- to three-hour radius. SHJ's sister hospital, Memorial Hospital Jacksonville, provides about one-third of its patients, while two-thirds come from both in and outside of the city of Jacksonville. "We've become a welcome resource in the medical community," notes Ford.

Less than five years after its repositioning, the hospital is financially strong, and employs more people than at the time it made the transition from a general acute care hospital to a long-term acute care hospital. The facility regularly receives high marks for patient and physician satisfaction. The long-term approach certainly has been effective for Specialty Hospital Jacksonville, which is now sailing into the future in very good health.

SHJ'S VENTILATOR WEANING SUCCESS RELIES UPON A MULTIDISCIPLINARY TEAM APPROACH THAT ENCOURAGES A COLLABORATIVE EFFORT BY ALL CAREGIVERS. THE HOSPITAL'S 24-HOUR-PER-DAY CARE BY REGISTERED RESPIRATORY THERAPISTS IS A KEY TO SUCCESSFUL OUTCOMES.

THE GOAL AT SHJ IS TO RETURN PATIENTS TO THEIR MAXIMUM FUNCTION. EVERY EFFORT IS MADE TO ENLIST THE SUPPORT OF FAMILY AND FRIENDS IN THE RECOVERY PROCESS.

EASTON, SANDERSON AND COMPANY

THE EASTON NAME IS WELL KNOWN IN THE STATE OF FLORIDA. OVER the years, many members of the family have made their mark in the commercial real estate and development markets, from Jacksonville all the way down to Miami. All told, the Easton family owns, leases, or manages more than 9 million square feet of space in Florida. Success seems to be hereditary in this highly competitive field.

The family became involved in commercial real estate and land development in Florida in 1971, when Samuel M. Easton Sr. and his sons purchased the Ambassador Hotel in downtown Jacksonville under the name Easton Land Development. Easton had previously been involved in the lumber and construction business, building 660 homes, but the new company was his first venture into real estate. The hotel did well, and led the family to form a commercial and industrial real estate company, which they called Easton Commercial Real Estate. After several years of success with this venture, Samuel M. Easton Jr. formed Easton, Sanderson and Company in 1979, with partner Wayne Sanderson.

FOCUS ON COMMERCIAL PROPERTIES

Easton, Sanderson's focus is strategic investments and property management of commercial properties. Office buildings and warehouse space make up the bulk of Easton, Sanderson's portfolio, but the company has also developed and managed several residential

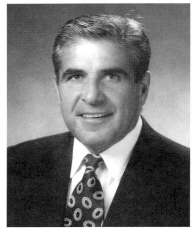

properties. Three condominium developments at St. Augustine Beach, just south of Jacksonville, were developed, built, marketed, and managed by the company. In total, Easton, Sanderson has managed more than 1,000 apartment and condominium units, along with more than 1.4 million square feet of commercial space. These numbers make Easton, Sanderson the fourth-largest property management company in the city of Jacksonville, with sales of more than $10 million annually.

The Eastons are committed to downtown Jacksonville, and the company has been active in the city's River City Renaissance Program, which aims to rejuvenate the downtown business district, among other goals. Easton, Sanderson has made a practice of purchasing older downtown office

EDWARD W. EASTON IS CHAIRMAN AND FOUNDER OF THE EASTON-BABCOCK COMPANIES, BASED IN MIAMI.

MEMBERS OF THE EASTON FAMILY HAVE MADE THEIR MARK IN FLORIDA'S COMMERCIAL REAL ESTATE AND DEVELOPMENT MARKETS. THE FAMILY'S BUSINESSES INCLUDE EASTON, SANDERSON AND COMPANY; THE EASTON-BABCOCK COMPANIES; AND EASTON-BABCOCK & ASSOCIATES, AMONG OTHER ENTERPRISES. PICTURED HERE ARE (FROM LEFT) MAC EASTON, WAYNE SANDERSON, MICHELLE HAM, LAURI SHEPRO, AND SAMUEL EASTON.

buildings, renovating them, and installing modern conveniences while maintaining their historical significance.

The Otis Elevator Building, a Jacksonville landmark since 1926, is an example of Easton, Sanderson's work downtown. After acquiring the building, the company invested considerable money in its renovation, restoring it to its original beauty while adding contemporary elements. More recently, Easton, Sanderson has purchased the Kress Building at 10 West Adams in downtown Jacksonville, another quality historic building, built in 1912 and now renovated for modern use. This type of reinvestment in existing buildings exemplifies the company's commitment to Jacksonville's downtown revitalization.

FAMILY TRADITIONS

Other members on the Easton family tree are involved in commercial real estate throughout the state. The Easton-Babcock Companies, based in Miami, include a development arm, a property management company, an investment division, and Miami's largest industrial brokerage firm. One of the company's most noteworthy projects is the 300-plus-acre International Corporate Park, a $250 million master-planned business park in west Dade County. The business was founded by Chairman Edward W. Easton in 1974, with President Calvin H. Babcock joining the firm in 1989. Easton-Babcock's portfolio includes properties throughout the state. In Jacksonville, the company is involved with riverfront properties, apartments, and warehouses.

Two of Edward's sons are following in their father's footsteps: Edward J. Easton is a broker at Easton-Babcock & Associates in Miami, and William "Mac" Easton works as a broker with his uncle, Sam Easton, at Easton, Sanderson.

Another member of the Easton clan involved in commercial real estate in Southeast Florida is Wayne Schuchts, the grandson of Samuel Easton Sr. Schuchts spent 12 years as an industrial real estate specialist in Jacksonville, and garnered two awards in the industry for several consecutive years. Twice he was named Broker of the Year by the local chapter of the National Association of Industrial and Office Properties (NAIOP). Schuchts has represented many Fortune 500 companies and a considerable number of Jacksonville-based companies in local and national representation assignments. Currently, he is in the process of opening his own business in Fort Lauderdale.

The Easton family has also established a tradition of giving back to the community through charitable works and civic service. Members of Easton, Sanderson in Jacksonville have been active in the local YMCA, the Catholic Church, the Jacksonville Chamber of Commerce, and the local Board of Realtors.

Experience, tradition, family values, honesty, and stability—these characteristics have all become associated with the Easton name in Florida. Through decades of solid business practice and responsible corporate citizenship, the Easton family has earned its title of First Family of Commercial Real Estate.

EASTON, SANDERSON HAS PURCHASED THE KRESS BUILDING AT 10 WEST ADAMS IN DOWNTOWN JACKSONVILLE, A QUALITY HISTORIC BUILDING, BUILT IN 1912 AND NOW RENOVATED FOR MODERN USE.

JACKSONVILLE TRANSPORTATION AUTHORITY

AS WITH MANY BUSINESSES AND ORGANIZATIONS IN JACKSONVILLE, the Jacksonville Transportation Authority (JTA) has its roots in the river. In the late 1940s, transportation was becoming an issue in the city. The growth on both sides of the St. Johns River into outlying areas made the need for a network of bridges and highways glaringly apparent. The Jacksonville Expressway Authority was created in 1953 to address these needs. This organization is the predecessor of today's Jacksonville Transportation Authority, which not only constructs the bridges and highways in Duval County, but also manages the city's growing mass transit system, which includes buses and the elevated and automated Skyway.

In 1971, responsibility for the bridges and highways was combined with mass transit. The Jacksonville Transportation Authority was created by merging the functions of the Jacksonville Expressway Authority and the privately owned bus service. Although several private bus companies had served Jacksonville since 1925, residents were not satisfied with the service, and operators reported growing losses each year.

While the decision to take over the city's bus service was controversial at the time, no one argued with the results, which were seen almost immediately. During the first month of operations, ridership increased by 19,000. JTA also lowered fares, purchased 45 new buses, and extended its service throughout the city. Today, the bus system includes a network of 165 buses, operating on 53 routes accommodating nearly 31,000 passenger trips on an average weekday.

SUPPORTING JACKSONVILLE'S GROWTH

At the same time, JTA also expanded the county's roadway system. One of its first projects under the new organization was to construct J. Turner Butler Boulevard on the city's Southside, which included the Arthur N. Sollee Bridge over the Intracoastal Waterway. Over the years, Butler Boulevard has become one of the city's busiest thoroughfares and home to many of Jacksonville's new businesses, office parks, and residential developments. This project was completed without using state or local funds; instead, bond issues secured by expressway tolls were used to support the city's transportation growth.

In 1989, local leaders championed a shift in JTA funding sources from tolls to a sales tax. Toll booths were torn down on bridges and expressways, and a half-cent sales tax was imposed to fund new JTA projects. The sales tax now provides an ongoing source of revenue, which may be bonded, to support the construction of roads and bridges in Duval County, as well as funding improvements to the bus system.

One JTA project in the late 1980s that has garnered attention is the Dames Point Bridge, which connects the city's Southside area with the Northside. This project was completed under budget, allowing JTA to use the

ONE OF THE 21 NEW NOVA BUSES, DELIVERED TO JTA IN MAY 1997, AWAITS PASSENGERS AT THE NEWLY EXPANDED REGENCY SQUARE SUPER BUS STOP.

THE DAMES POINT BRIDGE, WHICH OPENED IN MARCH 1989, INCREASED ACCESSIBILITY TO THE SOUTHSIDE AND BEACHES AREAS FOR NORTHSIDE RESIDENTS.

additional funds to complete other projects.

Examples of other engineering accomplishments include the interchange connecting AIA and Butler Boulevard; the reconstructed interchange at I-95 and Belfort Road; and the widening of Baymeadows Road to four lanes between San Jose Boulevard and Phillips Highway; and improvement of SR 9A, Heckscher Drive to US 17, from a two-lane to a four-lane divided roadway.

In mass transit, the authority has funded door-to-door services for the disabled through Intelitran Corp. In addition, passengers aged 60 and over ride JTA buses free. Commuter services have also been expanded to include Park-N-Ride and Express Flyer buses for residents of suburban areas. The ever-popular Jaguars Park-N-Shuttle, operating round-trip from seven locations to Alltell Stadium for home games, is a very attractive alternative for football fans who leave the driving to JTA.

KEEPING JACKSONVILLE ON THE MOVE

Perhaps JTA's most noteworthy project is the Skyway, an elevated, 2.5-mile automated monorail-type

transit system that links downtown destinations with high-volume parking facilities, and eventually with other mass transit modes. Introduced in 1989, the Skyway project began with service on a .7-mile guideway connecting the city's Prime Osborn Convention Center and the Omni Hotel on Bay Street. The system is being expanded by adding a segment connecting the downtown campus of Florida Community College of Jacksonville to the Southbank

crossing of the St. Johns River. Stations on this segment will be located at San Marco, Flagler Street, and duPont Center, south of Prudential Drive. When completed, the Skyway will be a major ingredient in the city's mobility, reducing traffic congestion and pollution in the central business district.

What does the future hold for the Jacksonville Transportation Authority? Miles N. Francis Jr., executive director, notes that JTA is a premier partner with the city. "Jacksonville and Northeast Florida are growing and progressing," says Francis. "We need to plan now for the next 15 to 20 years and address the area's future transportation requirements." JTA has begun this process by researching residential and business development trends in the area, and forecasting the resulting transportation challenges. Electric-powered commuter rail lines are one of the first answers to the increasing volume of commuter traffic for the burgeoning suburbs, coupled with ultramodern feeder buses to connecting neighborhoods. With a keen eye on the future, JTA plans to transport Jacksonville into the next century with state-of-the-art solutions.

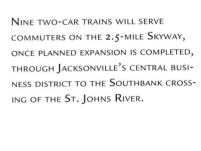

NINE TWO-CAR TRAINS WILL SERVE COMMUTERS ON THE 2.5-MILE SKYWAY, ONCE PLANNED EXPANSION IS COMPLETED, THROUGH JACKSONVILLE'S CENTRAL BUSINESS DISTRICT TO THE SOUTHBANK CROSSING OF THE ST. JOHNS RIVER.

MediaOne

XCITING THINGS ARE HAPPENING AT MEDIAONE. THE NATIONAL telecommunications company is an industry leader in state-of-the-art delivery of entertainment, Internet services, and business communications through a revolutionary broadband communications system. This new technology promises to bring customers the most advanced interactive capabilities that have yet become available to the general public and the business community.

The broadband system enhances traditional cable television service by providing the capability for many other services. MediaOne customers can tune into popular cable television channels, pay-per-view movies and special events, digital music channels that provide commercial-free music in a variety of styles 24 hours a day, and the fastest Internet service available to the home today.

Customers can choose from a variety of channel packages, and need not sign a contract or rent any equipment to access their entertainment service. As the broadband network continues to expand, more channels will be added, and customers will be able to use the broadband technology to get the most out of their entertainment service, with features such as parental controls and interactive programming guides. The broadband network also improves picture clarity and increases signal reliability.

The sophisticated broadband technology also makes two-way interactive communication possible at an amazing rate of speed, since the new cable has enormous capacity. MediaOne provides high-speed Internet access through a cable modem—up to 50 times faster than dial-up modems connected to home telephone lines. Connections and downloading waits are virtually eliminated, regardless of file size. Users can realize the full potential of sites throughout the World Wide Web, since complex files—such as videos, real-time CD-quality sound, and complex virtual reality games—can be transmitted much more quickly and effectively through the broadband cable.

Businesses can take advantage of MediaOne's cutting-edge capabilities through its Business Services division, which provides a single source for high-speed Internet access, local telephone service, and television and music services. Many businesses look to MediaOne for Web site hosting. The NFL Jacksonville Jaguars Web site, hosted by MediaOne, has been recognized for its innovative and useful approach, garnering a spot in *PC World* magazine's Top 100 Web Sites, and in *USA Today*'s Top Sites of the Week.

MEDIAONE IS AN INDUSTRY LEADER IN STATE-OF-THE-ART DELIVERY OF ENTERTAINMENT, INTERNET SERVICES, AND BUSINESS COMMUNICATIONS THROUGH A REVOLUTIONARY BROADBAND COMMUNICATIONS SYSTEM.

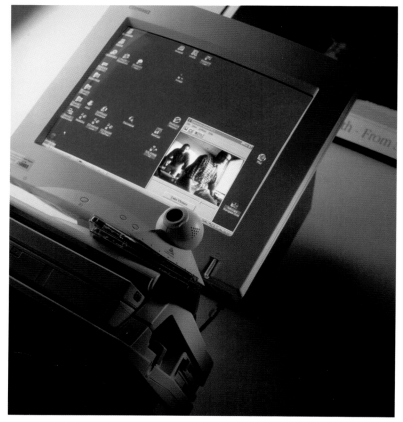

MediaOne can also create intranets for businesses, which link related users through Internet standards and protocols. Employees, suppliers, and other parties with whom a client company interacts on a regular basis can be connected through an intranet in a secure manner that maximizes productivity. This new capability makes telecommuting and multiple-site collaboration a practical and realistic option for forward-thinking businesses.

Although MediaOne is known for the futuristic possibilities it offers, the company remains committed to the old-fashioned value of serving the customer. Customer support is available 24 hours a day, seven days a week, for all MediaOne services. Technicians are guaranteed to arrive within a specified window of time, and MediaOne even offers complimentary at-home problem evaluations for customers having difficulty with the new technology.

While MediaOne is a relatively new name in Jacksonville, the company boasts a strong background in the telecommunications industry. MediaOne is a unit of US WEST Media Group, and is the nation's leading broadband services company, with more than 5 million subscribers in 19 states. In 1996, Continental Cablevision merged into US WEST Media Group, creating a multimedia powerhouse by fusing a premier telecommunications company with a state-of-the-art entertainment provider. Continental, founded in 1963 in Boston, was a legendary ground-breaker in the cable industry and grew from a start-up venture to become the third-largest cable firm in the United States, with assets in excess of $2 billion. Continental bought Jacksonville's 84,000-subscriber system from Area Cablevision in 1984. Continental invested nearly $17 million in improving the original cable system, which had been established in 1977. An active member of the Jacksonville community,

Continental supported many organizations over the years and received several marketing, customer service, and programming awards recognizing its efforts.

Some 20 years ago, Jacksonville residents did not have cable television service or computers in their homes, and the Internet did not exist. Today, all three have become household terms, and MediaOne has combined all three into one powerful telecommunications force, utilizing the phenomenal capabilities of its broadband cable system.

PGA TOUR

PONTE VEDRA BEACH IS KNOWN TO GOLF ENTHUSIASTS AS THE HOME of the Tournament Players Club at Sawgrass, the site of the annual PLAYERS Championship. But many do not realize that the national headquarters of the PGA TOUR also is located in this Northeast Florida community. In these offices, more than 400 employees work year-round to manage the many complex business aspects of this popular and profitable game.

While THE PLAYERS Championship, held annually in March, is the most visible aspect of the TOUR on the First Coast, it is only one component of the diverse operations managed from TOUR headquarters. PGA TOUR, Inc. actually consists of three professional golf tours: the PGA TOUR, the SENIOR PGA TOUR, and the NIKE TOUR. In addition to conducting a number of events, the organization cosponsors more than 120 other tournaments on all three tours.

But there is much more to the PGA TOUR than conducting golf tournaments. In the past 20 years, the TOUR has grown into a multimillion-dollar operation with interests in a variety of areas, such as the expanding network of Tournament Players Clubs and courses; PGA TOUR Productions, a video and television production company; and the new World Golf Village. "Since 1985," says Charles L. Zink, executive vice president and chief financial officer, "the PGA TOUR's businesses have grown enormously from a revenue and asset base of less than $50 million to a projected base of more than $500 million by the year 2000." The city of Jacksonville, located just northwest of Ponte Vedra Beach, has been a major beneficiary of this growth.

A HOLE IN ONE FOR THE FIRST COAST

The PGA TOUR's value in Jacksonville goes far beyond that of an ordinary employer. The First Coast also has greatly benefited from the TOUR's visibility, as the PGA TOUR and THE PLAYERS Championship have attracted national attention and dollars to the area. The additions in 1998 of the SENIOR TOUR's Liberty Mutual Legends of Golf event and the World Golf Village will only increase the TOUR's impact on the area.

"The PGA TOUR has been a shot in the arm for North Florida," says Jacksonville Mayor John Delaney. "The TOUR not only means increased business, prestige, and tourism for our area, but it distinguishes Florida's First Coast as an international golf mecca. Golf brings thousands of people to our community, who, once they get here, recognize everything else that North Florida has to offer."

CHARITIES—A "DRIVING" FORCE

The First Coast's charitable organizations also realize the benefits of the PGA TOUR's location. Since the game's early days, PGA TOUR events and charitable causes have been inexorably linked. It is a long-

FORMER PGA TOUR COMMISSIONER DEANE BEMAN (LEFT) IS PICTURED HERE WITH CURRENT COMMISSIONER TIM FINCHEM.

THE SIGNATURE HOLE OF THE TOURNAMENT PLAYERS CLUB AT SAWGRASS IS THE ISLAND GREEN, NUMBER 17.

PGA TOUR/SAM GREENWOOD

PGA TOUR/SAM GREENWOOD

standing TOUR policy that any TOUR-sponsored event must be structured as a not-for-profit organization and have a charity component. For example, THE PLAYERS Championship has benefited more than 50 worthy causes in the Jacksonville area, including a scholarship program and the TPC Village, a residential treatment center for adolescents with substance abuse problems. In Northeast Florida alone, the TOUR's year-round charitable contributions exceed $1 million annually.

Through the years, more than $300 million has been contributed to charities in communities across the country where TOUR events are played. Each tournament's sponsoring organization selects charities in its community to be the primary beneficiaries, a policy that keeps the funds at a local level. Since 1987, the TOUR has also named a Charity of the Year, chosen from the hundreds of organizations supported by TOUR events.

Funding also is raised through the efforts of PGA TOUR Charities, Inc., the TOUR's own charity arm; the Players Wives Association; and the players' individual efforts. The concept of charitable giving seems to be instilled in each TOUR member. Through the Player Volunteer Program, veteran TOUR members spend time at charities affiliated with TOUR events throughout the year. In addition, many players devote hours of their time to personal causes in their home communities, including Jacksonville. Staff members at the PGA TOUR National Headquarters in Ponte Vedra Beach also take the TOUR's mission to heart, devoting countless hours of their own time to a variety of charitable organizations in the Jacksonville area.

TEEING OFF: THE ORIGINS OF THE TOUR

Although professional golfers in the United States have competed against each other in tournaments since 1895, the players did not begin taking control until the late 1960s, when the TOUR's predecessor, the Tournament Players Division, was formed. The group named Joseph C. Dey as its commissioner in 1969, and established offices in Washington, D.C. Deane R. Beman took over as commissioner in 1974 and retained the title for 20 years. He was succeeded by the current commissioner, Timothy W. Finchem, in 1994.

Beman was largely responsible for bringing the PGA TOUR to Northeast Florida in 1979. He had a vision of creating an ideal tournament facility that eventually would become the permanent home of THE PLAYERS Championship. Introduced in 1974 as the Tournament Players Championship, the tournament initially was rotated among different courses.

Ponte Vedra Beach, just southeast of Jacksonville, attracted Beman's attention, and the TOUR began scouting the area. Finally, a deal was struck with a local family, the Fletchers, to purchase several hundred acres of land in Ponte Vedra Beach—for one dollar. In 1979, the PGA TOUR officially opened the location that eventually became the permanent home for both its headquarters and the tournament.

One of the things that attracted Beman to this area was the success of the annual Greater Jacksonville Open. Beman recognized the community support and volunteer commitment to this tournament each year, and he believed that the TOUR could tap into this resource to support its causes, as well.

THE TOURNAMENT PLAYERS CLUB (TPC) NETWORK

It is hard to believe that a place as beautiful as the Tournament Play-

NUMBER 18 PROVIDES A TOUGH FINISHING HOLE AT THE TOURNAMENT PLAYERS CLUB AT SAWGRASS (LEFT).

THE TPC VILLAGE IS ONE OF THE PRIMARY CHARITIES OF THE PLAYERS CHAMPIONSHIP. PLAYER INVOLVEMENT IS PERSONIFIED BY JACKSONVILLE NATIVE AND 1988 PLAYERS CHAMPIONSHIP WINNER, MARK MCCUMBER (RIGHT).

ers Club at Sawgrass was once known as Cabbage Swamp. But before the PGA TOUR came to town, this was an accurate description of the site. The property had actually been earmarked for a low-cost housing development. Many locals thought Beman and his supporters were delusional when they talked about turning the area into a world-class resort community.

Today, no one questions the TOUR's business sense. Thanks in large part to the presence of the Tournament Players Club at Sawgrass, Ponte Vedra Beach is one of the First Coast's most prestigious addresses. And the Tournament Players Club concept, introduced here, has blossomed into a network of nearly 30 clubs and licensed courses, including sites in Japan, China, and Thailand.

"Golf has become a desirable investment for companies, and PGA TOUR events are a highly attractive benefit that most other courses don't have," says Vernon Kelly, president of PGA TOUR Golf Course Properties, Inc., the PGA TOUR subsidiary that owns and/or operates Tournament Players Clubs. "What that does is help lower the risk and increase the upside, because of this unique benefit that differentiates it from the rest of the market."

For the first time in the history of the game, courses were developed with professional tournaments in mind. Visibility, hospitality, and television coverage issues were considered during the course design. It is estimated that the TPC Network saves tournaments about $9 million annually in rental fees once paid to other courses for tournament use. These savings are passed along to the players in larger purses and to the charities that benefit from TOUR events held on TPC courses.

The Game Seen round the World

Golf tournament attendance and viewership have reached all-time highs in recent years, reflecting the explosion of interest in the game. "The PGA TOUR is enjoying a period of unprecedented popularity and success," notes Finchem. Indeed, times have never been better for the PGA TOUR. Purse and charity levels are up, and the TOUR's total asset value exceeded $300 million in 1996. But Finchem is not one to rest on his laurels. The commissioner states, "Our challenge is to capitalize on the health of, and interest in, our game. Rather than basking in our current success, we need to use our achievements as building blocks for future growth."

Minority involvement in the business of golf has been low historically, but this is also changing, thanks in part to the TOUR's Minority Internship Program. Initiated in 1992, this program attracts "culturally diverse college students" for nine-week internships in a variety of the TOUR's business areas. The program has been extremely successful, with more than 20 percent of its participants landing positions in the golf or sports management industries after graduation.

The TOUR's momentum also is evident in the growth of the TOUR internationally. Television coverage of TOUR events in Europe and Asia has increased dramatically in recent years, further expanding golf's international base.

The TOUR has worked to develop international golfing events, such as The Presidents Cup. The PGA Tours International Federation was formed to bring the five major professional golf tours together to organize more of these events. The World Golf Championships will begin with three events—stroke play, match play, and an invitational—in 1999 and a team event in 2000. "The best players in the world want to play against each other more consistently," explains Edward Moorhouse, the TOUR's executive vice president and chief legal

PGA TOUR/ARCHIVES

THE NATIONAL HEADQUARTERS OF THE PGA TOUR AND THE TOURNAMENT PLAYERS CLUB AT SAWGRASS ARE IN PONTE VEDRA BEACH.

PGA TOUR/CHAD SPENCER

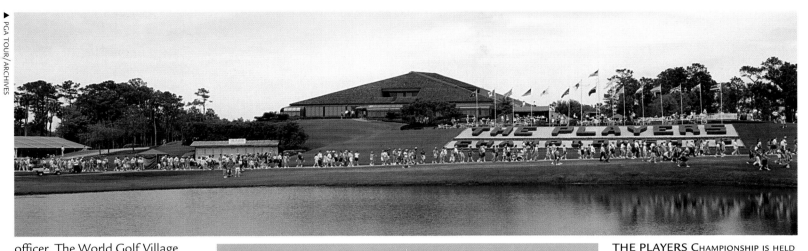

officer. The World Golf Village project also has brought all of the world's golf organizations together to develop this international shrine to the game and its best players.

WORLD GOLF VILLAGE

Officials call it the most ambitious project ever undertaken in golf. Located nine miles northwest of historic St. Augustine in St. Johns County, the 260-acre World Golf Village, Inc. is a separate, not-for-profit entity that has received the support of all major golf organizations from around the world.

The centerpiece of the Village is the World Golf Hall of Fame, designed by internationally renowned architect E. Verner Johnson. The Hall of Fame building totals 80,000 square feet, including 36,000 square feet of exhibits on the history and the future of the game. The complex also includes an International Golf Library and Resource Center, World Golf Resort and Convention Center, Vistana World Golf Village Resort, the Residences at World Golf Village, the Shops at World Golf Village, PGA TOUR Productions, three golf courses, a golf academy, and a Mayo Clinic family health care facility. Village officials estimate that the complex will attract more than 750,000 visitors in its first year alone. The combined annual financial impact of the game of golf in Florida reaches into the millions of dollars, and the World Golf Village will bring

even more tourist dollars to the state.

The First Coast will benefit from the World Golf Village's presence, as it has from the PGA TOUR's headquarters in Ponte Vedra Beach. "Other cities approached us," notes Ruffin Beckwith, executive director of World Golf Village, Inc., "but we wanted to keep it in this part of the country, and this part of the state."

The World Golf Village, THE PLAYERS Championship, the TPC at Sawgrass, and PGA

TOUR Headquarters all bring tremendous international attention to the Jacksonville area. But this quality organization contributes much more: the TOUR's business savvy, leadership, and generosity have made a huge impact on the First Coast that cannot be measured in dollars or ratings. In the years to come, the PGA TOUR will continue its leadership role in broadening the horizons of professional golf, bringing worldwide acclaim to its hometown.

THE PLAYERS CHAMPIONSHIP IS HELD EACH MARCH AT THE TOURNAMENT PLAYERS CLUB AT SAWGRASS.

THE TOWER OF THE WORLD GOLF HALL OF FAME, SCHEDULED TO OPEN IN MAY 1998, OFFERS A SCENIC VIEW OF THE SLAMMER AND THE SQUIRE GOLF COURSE AT THE WORLD GOLF VILLAGE.

LANDCOM HOSPITALITY MANAGEMENT, INC.

LANDCOM HOSPITALITY MANAGEMENT, INC. HAS ESTABLISHED a well-deserved reputation for excellence and integrity in the lodging industry. The company's success in operating hotels and resorts has been enhanced by the consistent performances of the properties that make up Landcom's portfolio, and these hotels continue to be leaders in their respective markets.

Landcom has crafted its growth by selectively developing relationships with respected financial entities and investors. The company's solid reputation is based on its commitment to responsive and flexible service to meet the needs of each hotel, hotel guest, and client.

A Dynamic Team
The foundation of Landcom is a committed group of dynamic individuals who reflect an entrepreneurial spirit. Landcom's team of professionals brings pride, advanced education, significant experience, and integrity to form a culture that emphasizes excellence and achievement. The formula for success is exceptional employees producing sustained financial performance. Landcom has the human resources and capabilities to develop and manage all types of hotels, conference centers, and resorts. Landcom has provided management and consultation to more than 50 hotels representing virtually every major franchise, including Sheraton, Hilton, Radisson, Holiday Inn, Hampton Inn, and Marriott hotels.

Under the leadership of Chief Executive Officer H. Kenneth O'Steen Jr., Landcom has become a highly respected player in the hospitality industry. O'Steen and the company's other principals and officers bring years of experience in lodging, real estate development, and finance.

Local Presence
One of Landcom's local hotels is the Marriott Residence Inn on J. Turner Butler Boulevard, Jacksonville's fastest-growing corridor. The Marriott Residence Inn is located in Deerwood Park, one of the area's most pristine office parks. Designed primarily for guests needing extended stays, this all-suite property features 120 suites that include full kitchens and other services. The ideal positioning of this type of lodging facility in a rapidly expanding business area makes the Marriott Residence Inn another successful addition to Landcom's portfolio.

Targeting another niche market, Landcom also developed and operates a Hampton Inn in Jacksonville's central business district. Hampton Inns typically provide moderately priced hotel services with an emphasis on guest satisfaction. The Hampton Inn Central I-95 on Prudential Dr. will provide the greatest price value and hotel experience to both weekday corporate customers and tourists visiting one of Jacksonville's many cultural or entertainment events, including the Jacksonville Jaguars' home games.

As the company approaches its 20th anniversary, the founders of Landcom have much to celebrate. Through careful planning and analysis, the company has established a reputation of success in its industry, and has compiled a portfolio of hotels that continues to get bigger and better.

MARRIOTT RESIDENCE INN IS LOCATED ON J. TURNER BUTLER BOULEVARD IN DEERWOOD PARK (TOP AND BOTTOM LEFT)

HAMPTON INN CENTRAL IS LOCATED ON PRUDENTIAL DRIVE (RIGHT).

The PARC Group, Inc.

FLORIDA'S FIRST COAST HAS BLOSSOMED WITH GROWTH IN RECENT years. New jobs have flourished in the Jacksonville area, and with them have come new residents who desire new homes. All of this is good news for companies such as The PARC Group, which specializes in the development of residential communities.

PARC (Planned Active Residential Communities) was established in 1989 by Roger M. O'Steen, the company's current president. As a developer in North Florida for nearly 20 years, O'Steen contributed to more than 30 residential neighborhoods and resort properties, including five golf course communities. This experience, coupled with knowledge gleaned as a principal in a number of other development companies and partnerships, provided the base to start The PARC Group.

It was a wise decision. The PARC Group has developed more than $100 million in properties since its inception, and currently has five active developments in the First Coast area, ranging from office parks to country club communities.

A Broad Range of Communities

The PARC Group is involved in several communities in the Jacksonville area, varying in scale, location, and style. Marsh Creek Country Club, located in historic St. Augustine in St. Johns County, is an exclusive, gated community that includes a country club and a very successful private golf course. The community will include 650 homes, ranging in price from $180,000 to more than $1 million. Another community in St. Augustine is Sea Place, an oceanfront development offering town homes and patio homes in the $175,000 to $400,000 range.

In Jacksonville, PARC is developing Timberlin Parc, a multiuse, planned community in the city's Southside area. The community includes single-family homes, apartment homes, an assisted living home, and the Timberlin Village shopping center.

Reedy Branch Plantation, another residential development in Jacksonville, includes more than 200 single-family homes ranging from $120,000 to $200,000. The Plantation features a park with a pavilion, a playground, and a community pool.

The PARC Group is also involved in commercial developments, such as San Pablo Office Park in Jacksonville. This exclusive, residential-style office park is in one of the city's fastest-growing business areas and features 12 office sites in classic, casual-style buildings.

The PARC Group prides itself in the quality of its developments, from the homes themselves to the amenities included in the communities. PARC strives to preserve the natural surroundings of the land it develops, while providing common outdoor areas such as parks and other community features. The group lavishes this attention on its homes as well, focusing on such essential elements as curb appeal, landscaping, and attractive entryway features.

Jacksonville and The PARC Group have grown together and continue to enjoy the benefits of success. Neither shows signs of slowing down.

CLOCKWISE FROM TOP LEFT: MARSH CREEK COUNTRY CLUB OFFERS A FULL RANGE OF AMENITIES IN A PRIVATE GATED COMMUNITY.

SAN PABLO OFFICE PARK IS IDEALLY LOCATED NEAR THE BEACHES AREA AND THE MAYO CLINIC.

PARC PROVIDES COMMON OUTDOOR AREAS, SUCH AS PARKS AND OTHER COMMUNITY FEATURES, IN ITS DEVELOPMENTS.

TIMBERLIN PARC IS LOCATED IN JACKSONVILLE'S HIGH-GROWTH SOUTHSIDE AREA.

Genesis Rehabilitation Hospital and Centers

WHEN A PERSON IS INCAPACITATED THROUGH ILLNESS OR INJURY, loved ones will accept nothing but the best for the patient's care. On the First Coast, Genesis Rehabilitation Hospital and Centers, based in Jacksonville, provides this care by offering an advanced, comprehensive approach to rehabilitation for

adults and children with physical disabilities, delivered in a warm, friendly setting. Genesis has gained a reputation as a national center of excellence in rehabilitation care.

Genesis' programs benefit patients who have been disabled as the result of a stroke, brain injury, spinal cord injury, orthopedic injury, or neurological disorders. The hospital is licensed for 127 beds to accommodate acute medical rehabilitation, and is accredited by the Joint Commission on Accreditation of Healthcare Organizations (JCAHO) and the Commission on Accreditation of Rehabilitation Facilities (CARF).

Many patients from acute care hospitals and nursing homes in Northeast Florida and southern Georgia, as well as more distant places both north and south, are referred to Genesis, as it is the largest rehabilitation facility in the Southeast. Currently, there are only a dozen freestanding rehabilitation hospitals in Florida, and only 184 in the entire country, making the type of care Genesis provides highly specialized.

CLOCKWISE FROM TOP:
THE NEW GENESIS REHABILITATION HOSPITAL OPENED IN 1994, REPRESENTING BOTH A CHANGE IN ITS NAME (FORMERLY MEMORIAL REHABILITATION) AND LOCATION.

GENESIS REHABILITATION IS HOME TO ONE OF THE MOST TALENTED AND RESPECTED GROUP PRACTICES OF PHYSICIANS IN THE AREA, HEADED BY PHYSIATRIST JAY HUSSAIN M.D.

"PEOPLE ARE WHAT REALLY MATTERS IN PHYSICAL REHABILITATION AND ALL ASPECTS OF HEALTH CARE," SAYS GENESIS PRESIDENT STEPHEN K. WILSON, SEEN HERE VISITING WITH A YOUNG PATIENT.

Dedicated to Rehabilitation

Rehabilitative hospital care has actually been available in Jacksonville since 1970, when Cathedral Rehabilitation Hospital opened in downtown Jacksonville as the area's only comprehensive rehabilitation hospital. The center was purchased by Memorial Medical Center in 1982, and renamed Memorial Regional Rehabilitation Center. Memorial relocated the rehabilitation hospital to its campus on University Boulevard in 1983.

The facility soon outgrew its space in the existing locale, and a construction project was begun to build a freestanding hospital next door. The brand-new Memorial Rehabilitation Hospital opened its doors in 1994, featuring state-of-the-art facilities. When Columbia/HCA Healthcare purchased Memorial Medical Center in 1995, the rehabilitation hospital remained an independently owned and operated nonprofit hospital under the new Genesis name. Today, Genesis Rehabilitation Hospital and Centers operates as part of Genesis Health, Inc., a Jacksonville-based health care system. Throughout all of Genesis' changes, the organization's original mission to rehabilitate the disabled has remained its primary goal.

Focusing on Skills

"Our goal is to enable patients to return to the functional world," explains Stephen K. Wilson, the president of Genesis. "We are focused on teaching them to be as independent as possible. This may include teaching them life skills, like brushing their teeth, getting dressed, and feeding themselves. But it also includes daily

activities like shopping for basic needs, using an automated teller machine, and driving a car."

To reinforce these skills, Genesis utilizes a replicated community environment known as Independence Square. Realistic settings have been constructed inside the facility, including sidewalks, curbs, stairs, and home and store-front simulation, enhanced with life-size photomurals of scenes from the First Coast. The concept is extended to recreational pursuits as well; the center includes a setting for shopping for groceries, making a purchase at a hardware store, performing banking transactions, boating, and putting on a green. Some patients even spend a few nights in one of the hospital's apartments just before discharge so they can practice the new skills they will soon be using in the outside world.

Genesis took the concept of community integration to a higher level during the construction of its newest building. Instead of using sterile, institutional names for each floor and wing, the units at Genesis were named for Jacksonville's neighborhoods and surrounding communities. This theme was reinforced by the street lamp signs in each hallway that contribute to the hospital's homelike atmosphere.

The case manager plays a vital role in the coordination of various aspects of each patient's care and well-being. The case manager is the link between the patient and the treating staff members, as well as an invaluable link to resources of the community. Staff members at Genesis also work diligently with family members to educate them about their loved one's disabilities and to make them a partner in the rehabilitation process.

In order to make the patient's transition into the real world a little easier, Genesis has established a number of outpatient medical

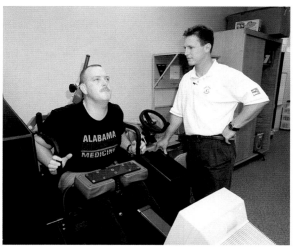

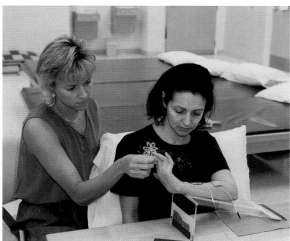

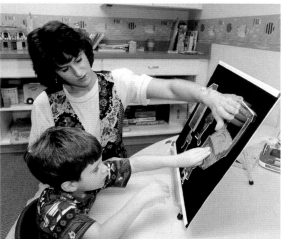

rehabilitation centers throughout Jacksonville and the surrounding areas. These centers allow patients to return home to their families and resume their lives, while continuing the work crucial to their long-term improvement. These centers also provide therapy services for children and adults whose recuperation from surgery or illness does not require hospitalization.

Genesis is a results-oriented environment, so it is no surprise that the hospital measures the success of its efforts diligently. A patient's condition and skill levels are assessed at admission, discharge, and 90 days after leaving the hospital. When these figures are compared to other medical rehabilitation facilities across the country, Genesis constantly ranks

in the top percentiles for clinical results and patient satisfaction.

Another important part of the Genesis Health System is the Genesis Health Foundation, conceived to support the quality of life for persons with disabilities in Northeast Florida and Southeast Georgia. The foundation supports Genesis Rehabilitation Hospital and other community projects relating to living with a disability, injury prevention, education, and understanding of rehabilitation. Grants are awarded quarterly to nonprofit organizations with qualifying programs that serve persons with disabilities.

Genesis Rehabilitation Hospital and Centers works to fulfill its mission of helping patients and their families start a new life after a disabling illness or injury.

GENESIS' PROGRAMS BENEFIT PATIENTS WHO HAVE BEEN DISABLED AS THE RESULT OF A STROKE, BRAIN INJURY, SPINAL CORD INJURY, ORTHOPEDIC INJURY, OR NEUROLOGICAL DISORDERS.

WAPE-FM, WFYV-FM, WKQL-FM, WMXQ-FM, WOKV-AM, and WBWL-AM

SIX RADIO STATIONS—WAPE-FM, WFYV-FM, WKQL-FM, WMXQ-FM, WOKV-AM, and WBWL-AM—form a broadcasting portfolio representing a variety of formats, and sharing a commitment to excellence that makes them leaders in their markets. Four FM stations and two AM stations in Jacksonville are under the leadership umbrella of President and General Manager Mark Schwartz. No stranger to success, Schwartz has more than 25 years of experience in radio, and he has been repeatedly nominated for honors such as General Manager of the Year and Radio Executive of the Year.

The flagship station in Jacksonville is WAPE-FM 95.1, known in the radio industry as The Big Ape. This station enjoys legendary status in broadcasting circles as a nationally ranked Top 40 station and recipient of many industry awards. After switching to FM in 1986, the station was able to re-

tain its position at the top of the Jacksonville market. In fact, soon after the change to FM, WAPE held the number one spot in the industry's Arbitron ratings books for 21 consecutive reports. WAPE-FM also received the radio broadcasting industry's national Gavin Award for Station of the Year for two consecutive years. WAPE's Contemporary Hit Radio format bills itself as Today's Best Music and continues to dominate its target audience.

WFYV-FM 104.5 is another strong member of this radio station family. The station, better known in Jacksonville as ROCK 105, features album-oriented rock, and is renowned for developing the talents of Lex & Terry, a team that went on to syndication through another sister station affiliate in Dallas. ROCK 105 has also been a

DON SMITH

CLOCKWISE FROM TOP LEFT: ALSO KNOWN AS THE BIG GUY, MARK G. SCHWARTZ IS PRESIDENT AND GENERAL MANAGER OF WAPE-FM, WFYV-FM, WKQL-FM, WMXQ-FM, WOKV-AM, AND WBWL-AM.

CAT THOMAS IS OPERATIONS MANAGER OF WAPE-FM, WFYV-FM, WKQL-FM, WMXQ-FM, WOKV-AM, AND WBWL-AM.

WAPE-FM AIRS *THE BIG APE MORNING ZOO* FROM 5:30 TO 10 A.M. DAILY, FEATURING (FOREGROUND, FROM LEFT) AMADEUS, ASHLEY KING, ANGIE, HOYLE DEMPSEY, EDEN KENDALL, AND (BACKGROUND) STEVE SUTTON.

DON SMITH

consistent leader in the Jacksonville ratings. The combination of WFYV and WAPE under one organization provides a significant opportunity to advertisers, as the two stations dominate the desirable age-18-to-49 demographic, as well as the age-25-to-54 demographic.

WMXQ-FM 102.9, known as MIX 103, features the Best Mix of the '70s, '80s, and '90s, which is delivered by personable, lively announcers who are heard by an estimated 100,000 listeners each week. MIX 103 is the only station of this format in the city, making it a natural leader in its target demographics, specifically men and women between 25 and 49 years of age.

The final FM station in this Jacksonville operation is WKQL-FM 96.9, known as COOL 96.9 FM. This station focuses on an exclusive oldies format, playing music primarily from the 1960s. Its Good Times and Great Oldies slogan hits home with the baby boomer generation, men and women between the ages of 35 and 54. The station guarantees uninterrupted half-hour blocks of music during certain hours, a feature that is popular with listeners and advertisers alike.

Rounding out the group's presence in Jacksonville are the company's two AM stations, WOKV-AM 690 and WBWL-AM 600...The Ball.

WOKV's news/talk format features local announcers and hosts, as well as nationally syndicated personalities, such as Rush Limbaugh, Ken Hamblin, and Dr. Laura Schlessinger. The station boasts the best AM radio signal (50,000 watts) in Jacksonville and consistently maintains its position as the highest-rated AM station in the market. WOKV received seven Associated Press state awards for broadcasting excellence in 1996, more than any other radio station in Florida.

WBWL-AM 600...The Ball is the newest member of the fam-

ily, coming on-line with its sports format in late 1996. The Ball presents All Sports with AttiTUDE, focusing on local sports. The station takes some unique approaches to the format, such as its *Bullpen* during midday hours. The *Bullpen* features a rotating schedule of local sportscasters and sportswriters who analyze local sports issues and respond to listeners' calls. WBWL also features nationally syndicated sports broadcasters, such as San Diego-based

Jim Rome. In the first six months of the sports format, WBWL received several state awards from the Associated Press, including the Best Sports Station of the Market.

These six stations are securely positioned in the Jacksonville market, with nearly every format style and demographic represented in the lineup. The combined impact of these six stations makes this supercluster a formidable force on the First Coast.

TOP: BILL RILEY (FOREGROUND) IS THE MORNING HOST FOR **WBWL-AM 600**...THE BALL, WHICH FEATURES A SPORTS/TALK FORMAT. MIKE MILLER (BACKGROUND) IS THE MORNING ANCHOR FOR **WOKV-AM 690**, WHICH FEATURES A NEWS AND TALK FORMAT.

BOTTOM: **WFYV-FM 104.5**, ALSO KNOWN AS **ROCK 105**, FEATURES THE LEX & TERRY MORNING SHOW FROM 6 TO 10 A.M., HOSTED BY LEX STALEY (LEFT) AND TERRY JAYMES.

PSS/WorldMedical, Inc.

As entrepreneur Patrick Kelly composed the mission statement for his new medical supply business, PSS/Physician Sales & Service, Inc., the goal was to create the first physician supply company to reach a national market. At the time of PSS' founding in 1983, most companies in this industry were locally or regionally based. But in slightly more than 10 years, PSS surpassed its original goal of national distribution and began to reach the global marketplace. Today, the company continues to grow and set new standards for the medical supply industry.

PSS/Physician Sales & Service began as a local medical supply company, providing equipment and supplies to doctors' offices in the Jacksonville area. By 1997, PSS—now the largest national physician-based medical supplier—had become one of three divisions of PSS/WorldMedical, Inc., a multifaceted international medical distribution company. PSS/WorldMedical's European division, WorldMed, Inc., distributes medical equipment and supplies in Belgium, France, Germany, and the Netherlands through three service centers. The third division, DI/Diagnostic Imaging, Inc., was formed in 1996. In its first year, DI/Diagnostic Imaging became the leading U.S. distributor of medical diagnostic imaging equip-

ment, supplies, and services to the acute and alternate care markets through 25 service centers.

Today, PSS/WorldMedical has 90 distribution/service centers that reach more than 103,000 medical facilities and physician offices. The company has grown from employing 20 people in 1983 to a current staff of more than 3,200 in the United States and Europe.

"Hypergrowing" the Company

Perhaps the best evidence of the strength of PSS/WorldMedical is the consistently high annual sales growth rate of its PSS/Physician Sales & Service division: more than 40 percent each year since its founding. An article profiling the company that appeared in the October 1995 issue of *Inc.* magazine characterized this type of pattern as "hypergrowth."

A combination of factors have led to the company's success. Same-day delivery service to doctors' offices has distinguished PSS from its competition. And by

investing in other service enhancements—such as computer systems, delivery trucks, and extensive training for sales staff—PSS has been able to continue its steady rise. Along the way, the company also has grown through strategic acquisitions, such as its merger in 1995 with Taylor Medical, which formerly had been one of the company's largest competitors.

PSS has also taken innovative approaches to motivating and training employees. The company traditionally has targeted recent college graduates for its sales force, focusing on their attitudes and desires rather than their lack of experience. A rigorous training program follows at a PSS branch location, where new hires learn the business from the ground up. After working two months at the branch, new employees move on to PSS University in Jacksonville.

Company officials estimate that PSS/WorldMedical spends nearly $10,000 on training for each new salesperson. This dedication to training results in an exceptional sales force. Working as consultants

Patrick Kelly, chairman and CEO of PSS/WorldMedical, logs a tremendous amount of airtime spreading the vibrant culture of PSS/WorldMedical (left).

PSS' mission is to provide service to every doctor in America, including the frozen reaches of the great north (right).

LANS STOUT

rather than as order takers, PSS/ WorldMedical salespeople are consistently rated highest in the industry for service, diagnostic sales, and new product rollouts. These types of results have caught the attention of many manufacturers and have given PSS the opportunity to develop exclusive or semiexclusive distribution agreements. For example, PSS recently developed an exclusive distribution agreement with Abbott Laboratories, a large medical manufacturer that had previously been a competitor. Through the agreement, both parties benefit from distribution cost savings and increased efficiency.

Focus on Fun
At PSS/WorldMedical, many people work very hard to make this kind of success happen. Kelly and other executives believe in making work fun whenever possible. Annual regional picnics, national sales meetings, and other corporate outings often revolve around sporting events, such as golf, volleyball, and other games designed to help staff members let off a little steam.

Employees keep their eyes on profits as well. The company's employee stock ownership plan (ESOP) and incentive stock option plan help employees remain focused on the bottom line, which, in turn, helps profits grow. Other bonus

incentive plans on the branch level add an element of competition between branches that enhances employee efficiency.

Community Involvement
PSS/WorldMedical supports many Jacksonville community organizations, including InRoads Minority Internship Program, American Lung Association, Dreams Come True of Jacksonville, Sulzbacher Center for the Homeless, American Heart Association, Jacksonville Chamber of Commerce, University of North Florida, Mercy Ships Jacksonville Advisory Board, Jacksonville Symphony, and Wolfson's Children's Hospital.

Also, Kelly and PSS/World-Medical support the Virginia Home for Boys in Richmond, where Kelly is a member of the Executive Committee. He was raised at the Virginia Home for Boys from the age of five until he entered Virginia Commonwealth University. Kelly is very active with the Virginia Home for Boys, including the establishment of the Amelia Meadow Educational

Trust Fund, which provides college education funding for high school graduates at the Home, and the Boys Home Foundation, which supports children's homes in America. Kelly was also recognized as Alumnus of the Year in 1992.

PSS/WorldMedical's success has not gone unnoticed. In addition to the article in *Inc.*, the company has been profiled in the *Harvard Business Review* and *Investor's Business Daily*. A book on PSS called *Faster Company* will be published in spring 1998. PSS/WorldMedical and Kelly have also been recognized as the Healthcare Entrepreneur of the Year for Florida, and in 1997, Kelly was a recipient of the prestigious Horatio Alger Award.

Now that PSS/WorldMedical is firmly established as not only a national, but an international medical supply company, Kelly is quick to pinpoint the company's next objective: to make PSS/ WorldMedical a billion-dollar company by the end of 2001. With the company's track record, this goal will be reached in 1998.

SAME-DAY DELIVERY SERVICE TO DOCTORS' OFFICES DISTINGUISHES PSS/ WORLDMEDICAL FROM ITS COMPETITION.

PSS/WORLDMEDICAL, INC. IS A MULTIFACETED INTERNATIONAL MEDICAL DISTRIBUTION COMPANY HAVING THREE DIVISIONS. (BELOW LEFT TO RIGHT) DI/ DIAGNOSTIC IMAGING, INC. AND PSS/ PHYSICIAN SALES AND SERVICE HANDLE U.S. MARKETS, WHILE WORLDMED, INC. IS THE COMPANY'S EUROPEAN DIVISION.

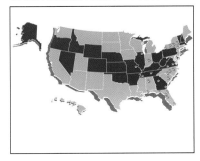

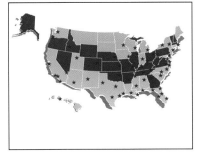

IMA Plus

THE INFORMATION TECHNOLOGY INDUSTRY IS NEARLY SYNONYMOUS with change. New enhancements and advancements are unveiled every day, often making yesterday's technology obsolete. At the same time, virtually all business solutions depend heavily upon computers to support a wide variety of functions. Because the relationship between business and technology is often so volatile, many businesses require the services of an experienced information technology consulting and programming services firm, such as IMA Plus.

IMA Plus is an acronym for Information Management Alternatives Plus, which was founded by William D. Fitzgerald in 1984. Fitzgerald recognized the need for a service-oriented company that could meet clients' system integration needs. "As companies position themselves strategically for the next century, the demand for information technology [IT] consulting services will continue to expand—making IT consulting one of the leading growth sectors of the future," explains Fitzgerald, president and chief executive officer of IMA Plus.

The prediction of growth certainly proved to be true for IMA Plus, as the company began with only two employees and today employs hundreds of business and technical professionals. IMA Plus has also experienced record earnings since 1995, with the company nearly doubling in size each subsequent year. This explosive growth has been recognized in *Inc.* magazine's annual Inc. 500, a listing of the nation's fastest-growing private companies, and the *Jacksonville Business Journal*'s

list of Northeast Florida's top 50 fastest-growing businesses. *Upside* magazine also included IMA Plus in its list of the top 100 private technology companies. In addition, IMA Plus has been recognized by the University of Florida and Florida State University business schools for outstanding leadership.

Fitzgerald chose Jacksonville as the headquarters for his new company based on the city's reputation as a business-friendly location. "Jacksonville has historically been known as the 'business city' in Florida," explains Fitzgerald. "It offers a very diverse marketplace of industries, such as health care, insurance, manufacturing, financial, and computer technology." Fitzgerald also notes Jacksonville's status as the largest financial center south of Atlanta in making the city a prime growth area for companies such as IMA Plus.

As the company has grown, its employees have also given back to the Jacksonville community. For example, IMA Plus and its employees regularly contribute time and money to the Leukemia Society, the Heart Association, the Boy Scouts of America, the Muscular Dystrophy Association, the Shriners Hospitals, and the Children's Miracle Network, among others. IMA Plus employees are also actively involved in various community groups, such as the Jacksonville Chamber of Commerce, the Rotary Club, and the Kiwanis Club of Jacksonville.

COMPREHENSIVE RANGE OF SERVICES
IMA Plus employs a comprehensive approach to its clients' information technology needs through five major areas of concentration: consulting, outsourcing, technical education, application development, and software technology resale.

IMA PLUS HAS EXTENSIVE EXPERTISE IN DEVELOPING SOFTWARE APPLICATIONS FOR VARIOUS INDUSTRIES. AN ESTABLISHED TRACK RECORD AND CLIENT SATISFACTION ARE EVIDENCE OF IMA PLUS' COMMITMENT TO PROVIDING QUALITY INFORMATION SYSTEMS (TOP).

THE COMPANY'S CONSULTING GROUP PROVIDES EXPERTISE IN CLIENT/SERVER METHODOLOGIES, COST/BENEFIT ANALYSIS, AUTOMATION PLANNING, AND NETWORK DESIGN AND INSTALLATION (BOTTOM).

CONSULTING

The consulting group provides expertise in client/server methodologies, cost/benefit analysis, automation planning, and network design and installation. IMA's staff members also advise clients on productivity improvement and project management through work flow analysis, change management, and business process reengineering.

In addition, IMA Plus can also function as a technical research firm, identifying and screening information technology professionals for businesses' human resources departments.

OUTSOURCING

IMA Plus also specializes in project outsourcing. The firm's outsourcing experts handle all aspects of software development, systems integration, network services, network implementation/support, and training.

Management of year 2000 conversion projects is another specialty that is in high demand as the new millennium approaches.

TECHNICAL EDUCATION

In addition, IMA Plus offers a comprehensive technical education

curriculum to its clients. The company maintains two complete education centers that are fully staffed with full-time professional technical trainers and equipped with state-of-the-art hardware. The Technical Education Services Center offers a series of curriculum methodologies to meet its clients' diverse needs. Courses can be selected by module, allowing employees to attend only a specific skill section, or they can be registered for an entire course.

IMA Plus also offers total transition curriculum planning, a method used to move groups of employees from one product, platform, or environment to another. This comprehensive approach includes important steps such as assessments of the needs, skills, and management goals of the transition. The training, whether delivered by the client's own training staff or IMA Plus trainers, can then be supported by mentors in the work environment to ensure successful information transfer.

APPLICATION DEVELOPMENT

IMA Plus has extensive expertise in developing software applications

for various industries. An established track record and client satisfaction are evidence of IMA Plus' commitment to providing quality information systems.

With a proven technical approach and development methodology, IMA Plus understands the complex issues surrounding the implementation of software solutions.

SOFTWARE TECHNOLOGY RESALE

The company rounds out its business lines with its software technology resale division, which distributes a variety of programming products that support a full range of services from client/server technology to legacy systems.

Looking forward, IMA Plus has no plans to slow down. The company intends to continue expanding and diversifying within the information technology industry, adapting to the requirements and needs of its clients. Notes Fitzgerald, "Based on our present rate of growth, we anticipate that we will continue to enjoy an explosive growth rate in the foreseeable future, utilizing a highly skilled and technical workforce."

Stein Mart

WHEN STEIN MART, NORTH AMERICA'S ONLY UPSCALE DISCOUNT specialty store, relocated to Jacksonville in 1984, the chain had only a handful of stores. Today, there are more than 150 stores in 26 states. Now in its 93rd year of business, the Stein Mart story began around 1905, when Sam Stein, a young immigrant, walked across Europe to board a ship for America in search of a new life. His travels led him through Ellis Island to New York, where he began a train ride that ended in Greenville, Mississippi. "It is a typical story," recalls his grandson, Jay Stein, current chairman and CEO. "He saw the bustling economy of the Mississippi Delta as an open door to opportunity." Sam Stein began selling notions and piece goods door-to-door, calling on wealthy cotton planters and tenant farmers alike. As this business grew, he traded his horse and cart for a small store in Greenville that soon grew to occupy a full city block.

In 1949, while liquidating excess merchandise in order to move from one location to another, Sam Stein's son, Jake, seized upon the realization that he could develop an entirely new business by discounting prices and, therefore, draw from an enormous customer base previously untapped. Jay Stein joined the family business full-time in 1967 and initiated the company's geographic expansion by opening its first branch store

in Memphis, Tennessee, in 1977. Additional stores were opened, first in the Southeast, and later nationwide.

BRAND-NAME CLOTHING, DISCOUNT PRICES

Jay Stein's vision of selling upscale merchandise at discount prices in an appealing, easy-to-shop environment became the blueprint for developing Stein Mart's highly successful chain of stores, currently employing more than 12,000 people. Since going public in 1992, Stein Mart's unique hybrid retailing philosophy has gained much attention from retail experts and consumers alike.

Like an upscale specialty store, Stein Mart stores have tasteful, innovative displays with designer and brand-name merchandise presented by lifestyle. Like a discounter, prices on seasonal accessories, shoes, unique home decor, fine linens, and top-quality clothing for men, women, and children are priced up to 60 percent below department store prices.

THE BOUTIQUE

While Stein Mart takes great pride in the high quality and unusual value of its merchandise, Jay Stein recognized the need for a department dedicated completely to the higher end of the designer market, from career-oriented separates to special occasion and formal dressing. The Stein Mart Boutique, introduced in response to this niche market, has since become a Stein Mart hallmark. This unique concept hinges on the "Boutique ladies" who staff the department.

The Boutique ladies work just one day a week, but their importance is immeasurable. Serving as local ambassadors for Stein Mart, they spread the Stein Mart word to their friends and their commu-

nity organizations. They provide important feedback to buyers and management on community preferences and market trends, and they serve as a test market for new merchandise. The Boutique ladies bring a high level of customer service to their positions by acting as personal shoppers and by recognizing new merchandise that suits the needs and tastes of individual customers.

An Active Member of the Community

Sam Stein was a visionary in his quest for a life in which future generations could draw upon the resources and values offered in this country. His son and grandson also embraced this vision, supporting the communities in which Stein Mart operates.

Stein Mart is proud of its long history of community involvement on both the corporate and the local level. Each Stein Mart store is encouraged to participate in local community causes and events, from programs with local school systems to holiday giving projects.

In Jacksonville, home to Stein Mart's corporate headquarters, the company focuses on the arts, education, and the needs of children. A good example is the support of arts-in-education initiatives such as the Arts-Infused Model School Program in local elementary schools. Administered through the Cultural Council of Greater Jacksonville, this innovative program has seen remarkable results, from improved reading and math test scores to increased parental involvement and decreased student absenteeism. Another example is Stein Mart's Holiday Giving Trees, a program through which the company offers a venue for more than 45,000 holiday gifts to be provided to children in foster care, group homes, and emergency shelters. In Jacksonville, The Children's Home Society works with Stein Mart on this important project.

The Bolles School, the Cummer Museum of Art and Gardens, and

Baptist Medical Center's Wolfson's Children's Hospital are but a few of the many community organizations that benefit from the generosity of Stein Mart and the Stein family. The company also underwrites public radio and television programming throughout the state of Florida, as well as in other markets throughout the chain. Stein Mart takes the spirit of stewardship so seriously that it sponsors the annual 12 People Who Care awards, which honor community volunteers—who are selected by their peers—and reward them with grants to further their important efforts.

Stein Mart's emphasis on community involvement starts at the top. Jay Stein is extremely active in local and national civic, charitable, and educational causes. Locally, he serves on the boards of the Barnett Bank of Jacksonville, the Bolles School, the National Conference of Christians and Jews, and the American Heritage Life Insurance Company. In addition, he has served as chairman of the Jacksonville Symphony Association and as cochair of the Mayor's Performing Arts Center Advisory Council during the building and opening of the Times Union Center for the Performing Arts. Stein is also a past member of the Mayor's Select Committee on Ethics in City Government. In 1993, he received the Humanitarian Award from the National Conference of Chris-

STEIN MART OFFERS TOP-QUALITY CLOTHING FOR MEN, WOMEN, AND CHILDREN, PRICED UP TO 60 PERCENT BELOW DEPARTMENT STORE PRICES.

THE STEIN MART BOUTIQUE OFFERS AN ARRAY OF LADIES' FASHION WEAR, RANGING FROM CAREER-ORIENTED SEPARATES TO SPECIAL OCCASION AND FORMAL DRESSING.

tians and Jews. Nationally, he is a trustee and member of the executive committee of the John F. Kennedy Center for the Performing Arts. He is currently vice chairman of the Hebrew Union College Board of Governors and was a founding member of the Holocaust Museum in Washington, D.C.

The Future

Stein Mart continues to grow into new markets around the United States. Stores are presently located as far west as San Jose and as far north as Milwaukee, and new stores are being opened at a rate of about 20 percent annually. Stein Mart's unique merchandising philosophy, its dedication to product quality and value, and its commitment to active involvement in its host communities will ensure the company's success in the next millennium.

The Stellar Group

RECOGNIZED AS ONE OF THE NATION'S FINEST FULL-SERVICE ARCHItecture/engineering and general contracting firms, The Stellar Group provides a diverse national clientele with comprehensive, single-source design, construction, and refrigeration services for industrial, commercial, and institutional facilities.

The industry's finest architects, engineers, construction management, and refrigeration professionals provide superior quality and schedule performance with exceptional value. The Stellar Group was founded with a commitment to superior performance and customer satisfaction. It employs a team approach that challenges every Stellar associate to excel.

Headquartered in Jacksonville, The Stellar Group now has a full-service western region office in Fresno, California. Parts and service operations are located in Jacksonville, Tampa, Memphis, Charlotte, Jackson, Birmingham, Modesto, Fresno, Grand Rapids, Seattle, and Dallas/Fort Worth. Service personnel are also located in the major metropolitan areas of Los Angeles, San Francisco, and Tracy, California; Miami; Atlanta; Savannah; and Indianapolis. Growing from $10 million in sales of design, construction, and refrigeration services in 1985 to sales of more than $200 million one decade later, The Stellar Group has maintained its commitment to supe-

rior customer service and now employs more than 600 people.

Recently Stellar was named First Coast 50 Company of the Year by the area's leading privately held companies for its dedication to the economy and community. In addition, The Stellar Group received awards of merit from the Associated Builders and Contractors' Excellence in Construction Awards for the construction of American Heritage Life Insurance Company, Coach Leatherware, Jacksonville Zoological Gardens, Fruit Cove Baptist Church, and YWCA.

Stellar employees are committed to the community that gave them their start. Local involvement includes working with Habijax, the Jacksonville Chapter of Habitat for Humanity; the Ronald McDonald House; and Dreams Come True, an organization for terminally ill children.

Stellar's major food projects in the Jacksonville area include A&H Seafood, Beaver Street Foods, Champion Brands, Industrial Cold Storage, and Sysco Foodservice.

Commercial and institutional project experience includes American Heritage Life Insurance Company, Deermeadows Baptist Church, Bethel Baptist Church, Fruit Cove Baptist Church, Epping Forest Yacht Club, Ponte Vedra Conference Center, San Jose Episcopal, Sun Trust Bank, Star Nine Building, The Stellar Group Corporate Offices, and YWCA. Stellar was also responsible for the African-themed transformation of the Jacksonville Zoological Gardens.

Some of Stellar's industrial distribution project experience includes Coach Leatherware; HGL Properties, Inc.; Maidenform; Michaels Stores; Perdue Office Interiors; Sally Beauty Company; U.S. Postal Service; and The Broadway Center.

Automotive dealership experience includes Brumos Motorcars, City Mitsubishi/Isuzu, Danny Sullivan Lexus, Mike Shad Ford, Nimnicht Cadillac, Nimnicht Chevrolet, Regency Dodge, and Stella Chevrolet.

The Stellar Group serves the food manufacturing, processing, and distribution industry nationwide, and has become one of the world's largest ammonia refrigeration contractors. Stellar's clientele includes companies such as Bar-S Foods, Burris Refrigerated Services, Kraft Foods, Pillsbury Bakeries & Foodservice, Tropicana Products, and United States Cold Storage.

In order to face the challenges of doing business in the next century, Stellar intends to work together with its customers to provide the highest-quality design, construction, and refrigeration services globally with the goal of earning repeat business.

ONE OF STELLAR'S INDUSTRIAL DISTRIBUTION PROJECTS INCLUDES HGL PROPERTIES, INC. (TOP).

THE STELLAR GROUP RECEIVED AN AWARD OF MERIT FROM THE ASSOCIATED BUILDERS AND CONTRACTORS' EXCELLENCE IN CONSTRUCTION AWARDS FOR THE CONSTRUCTION OF AMERICAN HERITAGE LIFE INSURANCE COMPANY (BOTTOM).

HE *JACKSONVILLE BUSINESS JOURNAL* IS AN ESSENTIAL TOOL FOR local businesses. Since its inception in 1985, the weekly publication has provided coverage of breaking news, government decisions, and emerging trends that affect the business community along the First Coast. ✳ Research shows that nearly 70 percent of its readers consider the *Jacksonville Business Journal* their primary source of local business news. The typical reader spends 30 minutes with each issue, and more than 70 percent say they peruse it more than once.

REACHING BUSINESS READERS

Each issue features a special section focusing on a specific industry and a section offering strategies for small businesses, along with public records, lists of the top 25 companies in a field, and recognition for those receiving promotions and awards. These regular features throughout the year place special emphasis on news in the categories of commercial real estate, residential development, high technology, human resources, professional services, hospitality, and health care.

The *Business Journal* has 68,000 readers in any given week and more than double that number in any given month. Each issue reaches the top 20 percent of the market—readers who are top decision makers and policy shapers at large and small businesses.

WORLD WIDE PRESENCE

The *Jacksonville Business Journal* can tap resources in 37 major markets across the country, where its parent company—American City Business Journals of Charlotte, North Carolina—operates weekly business newspapers.

Through its site on the World Wide Web (www.amcity.com/jacksonville), the *Business Journal* provides access to those 37 markets through an interactive search engine. The search feature allows Web users to type in a company name or key words—such as "economic development"—and immediately retrieve from each market all the stories containing the company name or key phrase.

The Web site also provides daily news updates from the First Coast and the top stories from each week's edition. Web users also may link to any of American City's weekly business newspapers or special Web journals on technology, real estate, health care, or hospitality.

The *Jacksonville Business Journal* is a community-minded business, organizing and sponsoring programs that honor the area's best in medicine and commercial contracting, 40 of the rising business stars, the fastest-growing local companies, and the area's largest private companies.

With its commitment to quality journalism and customer service, the *Jacksonville Business Journal* will continue to grow in circulation and influence, strengthening its reputation as the First Coast's definitive source for timely business news.

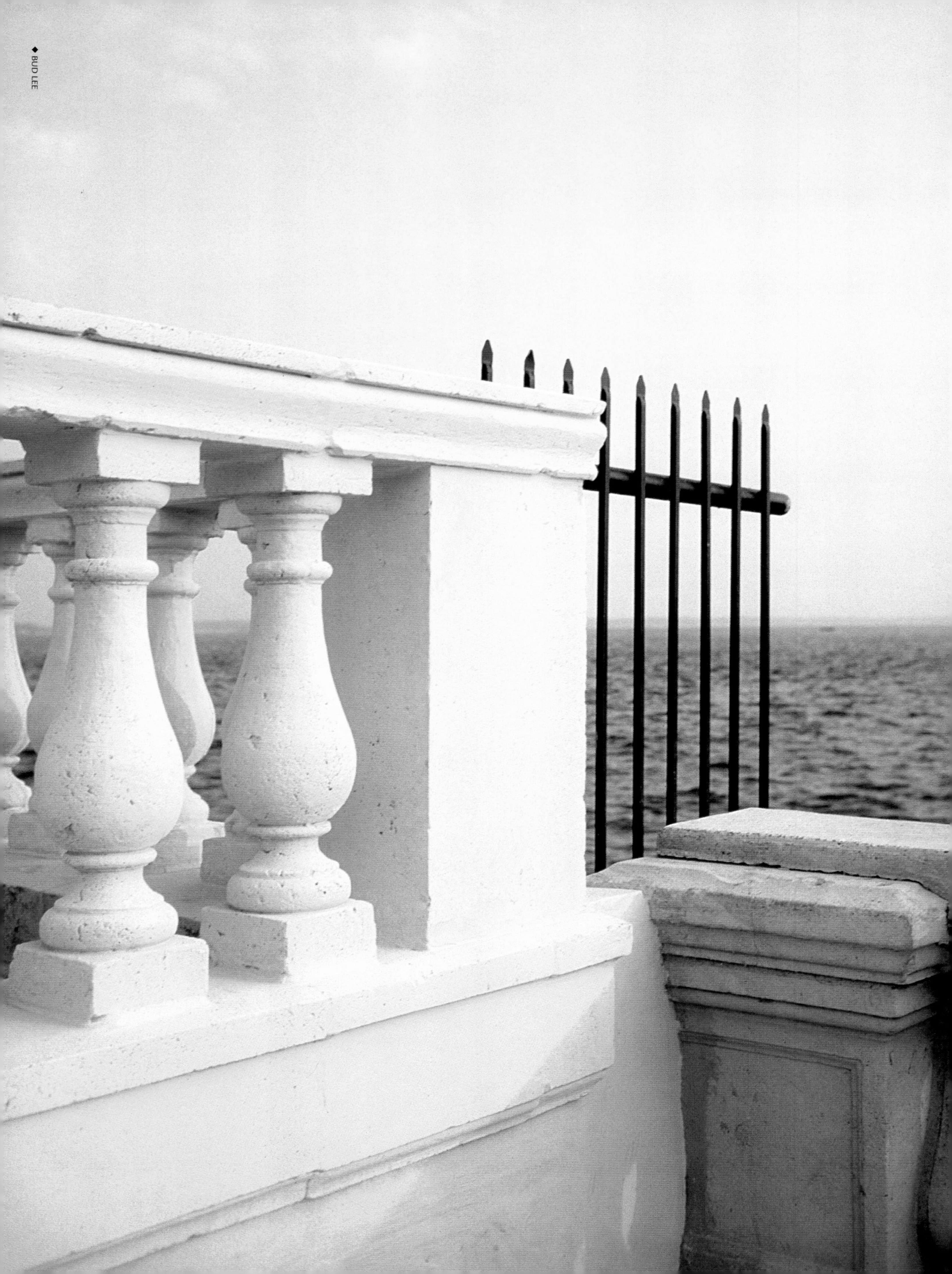

◆ BUD LEE

1986-1997

1986	Mayo Clinic Jacksonville
1987	Marriott at Sawgrass Resort
1987	Omni Jacksonville Hotel
1988	Vicar's Landing
1989	ATP Tour
1989	Pam Bingemann Realty, Inc.
1989	Merrill Lynch
1989	FOX 30 WAWS-TV Clear Channel Television, Inc.
1989	UPN 47 WTEV-TV
1990	CELL-TEL International, Inc.
1990	Cypress Village Retirement Community
1992	ALLTEL
1993	Arthur Treacher's Seafood Grille
1994	Champion HealthCare
1994	Compass Bank
1995	Institutional Asset Management Inc.
1995	Radisson Riverwalk Hotel
1996	HomeSide Lending, Inc.
1996	PrimeCo Personal Communications
1996	Wellspring Resources, LLC
1997	ABC25 WJXX
1997	Jacksonville Hilton and Towers

MAYO CLINIC JACKSONVILLE

AYO CLINIC HAS BEEN SYNONYMOUS WITH EXCELLENCE SINCE ITS founding in Rochester, Minnesota, in the late 1800s. There, Dr. William Worrall Mayo and his sons, William and Charles, laid the foundation for a medical center that has been called the only "brand name" in American medicine. More than 100 years later, the Mayo tradition of multispecialty team medicine expanded beyond the Midwest. In 1986, Mayo chose Jacksonville as the first-ever site for another Mayo Clinic. Since then, Mayo Clinic Jacksonville has become one of the cornerstones of Jacksonville's renaissance, bringing national and international attention to this city of the South.

WHY JACKSONVILLE?

Mayo Clinic had turned down offers from dozens of other cities, both in the United States and around the world, but a prominent Jacksonville resident, the late J.E. Davis, convinced the leaders at Mayo that the First Coast was an ideal location. Davis and his wife, Flo, had been patients at Mayo Clinic in Minnesota, and admired the institution's philosophy and reputation. His persistence, coupled with strong community support, led Mayo to branch out for the first time in its history.

"Jacksonville is an ideal location for a number of reasons," says Nancy Skaran, director of communications for Mayo Clinic Jacksonville. "Geographically, it allows us to attract patients all the way up the eastern seaboard and down into Latin America. Also, the quality of life in Jacksonville helps us recruit physicians and their families." Officials at Mayo also felt that Jacksonville was a business city, well positioned for growth, with excellent existing medical resources.

Davis and his family donated 140 acres of land on San Pablo Road for the construction of the original facility. Today, the campus spans 240 acres. The clinic has treated more than 200,000 patients since it opened its doors in Jacksonville in 1986, and has seen an increase in patient registrations each year. Mayo Clinic Jacksonville now employs 209 staff physicians and more than 1,200 support staff.

THE THREE SHIELDS

Mayo Clinic Jacksonville was founded on the same principles with which the Mayo brothers began their practice at the turn of the century: excellent patient care, leading-edge research, and innovative medical education. These three basic tenets are symbolized in Mayo's trademark three-shields logo, and all three elements are at work every day at Mayo Clinic Jacksonville.

Patients experience a whole new level of care at Mayo through its unique team approach to medicine. At many other medical centers, researchers often work in the labs while physicians use discoveries in clinical care, and the two roles rarely overlap. In Mayo's innovative system, medical staff are both researchers and physicians, spending time in both environments. This approach not only helps to close the gap between these two vital functions of health care, but also

THE EIGHT-STORY DAVIS BUILDING HAS MORE THAN DOUBLED IN SIZE SINCE MAYO CLINIC JACKSONVILLE OPENED IN 1986 (TOP).

MAYO PHYSICIANS NOW REVIEW DIGITAL IMAGES ON A COMPUTER WORKSTATION, RATHER THAN USING TRADITIONAL X-RAY FILMS (BOTTOM).

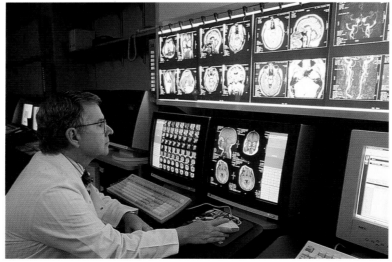

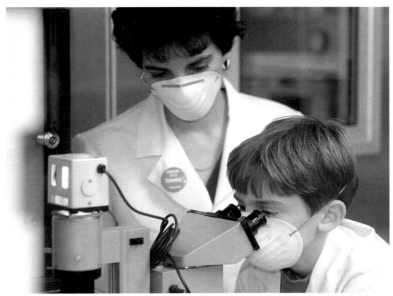

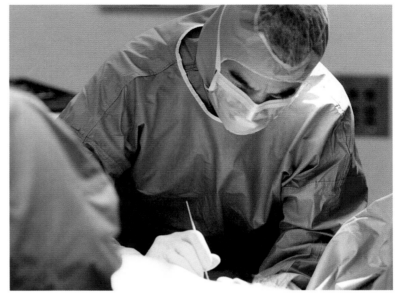

produces better results in both worlds.

While each patient has one physician who is primarily responsible for his or her care, specialists and other health care experts are also available on staff for diagnosis and treatment. Since all these professionals are part of the Mayo staff, the lines of communication are clear and free of red tape. The Jacksonville staff can even consult with Mayo staff in Rochester and Scottsdale via the clinic's sophisticated videoconference system.

Mayo Clinic Jacksonville participates in many research projects, including clinical trials for new drugs and protocols. However, the Jacksonville clinic has chosen to devote the majority of its research capabilities to solving the mystery of Alzheimer's disease, a progressive deterioration of the memory and other brain functions typically found in the elderly. According to Mayo, 2.5 million Americans already have Alzheimer's disease, and each year more than 300,000 new cases are diagnosed. Using state-of-the-art laboratory facilities—including molecular-modeling capabilities, 3-D computers, and robotics—researchers and technicians work to break the brain's intricate biochemical code.

Education, the third shield of the Mayo triad, is an element that the organization weighs equally with patient care and research. Mayo recognizes that education, in its many forms, is crucial to the continuation of the clinic's goals.

Since 1993, Mayo Clinic Jacksonville has offered its own independent residency programs, which attract medical students from across the country and all over the world. Mayo also offers numerous continuing medical education programs. In addition, Mayo participates in exchange programs with several international universities and medical centers, bringing visiting doctors to Jacksonville so they can share their knowledge and benefit from the wide range of experience within the Mayo organization.

At another level, Mayo recognizes that today's children are tomorrow's health care professionals. Each year, fewer and fewer American students choose careers in medical science. To counteract this trend, Mayo Jacksonville participates actively in area education initiatives. Mayo is in partnership with Alimacani Elementary School, serving on its advisory council and helping develop a vision for the school. The partnership also extends into the Blueprint 2000 program, in which students are introduced to medical and technical career opportunities through hands-on experiences. Mayo Jacksonville participates in the Alliance for Education program with Raines High School, providing internships for Raines teachers, helping to develop curricula, and offering support for special projects. In recognition of its dedication to education in Jacksonville, Mayo received the Duval County School District's Beacon Award in 1994 and a Business Recognition Award from the Florida Commissioner of Education in 1997.

Though hundreds of miles away from the plains of Minnesota, Jacksonville is carrying on in the tradition of innovative excellence that is Mayo. The Mayo brothers would have been proud to claim Mayo Clinic Jacksonville as their own.

CLOCKWISE FROM TOP LEFT: LOCAL ELEMENTARY SCHOOL STUDENTS ARE FREQUENT VISITORS TO THE LABS IN MAYO'S BIRDSALL MEDICAL RESEARCH BUILDING.

MAYO SURGEONS HAVE EXPERTISE IN 15 SURGICAL SPECIALTIES, AND MANY PROCEDURES ARE PERFORMED IN THE OUTPATIENT SURGERY CENTER ON THE MAYO CAMPUS.

DR. WILLIAM WORRALL MAYO (CENTER) AND SONS CHARLES (LEFT) AND WILLIAM FOUNDED MAYO CLINIC IN ROCHESTER, MINNESOTA, IN THE LATE 1800S.

Marriott at Sawgrass Resort

THE MARRIOTT AT SAWGRASS RESORT, LOCATED IN PONTE VEDRA Beach amid 4,800 acres of beautiful scenery, is just a short drive from downtown Jacksonville. Bordered by the Atlantic Ocean to the east and the Intracoastal Waterway to the west, this resort has something for everyone. ✳ Sports enthusiasts will be right at home at the Marriott at Sawgrass. The resort offers five golf courses, four driving ranges, and six putting greens. The Marriott at Sawgrass has received the prestigious Gold Medal for Excellence from *Golf Magazine*, and is consistently recognized by golfing publications and travel associations. The resort also provides 19 tennis courts in a variety of environments. Guests have access to the Association of Tennis Professionals (ATP) Tour International Headquarters, which features courts modeled after the surfaces of major international tournaments such as Wimbledon, the U.S. Open, and the French Open.

A Haven for Water Sports

Surrounded by water, the Marriott at Sawgrass is the perfect spot for water sports. The resort faces a two-and-a-half-mile beach and is encircled by more than 350 acres of freshwater lakes, ponds, and lagoons filled with an abundance of wildlife. The complex also features three swimming pools and two complete fitness facilities. For relaxation after exercise, guests can enjoy a wide array of superior spa services, including Swedish massages and revitalizing facials.

Even the youngest guest can join in the fun at the Marriott at Sawgrass. In fact, the Marriott was named one of the Top 50 Family Resorts by *Better Homes & Gardens*. The resort's popular Sawgrass Grasshopper Gang program organizes daily activities for children aged three to 12. Volleyball, horseback riding, nature trails, and miniature golf are all available.

Making Business a Pleasure

The Marriott at Sawgrass Resort is also a favorite spot for meetings and conventions. Its 508 guest rooms, suites, and golf villas, combined with a 40,000-square-foot meeting complex, make it the largest meeting facility between Atlanta and Orlando. The 5,100-square-foot Island Green Pavilion was recently added to the meeting complex to accommodate smaller functions. *Meetings & Conventions* awarded the resort its Gold Key and Gold Tee awards in recognition of the outstanding meeting facilities.

The interior of the hotel rivals the natural beauty that surrounds it. The lobby features a 70-foot, skylighted atrium and spectacular, panoramic views, complemented by exotic plants and palms. Lovely antiques, original artwork, and imported adoquine stone complete the mood of casual elegance.

This resort is a place where all members of the family can have the vacation of their dreams. It's no wonder that *Successful Meetings* called the Marriott at Sawgrass "a vacation paradise that everyone can enjoy."

CLOCKWISE FROM TOP LEFT: THE MARRIOTT AT SAWGRASS FEATURES THREE SWIMMING POOLS AND TWO COMPLETE FITNESS FACILITIES.

SURROUNDED BY WATER, THE MARRIOTT AT SAWGRASS IS THE PERFECT SPOT FOR WATER SPORTS. THE RESORT FACES A TWO-AND-A-HALF-MILE BEACH AND IS ENCIRCLED BY MORE THAN 350 ACRES OF FRESHWATER LAKES, PONDS, AND LAGOONS.

THE LOBBY OF THE MARRIOTT AT SAWGRASS RESORT FEATURES A 70-FOOT, SKYLIGHTED ATRIUM AND SPECTACULAR, PANORAMIC VIEWS, COMPLEMENTED BY EXOTIC PLANTS AND PALMS.

ATP Tour

N 1989, Ponte Vedra Beach became the headquarters for one of the world's most influential professional sports organizations: the ATP Tour, which serves as the governing body of men's professional tennis. The climate of the First Coast is conducive to playing tennis year-round, which makes Ponte Vedra Beach an ideal setting for the home of the worldwide men's professional tennis circuit.

In choosing Ponte Vedra as its headquarters, the tour "wanted to create an environment here, more of a campus setting," says Pete Alfano, vice president of communications. The facility includes a training center with tennis courts representing the major playing surfaces—hard courts and clay—of events around the world.

Origins of the ATP Tour

The open era of men's tennis began in 1968, when professionals were permitted to play all the major international tournaments. The Men's Tennis Council was the governing body of the sport in the 1970s and 1980s, while the players formed their own association, the Association of Tennis Professionals (ATP), in 1972. The players were represented on the board of the men's council, but in the late 1980s, the players did not believe that tennis was being properly marketed and promoted. Therefore, they sought a larger voice in how the game was run. When their demands were rejected, the ATP—under the direction of Hamilton Jordan, former chief of staff to President Jimmy Carter—decided to form its own circuit. The top 100 players in the world endorsed the decision, and the ATP Tour was organized in 1989.

The new tour was enthusiastically supported by tournament directors, who recognized the need for the sport to aggressively promote and market tennis worldwide. When the ATP Tour was launched in 1990 with 76 tournaments in 28 countries, the players and tournaments had formed a partnership unique in professional sports.

Game, Set, Match, Victory

Since 1990, the growth of the ATP Tour and men's tennis worldwide has been astounding. The Tour now includes 77 events in 34 countries, with prize money increasing from $38 million in 1990 to $61.7 million in 1997. Tour revenues are $55 million, representing steady growth since its inception.

Ponte Vedra Beach is home to Tour CEO Mark Miles, who succeeded Jordan in 1991, and most corporate functions. From its offices in Sydney, Australia, the ATP Tour also oversees European operations in Monte Carlo, as well as those in the Pacific Rim, Africa, and the Middle East. London is the home of the ATP Tour's broadcast and marketing office.

The ATP Tour supports what is truly the most international sport, with players from more than 50 countries. The Tour continues to expand its reach and increase exposure through a global television network composed of major broadcasters and innovative promotions.

Two of the Tour's objectives, as a new century approaches, are to increase the popularity of the sport and to reach a younger audience. The players' Kids' Fund Program, launched in 1995, is an initiative that has been well received by tennis fans and media worldwide. Tour players support this program by contributing 1.5 percent of their prize money pool each year and making hundreds of appearances to support the program—signing autographs, answering questions, and even trading forehands and backhands with young fans.

Through its outstanding facilities and diligent ongoing efforts, the ATP Tour will continue to broaden the scope of tennis for many generations of future players.

CLOCKWISE FROM TOP:
ATP TOUR'S FACILITIES IN PONTE VEDRA INCLUDE A TRAINING CENTER WITH TENNIS COURTS REPRESENTING THE PLAYING SURFACES—HARD COURTS AND CLAY—OF MAJOR EVENTS AROUND THE WORLD.

THE CLIMATE OF THE FIRST COAST IS CONDUCIVE TO PLAYING TENNIS YEAR-ROUND, WHICH IS IDEAL FOR THE HOME OF THE WORLDWIDE MEN'S PROFESSIONAL TENNIS CIRCUIT.

ATP TOUR ESTABLISHED ITS WORLD HEADQUARTERS IN PONTE VEDRA IN 1989.

◀ CYNTHIA LUM

OMNI JACKSONVILLE HOTEL

WHOLLY OWNED AND MANAGED BY OMNI HOTELS NORTH AMERICA of Dallas, the Omni Jacksonville has received the AAA four-diamond rating since its opening in 1987. The hotel boasts 354 guest rooms, including four luxury suites, and more than 14,000 square feet of meeting space. Guests can walk to the Jacksonville Landing festival marketplace, any number of downtown office buildings, and the newly renovated Times-Union Center for the Performing Arts. For added convenience, the property is connected to the Prime F. Osborn Convention Center via the city's Automated Skyway Express, a public transportation monorail.

Both business and leisure guests can experience the Omni's exceptional service, whether for business, a weekend getaway, or a conference. The Omni Jacksonville Hotel participates in several companywide programs that offer unique approaches to doing business. Planners of small meetings of up to 60 people can benefit from the Omni Express program, which provides the meeting planner with one consultant who will take care of all of the client's needs.

Another example is the Omni Select Guest Program, which provides exclusive, personalized service to frequent Omni guests. Amenities range from morning coffee and newspaper delivery to remembering that the guest prefers down pillows on the bed. Select guest preferences are stored in a national database, and details for these special guests are attended to before they arrive at the hotel.

The Omni welcomes guests and locals alike to one of Jacksonville's best restaurants, Juliette's. Named for the daughter of a steamboat captain who once navigated the St. Johns River, this Florida-style bistro serves breakfast, lunch, and dinner. Juliette's also is known for its Holiday Brunch, which has been voted Best in Jacksonville by *Folio Weekly* every year since 1992.

The property has been recognized with many industry distinctions, in addition to the four-diamond rating. The Omni Jacksonville is classified as Superior First Class by the *Official Hotel Guide*, and is listed in both the Best Places to Stay edition of *Florida* and *Frommer's Travel Guide*. The Omni has built its reputation as a fine hotel on its staff of associates, who are trained to anticipate their guests' every need. This second-to-none service is what has placed the Omni Jacksonville in the elite circle of top-notch hotels.

TOTAL QUALITY ADVANTAGE

The Omni began its quality journey in 1993. The hotel's executives

THE OMNI JACKSONVILLE IS WHOLLY OWNED AND MANAGED BY OMNI HOTELS NORTH AMERICA OF DALLAS, AND HAS RECEIVED THE AAA FOUR-DIAMOND RATING SINCE ITS OPENING IN 1987.

and associates worked together to implement a systematic and integrated approach to satisfying customer requirements. The framework of a quality management system allowed the hotel to align the realities of the everyday business with the key principles of customer, owner, and associate satisfaction. These values, also known as the Omni Trilogy, clearly define the culture of the Omni Jacksonville Hotel.

Each element of the trilogy is mutually inclusive and dependent on the others. Associate satisfaction drives defect-free delivery of superior service. Superior services, along with price-value and other variables, drive customer satisfaction. Customer satisfaction drives repeat business, which drives higher revenues. Superior financial performance allows the hotel to provide improved training, equipment, and benefits for associates.

The application of the trilogy as a business-building reality is accomplished through the Omni Service Tradition—the umbrella encompassing the interrelated programs and philosophies that lead to a quality experience. It involves all associates in continuously improving the hotel and the service it provides. Associates demonstrate their keen sense of

making things happen in several ways. They meet with the general manager on a monthly basis to monitor and track progress on process improvement initiatives in their department. On a daily basis, they respond to each "moment of truth" by empowering the hotel's chief tactic for building customer relationships, the Power of One. They reward and recognize fellow associates for delivering the Power of One by nominating them to be Omni Service Champions.

Finally, associates are asked to perform their responsibilities in accordance with the Omni Mirror Image Philosophy. This simple guideline of treating each other the way they treat guests reinforces the behavior expected in a quality-oriented hotel.

All of this focus on quality is apparently having a big impact on results. The most recent guest survey—taken annually at all Omni Hotels—rated the Omni Jacksonville Hotel highest in guest service and highest in number of guests most likely to return. However, it is not only the guests who are happy. The Annual Associate Opinion Survey also ranked the Omni Jacksonville as the premier Omni Hotel in terms of associate satisfaction.

These kinds of results and, more important, the efforts that take place to produce them, are why the Omni Jacksonville Hotel is considered a very special place. It has been recognized by Omni Hotels as a Best Practice Example for its implementation of quality and, in 1997, was awarded the Governor's Sterling Award for quality excellence. The Omni Jacksonville Hotel is the first and only hotel to achieve this distinction in the state of Florida, signifying that continuous improvement is a commitment that will keep the hotel a very special place for years to come.

CLOCKWISE FROM TOP LEFT:
THE ELEGANT LOBBY OF THE OMNI JACKSONVILLE HOTEL

THE OMNI JACKSONVILLE OFFERS MORE THAN 14,000 SQUARE FEET OF MEETING SPACE, INCLUDING THE LUXURIOUS FLORIDA BALLROOM.

THE HOTEL BOASTS 354 GUEST ROOMS, AND WAS AWARDED THE GOVERNOR'S STERLING AWARD FOR QUALITY EXCELLENCE IN 1997.

Vicar's Landing

Vicar's Landing is a resort-oriented life care retirement community in prestigious Ponte Vedra Beach, located just south of Jacksonville in St. Johns County. Members of Vicar's Landing enjoy not only the wide array of amenities available on the campus, but also many opportunities that the area has to offer, all of which collectively make this an ideal location for those enjoying their retirement years.

The idea to create a senior community in the area started among several members of Christ Episcopal Church in Ponte Vedra Beach in the late 1980s. They joined together to form Life Care Pastoral Services, Inc., a not-for-profit corporation, which is the sole owner of Vicar's Landing.

The community opened in 1988 and has been a rousing success from the first.

The campus is part of the Sawgrass community, which adjoins the Sawgrass Country Club, the Players Club, and the prestigious PGA Headquarters. This convenient location not only provides easy access to world-class golf and beaches, but also is only 10 minutes from the renowned Mayo Clinic in Jacksonville. Downtown Jacksonville to the north and historic St. Augustine to the south are only short, 30-minute drives away.

All the Amenities

Residents at Vicar's Landing take their pick of several comfortable housing options, including patio homes and apartments. Floor plans range from one-bedroom apartments to three-bedroom patio homes, fulfilling every lifestyle need. All homes and apartments have fully equipped electric kitchens, washers and dryers, smoke detectors, sprinklers, and emergency alert systems. Residents' monthly fees cover weekly housekeeping and linen service, as well as complete maintenance service for their home and the surrounding grounds. Pest control services are also included, as well as basic cable and all utilities, with the exception of telephone service. Twenty-four-hour security is provided throughout the grounds, allowing residents to relax with peace of mind.

There is much to enjoy at Vicar's Landing, as the community provides a full calendar of activities each month for its members. On-site programs—such as arts and crafts classes, creative writing groups, chorus, and exercise classes—are available to members. The complex also includes a heated pool, an art studio, a woodworking shop, bicycle paths, and a croquet court and putting green.

There are several world-class golf courses in the immediate area, and many residents take advantage of that opportunity. Outings to cultural events in the vicinity are another regular part of the Vicar's Landing schedule. Many

LIGHT STREAMS THROUGH THE PARLOR WINDOW AT VICAR'S LANDING, HIGHLIGHTING REFLECTIONS ON A POND AT TWILIGHT.

THE VICAR'S LANDING DINING ROOM PROVIDES AN EXCELLENT COURTYARD VIEW.

residents also take advantage of the abundance of fine resorts and clubs in the area, such as Sawgrass Country Club, the Lodge and Beach Club at Ponte Vedra Beach, and the Ponte Vedra Inn & Club.

With convenient access to a bank office, hair salon, travel agency, and gift shop—all of which are located on-site at Vicar's Landing—the campus is nearly self-sufficient. In addition, the community's fine dining room serves a full menu of selections for breakfast, lunch, and dinner. Other dining options within the community include the Pub at the Crossing, open for lunch and dinner, and the Lounge. Members can reserve private dining rooms for gatherings and parties, and the dining room staff provides catering service, both on-site and in members' residences.

LIFETIME HEALTH CARE

A reassuring aspect of the Vicar's Landing program is the availability of high-quality lifetime health care as needed. The Health Center includes a 60-bed, skilled nursing facility, with 52 private rooms and four semiprivate rooms. Also, 38 assisted living apartments serve those members who require daily assistance, but wish to continue as much of an independent lifestyle as possible. Health care is included in the monthly fee, and therefore usually does not call for any additional expense.

Vicar's Landing promotes good health at all times through its Wellness Clinic, which is staffed with a full-time nurse, and provides physician care one day per week. Specialists, such as podiatrists and dermatologists, are available for scheduled appointments. The Wellness Clinic provides a wide variety of proactive health care services, such as blood work, blood pressure and cholesterol testing, and hearing screening.

Additional life care assistance is also available through the Wellness Clinic's Assistance in Living program. Help with bathing, grooming, and dressing is provided to residents who need moderate assistance, but who are able to live on their own without

skilled nursing care. This approach allows the member to remain in a comforting environment surrounded by personal possessions and friends.

Vicar's Landing is a member of the Florida Association of Homes for the Aging, a group organized in 1963 to advocate high-quality care and living standards for the elderly. The group has been very successful in its efforts to pass supportive legislation on a state and federal level, and to support its members throughout the state.

Combining comfortable living accommodations, a full calendar of activities, and comprehensive health care, Vicar's Landing is truly an ideal location for the retirement years.

EQUAL HOUSING
OPPORTUNITY

Pam Bingemann Realty, Inc.

WHEN YOUR NAME IS ON THE DOOR, YOU'D BETTER BE GOOD AT what you do," says Pam Bingemann, who has proved that she is. As a result, she has her name on not one, but two doors in the First Coast Beaches area. Her general real estate brokerage firm, Pam Bingemann Realty, Inc., has established itself as a leader within the real estate community in fewer than 10 years of business.

WITH OFFICES IN JACKSONVILLE AND PONTE VEDRA BEACH, PAM BINGEMANN REALTY, INC. HAS ESTABLISHED ITSELF AS A LEADER WITHIN THE REAL ESTATE COMMUNITY IN FEWER THAN 10 YEARS OF BUSINESS.

TIME-TESTED REPUTATION

Bingemann, a lifelong resident of the First Coast, has more than 20 years of experience as a Realtor®. She worked for some of the largest brokerage firms in the area, including Arvida, a local resort community developer. Arvida developed the Jacksonville Golf and Country Club community, and Bingemann opened the office there and represented the developer for some time. In 1981, Arvida opened a general brokerage office in Neptune Beach and asked Bingemann to manage it. After several years, she bought out Arvida's North Beach operation and established Pam Bingemann Realty, Inc. in 1989. In 1996, a second location was added in Ponte Vedra Beach, one of the First Coast's most affluent communities.

Bingemann felt confident breaking out on her own, as she built her business on her greatest strength: residential real estate. The company also has some involvement in smaller commercial properties and vacant land, but focuses primarily on the upscale communities in the Jacksonville and Beaches area.

According to Bingemann, the business has grown and prospered, thanks to the experienced and caring Realtors on her staff. This group of professional, full-time sales agents recognizes that choosing a home is a very personal, and often emotional, decision. "We offer personalized service, and all of our associates are long-term residents who are actively involved in the community," says Bingemann. She is also proud to note that they are members of RELO®, the prestigious international relocation network, and have a corporate and military relocation division. Today, the staff includes more than 34 associates, and the company records in excess of $40 million in sales last year.

While busy building her business, Bingemann has also been occupied with professional and civic organizations, often in leadership roles. She was the president of the Northeast Florida Association of Realtors (NEFAR) for 1997, and remains on the board of this organization of more than 3,000 members. In this position, she worked to increase public awareness of the qualifications of a Realtor versus a real estate licensee, and to mesh the smaller chapters in the area into a unified NEFAR with much more power and strength in its membership. She is also a member of the National Association of Realtors and director of the Florida Association of Realtors. Personally and professionally, Bingemann also gets involved in a variety of community and charity efforts, ranging from fund-raising for the local library or community theater group to volunteering at the area's soup kitchen.

Bingemann's success has not gone unrecognized. She has received Realtor of the Year honors several times, and in 1995, she was named Small Business Leader of the Year by the Beaches division of the Jacksonville Chamber of Commerce. Many other organizations have also recognized Bingemann's efforts on behalf of the Beaches community and the real estate profession.

Bingemann plans to continue to grow her business, possibly opening more offices in the future. She notes the area's strong growth and continued expansion as prime contributors to a healthy real estate market. Those external factors, combined with her experience and dedication to the region, add up to happy home buyers and a successful business for Pam Bingemann Realty.

ERRILL LYNCH IS A LEADER IN THE FINANCIAL SERVICES INDUSTRY, providing world-class financial management and planning services to a wide variety of clients, including individuals, corporations, institutions, and governments. ✳ The company employs more than 52,000 people in 40 countries. Merrill Lynch

prides itself on being recognized and admired for its leadership excellence and business philosophy, and is guided by the following principles: Client Focus, Respect for the Individual, Teamwork, Responsible Citizenship, and Integrity. Its dedication to quality excellence and its dynamic work environment set it apart both in the industry and in Jacksonville as well.

Merrill Lynch, Pierce, Fenner & Smith Inc. (MLPF&S)—one of only four service companies in the country to receive a site visit in 1996 from the Malcolm Baldrige National Quality Award examiners—has branch offices in downtown Jacksonville, in Ponte Vedra Beach, and at Merrill Lynch's Southpoint campus. MLPF&S Financial Consultants provide comprehensive personalized service and financial advice to help clients build sound financial plans.

Since 1989, Merrill Lynch has made the commitment to expand and relocate key business operations to Jacksonville, and presently employs approximately 2,000 people in the city. The first business unit to relocate to the area was Merrill Lynch Credit Corporation (MLCC). Offering a wide variety of home financing, personal credit, investment financing, and business financing products, MLCC has been instrumental in expanding the firm's Domestic Private Client business from traditional asset management to total balance sheet management. Its Total Quality Management approach helped MLCC receive the 1996 Florida Governor's Sterling Award for Quality and the 1997 Malcolm Baldrige National Quality Award for business excellence and quality achievement.

Merrill Lynch Insurance Group Services, Inc. (MLIGS) relocated to Jacksonville in 1990, and established a similar record of success. This division is a subsidiary of Merrill Lynch Insurance Group, which provides retirement and estate planning services through variable annuity and variable life products, with more than $13 billion in assets under management. MLIGS received the Florida Governor's Sterling Award for Quality in 1995, as well as the Rochester Institute of Technology and USA Today Quality Cup and the Florida Sterling Team Showcase Award.

Adding to Merrill Lynch's list of award-winning Jacksonville divisions, Merrill Lynch Financial Data Services (MLFDS) moved its operations to the city in 1992. MLFDS provides record-keeping, financing, clearance, settlement, and transfer agency operations for more than 5,200 mutual funds and money market products sold by Merrill Lynch worldwide, serving 14.6 million accounts. With total assets exceeding $270 billion, Merrill Lynch's mutual fund and money market business continues to rapidly expand. In 1997, the division received the Florida Sterling Team Showcase Award.

These award-winning business units are supported by Merrill Lynch Private Client Systems Group, a division of Global Systems & Technology. Its developers and analysts understand the dynamics of today's business environment and provide systems analysis, development, and maintenance in mainframe and client-server environments, while linking local technology to Merrill Lynch's domestic and international systems.

Merrill Lynch recently announced the relocation of the Group Employee Services (GES) division to Jacksonville. GES provides employee-sponsored benefits and defined contribution plans to more than 200 of the Fortune 500 companies across the United States. Several other corporate divisions—including Accounting Services, Human Resources, Purchasing, and Telecommunications—have also moved to the Jacksonville Southpoint campus.

To support Merrill Lynch's award-winning service, the company also dedicates itself to being a world-class community citizen, offering thousands of volunteer hours each year for Jacksonville-based nonprofit organizations and educational partnerships with local schools and universities. Merrill Lynch strongly supports efforts to improve the Jacksonville community and encourages employees to take active roles in addressing community needs.

As a major employer and business leader of Florida's First Coast, Merrill Lynch is committed to providing the superior products and services that clients have come to expect from the premier planning-based financial management firm of choice.

CLOCKWISE FROM TOP:
MERRILL LYNCH HAS BUILT AND SUSTAINED A CULTURE IN WHICH LEARNING IS THE NORM AND INTELLECTUAL STIMULATION A CONSTANT.

MERRILL LYNCH'S SOUTHPOINT CAMPUS IS EASILY ACCESSIBLE FROM ALL AREAS OF THE CITY.

MERRILL LYNCH'S WORLD-CLASS BUSINESS PHILOSOPHY IS GUIDED BY ITS PRINCIPLES.

FOX 30 WAWS-TV
Clear Channel Television, Inc.

ALTHOUGH MANY INDUSTRY EXPERTS SCOFFED WHEN THE FOX television network was launched, few can criticize its current success. FOX has become "the fourth network," and is making its mark with the acquisition of National Football League coverage and the creation of Emmy-award-winning shows.

FOX 30 WAWS-TV in Jacksonville is no exception to the FOX success equation. The television station, serving 13 counties in northern Florida and southern Georgia, is near the top of all affiliates nationwide and continues to grow and evolve.

WAWS is owned by Clear Channel Communications, an innovative communications company that owns radio and television stations around the world, as well as an outdoor advertising division. Clear Channel, based in San Antonio, has one of the largest FOX affiliate groups in the nation, with seven FOX stations in its 1997 portfolio. The company is known for its shrewd business deals, which result in a very healthy return on investment. Clear Channel stations typically perform well above the industry average, with that margin increasing every year since 1991.

An Industry Leader

FOX 30 WAWS-TV became part of the Clear Channel family in 1989. Though the station was a new FOX affiliate at that time, it had been on the air as an independent station since 1981. Clear Channel recognized the opportunity to gain entrance to the growing First Coast market. "Clear Channel saw the potential in North Florida's growth," notes Josh McGraw, vice president and general manager of WAWS.

The Jacksonville station has been a major contributor to Clear Channel's success. WAWS-TV is consistently at the top in the city's market area for the most desirable demographic groups in both the prime-time and the 6 to 8 p.m. slots. The station is usually ranked in the top 20 FOX affiliates nationwide, and has been named to the network's #1 Club. FOX bestows this designation on affiliates that win the prime-time ratings war among all network affiliates in their local markets.

WAWS-TV is not resting on its laurels, however. The station recently moved into a new, 59,000-square-foot facility. In 1997, the station began producing and broadcasting its own news program, which airs at 10 p.m. Management plans to expand and develop the news coverage, and is considering the addition of a morning newscast in the future.

FOX 30 is actively involved in the local community, providing support and assistance to Easter Seals, Big Brothers and Big Sisters, the Florida/Georgia Blood Alliance, and the American Cancer Society. FOX 30 is also the home of the annual Jerry Lewis telethon.

FOX 30 is involved in a variety of events and activities in the city throughout the year, including the annual Beaches Festival, the Ham Jam festival, the Entrepreneur and Small Business Expo, and the Hooters Jordan Professional Golf Tournament.

The station is particularly popular with children, as it is home to many leading cartoons. Equally popular is the station's Kids' Club, which boasts more than 50,000 members. The host of the Kids' Club, Safari Sam, leads local kids in community outreach events and public service projects, and serves as host during the children's programming times. These programming hours also feature vignettes addressing topics relevant to children, such as health and safety, antidrug information, social issues, and environmental concerns.

FOX 30 WAWS-TV in Jacksonville—which joined the Clear Channel Communications family of stations in 1989—serves 13 counties in northern Florida and southern Georgia (top).

The station is usually ranked in the top 20 FOX affiliates nationwide, and has been named to the network's #1 Club, which designates stations that win in their local ratings wars (bottom).

UPN 47 WTEV-TV

THE TELEVISION INDUSTRY HAS BEEN REVOLUTIONIZED IN RECENT years by the onslaught of cable channels, direct broadcast satellites (DBS), and new broadcast networks. One of the new networks that has managed to emerge on top is the United Paramount Network, known as UPN. Launched in 1995, the

network now has more than 150 affiliates nationwide and continues to grow.

Jacksonville is home to UPN affiliate UPN 47 WTEV-TV. The station broadcasts popular sitcoms in syndication, movies, sports, and a growing list of the network's own prime-time programs to more than 20 counties in northern Florida and southern Georgia. The signal reaches as far north as to Brunswick, Georgia; south to Flagler County; and west to Lake City. More than 15 cable companies broadcast WTEV, bringing it into the homes of more than 300,000 subscribers in its market. WTEV is typically ranked among the top nationwide UPN affiliates in the crucial 18- to 49-year-old demographic, making it a very successful entrant in this competitive industry.

In September 1997, UPN 47 launched a 6:30 p.m. newscast.

The growth of Jacksonville and the resulting traffic makes it hard to get home by 6 p.m. While the other networks air national news, UPN 47 offers the only local news at 6:30 p.m.

A Strong Local Presence

WTEV-TV has been on the air in Jacksonville since 1980 and has been an independent station for the majority of that time. Joining the UPN family in February 1995, the station is now operated by Clear Channel Communications under a local marketing agreement. Clear Channel is owner and operator of Jacksonville's FOX affiliate, WAWS-TV, and an international player in radio and television broadcasting. An agreement with WTEV-TV ownership group RDS Communications allows both stations to benefit from economies of scale while not violating the Federal Communications

Commission's regulations about television broadcasting duopolies. WTEV shares office and studio space with WAWS in Clear Channel's new broadcast center located on the city's south side, where more than 110 employees work to help both stations grow and prosper.

CELL-TEL International, Inc.

THE **CELL-TEL** INTERNATIONAL STORY IS A CLASSIC AMERICAN entrepreneurial success story. Built from the ground up through hard work and determination, CELL-TEL has blazed a trail in the cellular equipment industry as an international clearinghouse for refurbished cellular systems, network infrastructure equipment, and ancillary parts. CELL-TEL pioneered the way with its vast and diverse inventory of quality-tested products, knowledgeable sales and engineering staff, and the most experienced technical services team in the cellular industry.

CELL-TEL was founded in 1990 by Elizabeth A. Wilson, an electronics engineer with more than 20 years' experience in the telecommunications industry. After completing her enlistment in the U.S. Navy, Wilson entered the private sector in aviation and electronics, which led her to the Kennedy Space Center in Florida, where she worked as a space shuttle test team member and worked on board the shuttle *Orbiter* as a systems test engineer. Later, she worked in the Midwest with one of the cellular industry's fastest-growing service providers.

After two years of building cell sites in the Midwest, Wilson returned to the Jacksonville area, where she uncovered an opportunity with an industry associate to market some used cellular equipment. Inquiries to industry contacts throughout the United States revealed an unsatisfied need for a used systems and equipment supplier. Wilson's initial investment in this small project not only reaped a handsome profit, but also helped her capitalize on a totally new business opportunity; thus, CELL-TEL International, Inc. was born.

Originally operated from Wilson's home, the company soon generated enough cash flow to command its own offices. Today, CELL-TEL averages $7 million to $10 million in annual sales, employs a full-time staff of 25, and continues to grow and prosper.

PROVIDING EXPERIENCE AND KNOWLEDGE

Elizabeth Wilson and her staff are empowered by a strong collective background in engineering, which differentiates CELL-TEL's service from that of its competitors. This proven experience and knowledge provide proactive service with a warranty program that is unsurpassed in the industry. Any piece of equipment acquired from CELL-TEL is guaranteed for at least 90 days, or it is replaced free of charge within 48 hours. Such fast, responsive service has earned CELL-TEL a large list of domestic and international clients.

CELL-TEL also offers a huge on-hand inventory that is computerized for easy tracking and retrieval of parts. In addition, the system tracks and locates equipment and parts throughout the wireless voice and data telecommunications industry.

CELL-TEL is fully integrated with technologies such as code division multiple access (CDMA) and time division multiple access (TDMA) wireless systems, enhanced

CELL-TEL INTERNATIONAL, INC. WAS FOUNDED IN 1990 BY ELIZABETH A. WILSON.

CELL-TEL INTERNATIONAL'S HEADQUARTERS ARE LOCATED IN JACKSONVILLE.

specialized mobile radio (ESMR) systems, and personal communications systems (PCS). The company recognizes the need to stay on top of emerging wireless technologies in order to remain competitive.

Through its established network of domestic and international contacts, CELL-TEL can help clients market new, used, obsolete, and spare equipment, turning it into working capital with a higher return on original investment. The company even provides de-installation, packaging, and transportation services, and can handle installation and reconditioning for selected manufacturers.

Rapid Deployment Cellular Communications Center (RD3C)

One of CELL-TEL's latest developments is the design, manufacture, and marketing of the Rapid Deployment Cellular Communications Center (RD3C), a custom-built mobile cellular system used for emergency communications, disaster recovery, and special events. Each RD3C can also be used as a temporary cell site to expand existing coverage until more permanent solutions can be developed or built. Originally designed for CELL-TEL's U.S. military clients, the RD3C is compatible with all types of wireless equipment, trunking systems, and standard radio telephone systems.

Other Business Interests

The success of CELL-TEL has allowed Wilson to develop other business interests that reflect her diverse background. One example is the Extra Experience, an aerobatic flight team established in 1995. Utilizing the Extra 300 world-class aircraft, the Extra Experience team provides aerobatic, emergency maneuver, and spin training, as well as passenger rides for those who want to experience the thrill of rolling through the air at 420 degrees per second. Wilson is one of the group's four professional

pilots, and enjoys introducing others to flying, a passion she has pursued since her teenage years.

Another business interest for Wilson is Tin Lizzy's, a full-service catering company founded in 1996, focusing on the executive catering market and specializing in mobile catering service to movie and television production sets. North Florida is host to a number of television and motion picture shoots, and Wilson realized that a mobile catering venture would be welcomed and could prove lucrative. A full commercial kitchen was constructed in a por-

tion of CELL-TEL's warehouse facility, and Tin Lizzy's took off under the direction of General Manager Alex Orban, an experienced chef and restaurant management professional.

In fewer than 10 years, Elizabeth Wilson has established three successful and diverse businesses in Jacksonville. All are welcome additions to the city's business community, adding variety to the traditional industries located in the region. The growth and success of all three enterprises demonstrates that the American dream is still alive and well in Jacksonville.

ALEX ORBAN IS GENERAL MANAGER OF TIN LIZZY'S, A FULL-SERVICE CATERING COMPANY FOUNDED IN 1996 BY ELIZABETH WILSON.

THE EXTRA EXPERIENCE, AN AEROBATIC FLIGHT TEAM, WAS ESTABLISHED BY ELIZABETH WILSON IN 1995.

CYPRESS VILLAGE RETIREMENT COMMUNITY

CYPRESS VILLAGE IS A PLACE THAT EXEMPLIFIES WHAT RETIREMENT ought to be. This vibrant community for people 55 years of age and older allows residents to reap all the rewards of active, independent living, while providing freedom from the drudgery of home maintenance and other chores. Cypress Village offers seniors many things, but perhaps the most important advantage the community provides is the opportunity to make choices about how to spend one's retirement years.

FREEDOM OF CHOICE

From the very moment the decision is made to become a part of Cypress Village, choices abound. Residents are offered a wide range of housing options, including conventional, equity-owned homes as well as apartments available on a lease basis. The purchase of equity properties is handled the same way tradi-

THERE ARE ENDLESS ACTIVITIES, BOTH INDOOR AND OUTDOOR, AT CYPRESS VILLAGE. A FULL-TIME ACTIVITIES DIRECTOR HELPS RESIDENTS PLAN EACH AND EVERY DAY.

tional real estate transactions are handled. Apartments require a refundable entrance fee—which is equivalent to the market value of the unit—followed by a monthly fee thereafter. A variety of floor plans—which include studio and one- and two-bedroom arrangements—can accommodate nearly every need. In addition, some two-bedroom plans also include a den, and all equity homes come with a garage or carport.

Home owners may select the colors and materials used in the construction of their homes or apartments, just as they would in any other new housing development. But the homes at Cypress Village offer additional perks, including complete maintenance of each home's interior and exterior, as well as lawn care and pest control. Additional services such as laundry and housekeeping are available if desired. Residents can choose to take as many meals as they wish in the restaurant-style dining room, or they can prepare their own in fully equipped kitchens.

All apartments feature covered balconies, and many offer lovely views of Lake Cypress. Apartment residents enjoy housekeeping and flat linen service, as well as a flexible dining plan for meals in the lovely lakefront dining room. When the resident needs to make other arrangements, 75 percent of the entrance fee is refundable. Whether a house or an apartment is chosen, both options allow residents the freedom and independence to pursue their interests and hobbies.

CONVENIENCE: THE MOST TREASURED AMENITY

Security and convenience are two of the other benefits of living in Cypress Village. The campus is patrolled 24 hours a day, and each residence is equipped with an around-the-clock emergency alert system. While residents are encouraged to keep their own vehicles, either in their home garages or in the community's parking garage, there is also a Cypress Village shuttle that makes regular visits to nearby shopping areas.

There is hardly a reason to leave the campus, with so many conveniences located within the

Village. An indoor pool, a beauty/barber shop, a bank office, a café, and a convenience store can all be found in Cypress Village. The planners of this community overlooked few details; large common areas and guest rooms are even available for residents welcoming out-of-town guests.

If some seniors can't imagine how they will fill their days during retirement, they won't wonder for long at Cypress Village. The community employs a full-time activities director, who works with residents to plan a weekly calendar of activities with broad appeal. Typical monthly events include a matinee at an area theater, weekly poker night, ballroom dancing, and numerous social events. There are also planned travel excursions and day trips, exercise classes, religious services, a computer club, and ceramics classes. Residents also enjoy the beautifully maintained croquet lawn, putting green, bike paths, and nature trails winding through the campus. Just minutes away from Cypress Village, beautiful beaches and world-class golf await, including Windsor Parke Golf Club, which borders the complex.

On-Site Health Care

The Cypress Village campus also includes a leading health center for seniors, complete with assisted living apartments, a skilled nurs-

ing center, and an Alzheimer's care and research center. An adult daily care program is also available. The Alzheimer's program is nationally recognized and benefits from a research association with Mayo Clinic Jacksonville. This branch of the world-renowned Mayo Clinic in Rochester, Minnesota, is located right next door to Cypress Village, offering residents the convenience of world-class care in their own backyard.

Cypress Village is sponsored by the National Benevolent Association of the Christian Church (Disciples of Christ), more commonly known as the NBA. This organization, founded in 1887, is based in St. Louis, and has become one of the premier providers of care communities for seniors and disabled persons. The NBA oper-

ates 79 facilities in 27 states, with more than 10,500 residents nationally. The American Senior Housing Association ranked NBA as the 12th-largest owner of senior housing properties in the country, and 14th-largest in the listing of senior property managers. The organization is fiscally strong as well, with assets in excess of $271 million and an investment grade rating from both Fitch and Moody's.

The NBA's senior communities all operate around the guiding principle that the community belongs to the residents. At Cypress Village, programs are resident initiated and resident oriented; changes and additions are frequently made in response to input from the people who live there. It's all part of the NBA's motto, "What we do best is care."

CYPRESS VILLAGE RESIDENTS CAN ENJOY LAKEFRONT DINING OR UTILIZE THEIR OWN KITCHENS.

GARRY MCELWEE

ALLTEL

ALLTEL IS A CUSTOMER-FOCUSED INFORMATION TECHNOLOGY COMpany dedicated to providing residential and business customers with high-quality, state-of-the-art technology and services that meet their individual needs and lifestyles. ALLTEL's wireline and wireless communications operations serve 2.7 million customers in 14 states, while its information services operations provide information processing, software, and services to financial and telecommunications clients in 45 countries.

As one of the nation's leading information services and telecommunications companies, ALLTEL has ideally positioned itself to grow with the City of Jacksonville. ALLTEL is a Fortune 500 company, a Forbes 500 company, and is listed in Standard & Poor's 500 index. With more than 1,100 employees, ALLTEL is the 18th-largest private employer in Jacksonville.

A Full-Service Provider

As the choices for communications services have grown more complex, customers have increasingly been looking for one reliable and technologically advanced provider to meet their communications needs. ALLTEL has responded to these needs with plans to combine its wireline and wireless communications services in order to provide customers with a full complement of communications and information services.

With the announcement of these plans, Jacksonville was selected as the home for ALLTEL's management center for the Southeast market. ALLTEL now offers customers in Jacksonville an array of telecommunications products and services, including personal communications service (PCS), paging and long-distance services, and Internet access.

In addition to telecommunications and information services, ALLTEL operates a directory publishing company and a communications and data equipment supply business. Since 1992, Jacksonville has been home to ALLTEL's mortgage operations, the nation's leading provider of software and data processing services to the real estate lending industry.

Commitment to Jacksonville

During a relatively short time frame, ALLTEL has demonstrated its commitment to the health and vitality of the community at large. ALLTEL's Jacksonville employees have been the leaders in per capita contributions to the United Way for nine of the last 10 years.

To add another stake toward its commitment to Jacksonville, ALLTEL entered into an agreement with the Jacksonville Jaguars and the City of Jacksonville to purchase naming rights for what is now known as ALLTEL Stadium. History was made on May 27, 1997, when the Jacksonville City Council approved the 10-year agreement that made it official. The Jaguars now play at ALLTEL Stadium.

ALLTEL summed up the company's commitment to Jacksonville in a full-page ad in the *Florida Times-Union* following the stadium agreement: "To grow with this city and be a part of it is an honor. To share the glory with the Jaguars is a privilege."

ALLTEL STADIUM IS THE PROUD HOME OF THE JACKSONVILLE JAGUARS.

Champion HealthCare

ABSOLUTE DEDICATION TO QUALITY PRODUCTS ADMINISTERED WITH nothing less than the finest possible service in an environment that reflects the highest degree of respect for every human being": This is the mission statement of Champion HealthCare, Northeast Florida's newest health maintenance organization.

Determined to differentiate itself in its competitive industry by providing warm, friendly, and respectful service to its customers, Champion HealthCare's emphasis on service is welcomed by patients and physicians alike.

Founded in 1994 with headquarters in Jacksonville, Champion HealthCare planned extensively before unveiling its professional health care concept to Florida businesses and residents. Champion's solid planning ensured a warm welcome in Northeast Florida's health care circles—Champion has joined one of Jacksonville's most respected health care organizations, the Baptist/St. Vincent's Health System, and the nation's largest health care group, Columbia Health Care.

Champion's comprehensive network of area physicians, specialists, and hospitals covers nearly every health care need, and all remain committed to the Champion philosophy. The goals include providing easy access to care for all members, as well as open, responsive communication with member physicians and providers. Champion also feels that it is uniquely suited to serve the specific needs of northern and Central Florida residents, as the demographics of this region vary significantly from other parts of the state.

Although the company is relatively new, it is supported by extensive financial resources. This strong foundation, provided by local investors and recognized institutional investors, allows Champion to back up its philosophy with top-notch infrastructure and staff. Champion's local board of directors is composed of experienced physicians and other health care professionals

who are committed to quality and performance.

Service with Respect

Champion's commitment to respect and service is translated into concrete experiences, such as rapid claims handling, flexible benefit packages, and extensive member education programs. The organization utilizes sophisticated information management systems to efficiently manage data and to maintain the most current and useful information for its members and affiliated providers. Seminars and classes on a variety of topics are sponsored by Champion; other specialized programs, such as the Winning Beginnings maternity management program, provide customized information and guidance for members with special health care needs.

Proactive health care is an important element in the company's approach. Champion aims to be a true health maintenance organization. Participating physicians are encouraged to develop a relationship with their patients, and all members' health records are tracked diligently. If and when

more serious situations arise, patients receive more effective, efficient care thanks to the complete and thorough health care histories available within the Champion network.

In 1997, based on the company's wide array of choices and willingness to work with the business community, the Jacksonville Chamber of Commerce selected Champion as the certified health care provider for Chamber members. This is just one example of Champion's success in accomplishing its mission statement, and proof that Champion HealthCare will be an important part of Northeast Florida for many years to come.

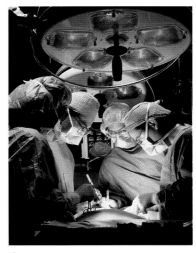

CLOCKWISE FROM TOP LEFT: BASED IN JACKSONVILLE, CHAMPION HEALTHCARE IS UNIQUELY SUITED TO SERVE THE SPECIFIC NEEDS OF NORTHERN AND CENTRAL FLORIDA RESIDENTS.

CHAMPION HEALTHCARE'S COMPREHENSIVE NETWORK OF AREA PHYSICIANS, SPECIALISTS, AND HOSPITALS COVERS NEARLY EVERY HEALTH CARE NEED.

CHAMPION OFFERS A NUMBER OF SPECIALIZED PROGRAMS—SUCH AS THE WINNING BEGINNINGS MATERNITY MANAGEMENT PROGRAM—THAT PROVIDE CUSTOMIZED INFORMATION AND GUIDANCE FOR MEMBERS WITH SPECIAL HEALTH CARE NEEDS.

Arthur Treacher's Seafood Grille

WHO IS ARTHUR TREACHER?" MANY PEOPLE ASK THIS QUESTION. THE real Arthur Treacher was a British actor known for his butler roles in movies and his stint as Merv Griffin's sidekick on his popular 1970s afternoon talk show. The actor died in 1975, only six years after the restaurant chain was founded.

Originating in Columbus, Ohio, Arthur Treacher's Fish & Chips was at one time a large presence throughout the United States and Canada, with more than 800 locations. The restaurant was known for its menu of British-style fish and chips and other deep-fried seafood dishes. However, a series of ownership changes in the 1980s resulted in lagging franchisee morale and

a lackluster image with consumers. In the early 1990s, a new investor group, led by a new chairman of the board, Bruce Galloway, saw an opportunity to revitalize the Arthur Treacher's chain and enhance its presence across the United States.

In 1993, Arthur Treacher's, Inc. acquired a new image, a new strategy, and a new headquarters. The management team decided Jacksonville was the perfect place for the seafood chain to start fresh. "Jacksonville was well on its way to establishing itself as a city on the move, and it was a perfect fit with a company that was also on the move," explains President and CEO R. Frank Brown, who joined the investor group in mid-1996.

Arthur Treacher's new leadership is revamping almost every aspect of the nearly 30-year-old company, and has already seen significant early success. Stock

prices have more than doubled in the 1996-1997 fiscal year, same-store sales have increased over the prior year, and the cost of goods has been dramatically reduced. These successes are due in large part to the efforts of Brown, a veteran of the restaurant business who was formerly the president of Captain D's, a seafood restaurant chain owned by Shoney's, Inc.

Building an Image

Brown has taken several steps in a very short time to improve the company. In addition to evaluating suppliers, renegotiating leases, and hiring new marketing and advertising staff, he has also taken important steps to improve relations with franchisees as well as develop a vision that will guide Arthur Treacher's into the future.

But the most exciting change implemented by Brown is the new Seafood Grille concept. Arthur

THE SEAFOOD GRILLE CONCEPT WAS TEST-MARKETED IN 1996 AND WAS INTRODUCED TO SELECTED RESTAURANTS LATER THAT YEAR. THE LOCATION AT THE AVENUES MALL FOOD COURT ON JACKSONVILLE'S SOUTHSIDE WAS THE FIRST TO UNDERGO THIS TRANSFORMATION.

Treacher's menu now includes lighter, more healthful items, such as freshly prepared grilled seafood and chicken, as well as new vegetable selections. The Seafood Grille concept was test marketed in 1996 and was introduced to selected restaurants later that year. In fact, the Arthur Treacher's location at the Avenues Mall food court on Jacksonville's Southside was the first to undergo the transformation.

Response to the change has been positive, and the company is continuing the Seafood Grille expansion at all of its locations. "As the population has become increasingly aware of their wellness, their eating habits have evolved," explains Brown. "Our offerings of food items need to reflect consumers' desires." In conjunction with the menu change, Arthur Treacher's restaurants are beginning to provide customers with nutritional information on menu items, detailing caloric, fat, and cholesterol content.

Another major decision that changed the direction of Arthur Treacher's was that of forgoing franchisee expansion in favor of the development of more corporate-owned and -operated sites. Prior to 1996, most of Arthur Treacher's restaurants were franchises. Since the new management took the helm, the company has actively pursued opportunities to purchase these franchises. In late 1996, the company acquired its largest franchisee, MIE Hospitality, Inc. This acquisition was significant because MIE Hospitality, Inc. owned the firm's territorial/developmental rights in Pennsylvania, Delaware, New Jersey, and most of New York. MIE Hospitality, Inc. also owned and operated 32 restaurants in these markets. During this period, Arthur Treacher's also purchased six other franchises. The chain now consists of nearly 200 restaurants, only 60 of which are franchises.

In the future, the goal of Arthur Treacher's is to have 350 restaurants by the year 2000, with 40 percent of those locations under company ownership and control. The restaurant chain will continue to focus on its principal existing markets in Florida, Ohio, Michigan, Texas, and Ontario, and also will

ARTHUR TREACHER'S MENU NOW INCLUDES LIGHTER, MORE HEALTHFUL ITEMS, SUCH AS FRESHLY PREPARED GRILLED SEAFOOD AND CHICKEN, AS WELL AS NEW VEGETABLE SELECTIONS.

see expansion into areas where the brand has had a strong presence in the past. These areas include Maryland; Illinois; Washington, D.C.; and the New England states.

The business community has reacted favorably to the changes at Arthur Treacher's. Stock prices have increased, and profitability and sales continue to rise. All signs indicate that the new management at Arthur Treacher's has the company in the swim once again.

Compass Bank

COMPASS BANK HAS BEEN NAVIGATING A STEADY PATH OF GROWTH in Jacksonville since arriving in 1994. In that year, Compass Bancshares, headquartered in Birmingham, Alabama, acquired two banks in Jacksonville with the purpose of establishing a presence in the profitable First Coast region. Compass Bancshares, a multibillion-dollar, multistate bank holding company, operates more than 220 Compass Bank offices in Alabama and Texas, as well as locations in Jacksonville and in Florida's panhandle region.

Since the acquisition of First Performance National Bank and offices of Anchor Federal Savings Bank in 1994, Compass has added several other Jacksonville banks to its family, including CFB Bancorp, Inc. and Enterprise National Bank, and has set up its Florida headquarters in the area. In just a few short years, Compass Bank has strongly established itself in Florida, with more than $1 billion in assets. Since entering the attractive First Coast area just three years ago, Compass has grown to rank third in market share.

Bennett Brown, Compass Bank's city president for Jacksonville, believes that Compass has been successful in Jacksonville as a result of the experienced, dedicated local people who work there.

COMPASS BANK'S NEW, FIVE-STORY, 85,000-SQUARE-FOOT HEADQUARTERS BUILDING WILL OPEN IN MAY 1998 AT THE CORNER OF J. TURNER BUTLER BOULEVARD AND GATE PARKWAY. THE FACILITY WILL FEATURE A FULL-SERVICE BANKING CENTER WITH FIVE DRIVE-UP TELLER LANES (TOP).

COMPASS EMPLOYEES MAKE THE DIFFERENCE IN FULFILLING THE COMMITMENT TO EXCELLENCE IN SERVICE. AS THE COMPANY'S SLOGAN INDICATES, "WHERE THERE'S COMPASS, THERE'S A WAY!" (BOTTOM).

"Our staff has a wealth of experience in the local marketplace, and a major commitment to the Jacksonville area," says Brown. Compass employs more than 250 people on the First Coast, and the majority of them have many years of experience in their banking specialties. Those specialties cover a full range of banking services, including retail mortgages, construction financing, consumer and small-business lending, corporate banking, and private banking. Compass also provides investment services, asset management, and international banking to further enhance its financial service offerings.

Brown also stresses that while the Compass name may be relatively new to Jacksonville, the bank's local roots run deep through its acquired institutions. "This is an example of the principle that the sum of the parts is stronger than the individual components," notes Brown. Those parts are coming together in a new corporate head-quarters building on J. Turner Butler Boulevard on the city's Southside. The new building promises to allow growing room for the bank, as it continues to expand on the First Coast and throughout the state of Florida.

Community involvement has always been a priority for Compass and its employees, and that is not expected to change despite the bank's rapid growth. "We have always been heavily involved in the community, and will continue to be," states Brown. Compass supports many local organizations, such as Wolfson's Children's Hospital, the Jacksonville Symphony, and HabiJax, the Jacksonville chapter of Habitat for Humanity.

Compass Bank has charted a clear course for success in Jacksonville. With increasing revenues, expanding services, and experienced employees with local backgrounds, Compass looks forward to being an important part of Jacksonville's bright future.

RADISSON RIVERWALK HOTEL

THE RADISSON RIVERWALK HOTEL IS A FAMILIAR PART OF Jacksonville. Originally constructed in 1980, the property took the Radisson name in 1995. A total renovation project began soon after, which encompassed nearly every inch of the property, from the 322 guest rooms and 13 luxurious suites to the more than 25,000 square feet of meeting space. Today, the Radisson boasts a gracious lobby with a fountain and marble floors, a 24-hour fitness center, a state-of-the-art amphitheater, and an on-site business center.

The Radisson is in an ideal location, positioned at the east end of the Riverwalk—a 1.2-mile boardwalk connecting restaurants, museums, shops, and marinas along the mighty St. Johns River. The Radisson is within walking distance of excellent dining and nightspots in the Jacksonville area. Water taxis take guests for a relaxing ride across the St. Johns to more shopping and dining opportunities. In addition, the property is convenient to major business centers and interstate highways.

BUSINESS OR PLEASURE

Jacksonville attracts both business and leisure travelers, and the Radisson Riverwalk is a popular choice with both groups. The attractive pool with terrace seating; two lighted, hard-surface tennis courts; and the brand-new fitness center are perfect for relaxation. For the businessperson, each guest room features data port access and a voice mail system. The Business Center, located in the lobby, provides access to personal computers, printers, facsimile machines, and copiers.

The Radisson is also a favorite spot for conventions, meetings, and social events in Jacksonville. In addition to offering the biggest ballroom in the city, the hotel has an impressive new amphitheater, which seats 100 and offers individual data ports, 18-hour chairs, and a built-in audiovisual system. All meeting space is located on the hotel's ground level, making it easily accessible for those with physical challenges. The property boasts a separate Convention Center entrance, with large reassembly areas and ample designated parking.

HOTEL OF THE JAGUARS

The Radisson Riverwalk Hotel enjoys its status as the official hotel of the Jacksonville Jaguars, the city's NFL franchise. The hotel offers popular packages for Jaguars fans during the football season, including pre- and postgame buffets and happy hours. The team has also participated in panel lunches, allowing fans and the media to meet and discuss the national pastime with Jaguars players.

The Radisson Riverwalk has made its mark on Jacksonville. The hotel's management credits this fact to its staff of outstanding people. "There are many hotels in Jacksonville," says Charlette Tuiccillo, director of sales and marketing, "but none can offer the location, quality, and service that we provide at the Radisson."

CLOCKWISE FROM TOP LEFT: THE RADISSON IS IN AN IDEAL LOCATION, POSITIONED AT THE EAST END OF THE RIVERWALK—A 1.2-MILE BOARDWALK CONNECTING RESTAURANTS, MUSEUMS, SHOPS, AND MARINAS ALONG THE MIGHTY ST. JOHNS RIVER.

THE RADISSON BOASTS A GRACIOUS LOBBY WITH A FOUNTAIN AND MARBLE FLOORS, A 24-HOUR FITNESS CENTER, A STATE-OF-THE-ART AMPHITHEATER, AND AN ON-SITE BUSINESS CENTER.

THE RADISSON RIVERWALK HOTEL OFFERS 322 GUEST ROOMS AND 13 LUXURIOUS SUITES. FOR THE BUSINESSPERSON, EACH GUEST ROOM FEATURES DATA PORT ACCESS AND A VOICE MAIL SYSTEM.

Institutional Asset Management Inc.

THE FOUNDERS OF INSTITUTIONAL ASSET MANAGEMENT INC. WERE trained as an engineer and as an economist. With that background, it is not surprising that Institutional Asset Management is an organization supported by sound economic principles and leading-edge technology. The firm has broad exposure managing financial assets for organizations, as well as for that most important institution—the family. Clients include municipalities, credit unions, public and private corporations, labor unions, professional service firms, and foundations.

The imbedded emphasis on sound economic principles is fundamental to every investment decision. The typical portfolio investment of Institutional Asset Management is a leader in its industry with a record of superior performance and pricing elasticity. Shares are acquired at an earnings multiple of less than their growth rate and the market in general. This is true with both domestic and foreign equities.

Economic analysis, coupled with a concentration on quality, has helped the firm achieve above-market results with below-market risk, which is the Holy Grail of investment management.

To keep clients abreast of their portfolio results, the firm reports quarterly results on a net-of-all-costs basis, which is not the common practice in the investment management industry.

The technology focus includes the ability to communicate rapidly between the firm, clients, and information providers, which enables all parties to function efficiently and to be fully informed in an environment of rapidly changing information.

The firm pays significant attention to the difference between client accounts that are taxable versus those that are tax-deferred. This approach has a tremendous advantage for the typical taxable account. A mutual fund, by law, must pass all short- and long-term gains through to the shareholders. At Institutional Asset Management, a taxable client, with the aid of a portfolio manager, can control its tax situation more precisely.

Institutional Asset Management fully appreciates the financial and psychological aspects of its clients' experiences with the firm, and makes continuing efforts to measure client experience from a risk-reward relationship to client objectives.

Even though the investment activity is the primary focus of each account, cost control is also paramount. Because of the firm's

THE BULLS AND THE BEARS ARE ALWAYS IN A TUG-OF-WAR WITH THE BEST MINDS IN THE WORLD IN A TIME-SENSITIVE ENVIRONMENT.

FORREST TRAVIS (LEFT), PRESIDENT, AND MARK TRAVIS, CHIEF INVESTMENT OFFICER, DISCUSS STRATEGY FOR A CLIENT'S ACCOUNT.

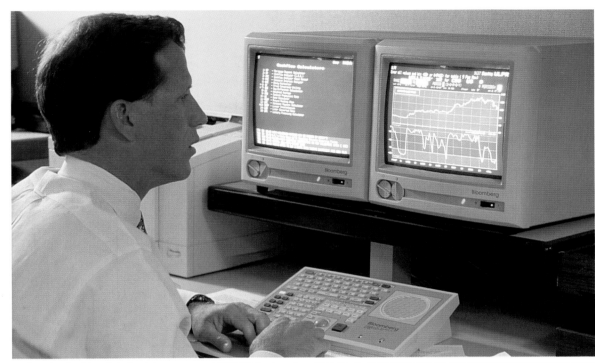

technological lead, it is able to transact business with every major securities firm at extremely competitive rates.

The long-term objectives of Institutional Asset Management include the integration of fine minds and leading-edge technology in an efficient, highly technical organization that is able to deliver objective investment management excellence. The growth of its employees, client assets, and strong referrals from satisfied clients offers tremendous advantages to the firm and to each client.

The principals and most of the firm's employees are long-time residents of Jacksonville, and are strongly committed to the city with multiple civic involvements that include educational, health, conservation, and athletic organizations. They think of Jacksonville as a marvelous place that has only recently been discovered by the national media.

As Jacksonville grows and develops into the front ranks of American cities, Institutional Asset Management plans to be in the front ranks, leading the way with superior results in investment management.

HomeSide Lending, Inc.

APPLYING FOR A MORTGAGE IS GENERALLY PERCEIVED AS A PROCESS that is tedious and frustrating, full of red tape and last-minute crises. But Jacksonville-based HomeSide Lending, Inc. has been changing this perception by following its mission: Meeting the needs of customers, employees, and shareholders by provid-

HOMESIDE LENDING, WHOSE MAIN OFFICE HAS BEEN LOCATED IN JACKSONVILLE SINCE 1996, IS NOW ONE OF THE NATION'S LARGEST ORIGINATORS OF HOME LOANS (TOP).

MORE THAN 130 CUSTOMER SERVICE REPRESENTATIVES HANDLE CUSTOMER INQUIRIES. CUSTOMERS CAN ALSO ACCESS A SOPHISTICATED 24-HOUR LOAN INFORMATION SYSTEM VIA TELE-PHONE (BOTTOM).

ing the best home financing available. HomeSide Lending, Inc., created in 1996, is now one of the nation's largest originators of home loans.

Making outstanding customer service a major focus, the company has a stated goal: To make getting a mortgage as convenient, timely, and cost-effective as possible. HomeSide's Loans-by-Phone service, which provides a fully automated mortgage application

process accomplished entirely by telephone and mail, provides dramatically improved service for new mortgage customers. In addition, with more than 130 customer service representatives standing by to answer inquiries and 24-hour access to loan information via a sophisticated telephone information system, HomeSide delivers top-notch service after loan closings. Not surprisingly, HomeSide's servicing is consistently ranked among those of the top echelon of companies in industry surveys.

HomeSide's superior efficiency is also evident in its back-shop operations. With accuracy ratings of close to 99.9 percent in its Investor Services, Cashiering, and Escrow departments, HomeSide ranks among the top lenders in the industry. The Mortgage Bankers Association's (MBA) delinquency average is consistently surpassed by HomeSide's default-management system. HomeSide's Loss Mitigation area, which helps borrowers avoid foreclosures, was the recipient of Fannie Mae's Top Gun award.

HomeSide's success can be attributed to several factors, an important one being the company's innovative use of technology. Utilizing the latest in client-server technology, HomeSide uses centralized loan processing to decrease errors and improve efficiency. Automated underwriting systems and state-of-the-art communications systems allow customers to apply for a loan, receive servicing assistance, and get prequalified for a mortgage via the telephone and the company's Internet address, www.homeloan.com.

HomeSide offers a variety of product options, including conventional, FHA, VA, fixed-

and adjustable-rate mortgages, and extendable-term balloon loans, as well as other special financing options. Customers can lock in their interest rates for up to 180 days and can take advantage of the unique Float Down Protection program. This program allows customers to lower their interest rates, even after locking in, if the market improves prior to their closings.

HomeSide Lending is also one of the nation's leading wholesale lenders, with multiple delivery channels that include correspondent, broker, and co-issue lending. Through these programs, HomeSide provides mortgage capital to more than 600 financial institutions and 1,500 mortgage brokers nationwide.

HomeSide carries its service commitment to its employees and the community as well. A tuition-reimbursement program provides opportunities for employees to enrich themselves through education. Frequent company social activities, such as picnics and award programs, keep morale high. Employees regularly volunteer for such organizations as the March of Dimes, United Way, and HabiJax, Jacksonville's branch of Habitat for Humanity. HomeSide also participates in an apprenticeship program that teaches leadership and business skills to high school and college students.

HomeSide's goal is to continue to expand its reach into the mortgage banking business, while continuously seeking new ways to improve the lending process. With a clear focus on customer service, efficient processing, and selective investment in technology, HomeSide will continue to be a leader in mortgage lending.

PrimeCo Personal Communications

PRIMECO PERSONAL COMMUNICATIONS WAS CREATED IN 1994 as a limited partnership among four major players in the communications industry: AirTouch Communications, Bell Atlantic, NYNEX, and US WEST Media Group. The parent companies' goal was to create a company that would provide the latest in quality, dependable wireless communication products and services, while at the same time simplifying the process so customers would easily understand how to use the services to their best advantage.

Since coming to Jacksonville in 1996, PrimeCo has been very busy. The Jacksonville office is regional headquarters for an area that stretches as far south as St. Augustine, west to Panama City, and north into southern Georgia. The communications company is expanding rapidly, with plans to serve eight major areas in the region, including Tallahassee, Pensacola, and Gainesville.

High Technology

One of the major selling points at PrimeCo is the availability of code division multiple access (CDMA) technology, a type of digital communication that provides increased network capacity while delivering sound quality comparable to a traditional wireline telephone. While most wireless communications companies have made the switch from analog to digital, few are offering the increased benefits of CDMA. This transmission technology provides additional levels of fraud and privacy protection, as well as longer battery life.

PrimeCo offers a wide range of other convenient features as well, including a 30-day, money-back guarantee, and 24-hour customer service and technical support. Call management is made simple with services such as voice mail, call forwarding, call waiting, and text messaging. Perhaps the most unique benefit of PrimeCo's wireless service is the company's cost-control services, which help customers better manage costs through improved billing and account management. No long-term service contracts or activation fees are required either, which adds to the economy and flexibility of wireless service.

Community Outreach

As part of PrimeCo's corporate mission, the company invests a great deal of time and resources in volunteering in and contributing to the communities in which it operates. When PrimeCo came to Jacksonville, employees threw a Halloween party for foster children at the Children's Home Society, delivered teddy bears to sick children at Nemour's Clinic and Wolfson Children's Hospital, delivered pet food and other items to the Jacksonville Humane Society, and donated wireless phones and 1,200 minutes of airtime to HabiJax, the local chapter of Habitat for Humanity. The company also commemorated National Food Bank Week by donating turkeys to several food banks in the Jacksonville area. These efforts have been continued in the community long after the company's grand opening, as part of PrimeCo's corporate culture, which encourages volunteerism and "contagious acts of kindness."

UTILIZING THE NEXT-GENERATION CDMA TECHNOLOGY, PRIMECO PERSONAL COMMUNICATIONS PROVIDES WIRELESS SERVICES WITH SUPERIOR VOICE QUALITY AND ENHANCED SECURITY (TOP).

THE JACKSONVILLE PRIMECO OFFICE IS REGIONAL HEADQUARTERS FOR AN AREA THAT STRETCHES AS FAR SOUTH AS ST. AUGUSTINE, WEST TO PANAMA CITY, AND NORTH INTO SOUTHERN GEORGIA (BOTTOM).

WELLSPRING RESOURCES, LLC

WELLSPRING RESOURCES PROVIDES COMPLETE ADMINISTRATION OF employee benefit and human resource programs for America's largest employers. Established in 1996 as a joint venture between two business powerhouses—Watson Wyatt Worldwide and State Street Corporation—Wellspring has established itself as a leader in the industry. Prior to that date, Wellspring operated as a wholly owned subsidiary of Watson Wyatt under the name Wyatt Preferred Choice.

PROVIDING VALUABLE SERVICES

Wellspring has been able to grow so quickly because large corporations value the services it provides. Ultimately, Wellspring acts as the human resources department for its clients, handling all aspects of human resource programs: pension and 401(k) plans, retiree payroll, health care plans, flexible benefit plans, and other human resources programs. Although these sensitive and personal issues are handled by an outsider, employees experience higher levels of customer service and better access to information than they did when the benefit programs were managed in-house, and many like the confidentiality of an outside benefits administration provider. Once freed of their administrative burdens, client human resources professionals can concentrate on human resources strategy, tying programs to business objectives.

Wellspring utilizes the latest in self-service technology in order to provide employees and retirees with access to their benefit information in a convenient, helpful, and efficient manner. In addition to a toll-free 800 number, Wellspring offers Internet/intranet access, through which employees can check their current benefit status, enroll for or make changes to their benefits, enroll in training classes, and check job postings. They can even do pension modeling exercises before making decisions regarding early retirement by logging onto their company's intranet anytime from a PC at work, at home, or while traveling. This visual, interactive technology is easy to use and enhances the basic capabilities of the state-of-the-art voice response tools Wellspring also provides.

Wellspring's services are delivered using its three-tier client/server architecture via the company's state-of-the-art data center. This system structure enables rapid changes in benefit plan design and access. It is one of the most advanced, flexible systems on the market today. In addition, Wellspring maintains a site on the World Wide Web (www. wellspringres.com) for those wishing to learn more about its services.

CHOOSING JACKSONVILLE

Watson Wyatt, headquartered in the Washington, D.C., area, and the Boston-based State Street chose Jacksonville for many reasons. "Jacksonville has become a customer service hub," explains Jonathan Palmer, Wellspring CEO. "As a result, Jacksonville offers an outstanding pool of experienced customer service personnel, and the city is very business friendly."

The company's growing employee base is housed at its two major locations in the city. Other workers are employed at Wellspring's site in Bethesda, Maryland. Wellspring hopes to continue its rapid growth in Jacksonville, as it continues to expand its client base among the nation's Fortune 500 companies.

Technological innovation and excellent customer service personnel form the foundation for efficient and cost-effective service for Wellspring's clients and their employees.

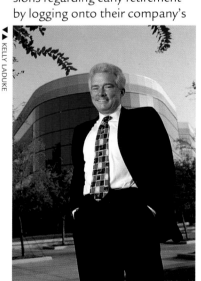

ABC25 WJXX

WJXX BEGAN BROADCASTING IN JACKSONVILLE AS THE ABC TELEVISION Network affiliate on February 9, 1997. Owned and operated by Allbritton Communications, WJXX was built to provide the Jacksonville community the very best in local broadcasting. WJXX quickly built a reputation of excellence based on an unwavering

commitment to the community. In Jacksonville, WJXX offers the most sophisticated and relevant news found anywhere in the city. The station also enjoys numerous partnerships with civic and charitable organizations designed to enhance the lives of people in Jacksonville.

The Allbritton Communications Company was founded in 1973 by Joe L. Allbritton. It has remained a family company since its conception. The company, which was launched with the initial purchase of three television stations and a Washington, D.C., newspaper, has grown steadily over more than two decades and has established a formidable presence in broadcasting nationwide. The communications company operates television stations in eight cities from Washington, D.C., to Tulsa, Oklahoma. Under the leadership of Robert L. Allbritton, Joe L. Allbritton's son, the company has grown to be the 25th-largest television broadcast company in the United States.

EMPHASIS ON QUALITY

Excellence in local news is a hallmark of WJXX. The company is committed to quality and integrity in professional news reporting. WJXX has been recognized for producing outstanding local news and informational programs that make a difference to viewers.

WJXX recruits its staff from a nationwide pool of applicants to create a first-class broadcast operation. WJXX's sister station, WBSG TV-21, broadcasts from Brunswick, Georgia, reaching the southern Georgia market. Each station airs its own local newscasts during certain time periods, providing viewers with news that is the

EXCELLENCE IN LOCAL NEWS IS A HALLMARK OF WJXX. THE COMPANY IS COMMITTED TO QUALITY AND INTEGRITY IN PROFESSIONAL NEWS REPORTING.

WJXX ENJOYS THE MOST TECHNICALLY ADVANCED FACILITY IN TOWN: A 28,000-SQUARE-FOOT COMPLEX ON A.C. SKINNER PARKWAY, ON THE CITY'S SOUTHSIDE.

most relevant to their community. The relationship between these two stations is unique to the market and clearly symbolizes the company's unparalleled commitment to this dynamic region.

WJXX also enjoys the most technically advanced facility in town: a 28,000-square-foot complex on A.C. Skinner Parkway, on the city's Southside. The station's 115 employees moved into this

state-of-the-art building in the fall of 1997. "This is a station for the 21st century," says WJXX President and General Manager Leonard L. Firestone. "We have been blessed with digital equipment and vast operational resources."

WJXX is committed to Jacksonville. The Allbritton family is extremely proud to serve the Jacksonville community and anticipates many years of valuable news and programming contributions.

Jacksonville Hilton and Towers

AS JACKSONVILLE HAS GROWN, COMPANIES HAVE FLOCKED TO THIS business-friendly city. As a result, the demand for downtown hotels has expanded, as well. MHI, L.L.C., a hotel management company based in College Park, Maryland, recognized this need and took advantage of an opportunity in downtown Jacksonville, opening the Jacksonville Hilton and Towers on the city's south-bank riverfront.

Though the hotel didn't actually open its doors until March 1997, work began 16 months beforehand to ensure a smooth transition and a clear focus for this 291-room property. The hotel underwent $16 million worth of extensive renovations, and the management team conducted extensive market research to determine the needs of the community and to plan Hilton's approach to those needs. Their efforts were rewarded when the Hilton Hotel Corporation bestowed its most prestigious designation, the Towers Class, on the Jacksonville hotel. Only a small percentage of Hilton's huge international network has been granted this recognition. The Towers Class represents an exceptional level of service that the Jacksonville property is only too happy to provide. Also, in October 1997, the hotel received AAA's four-diamond award.

An Upscale Business Hotel

The Hilton's new management recognized a need in Jacksonville for an upscale hotel that focused on the needs of the business traveler. "Corporate growth in Jacksonville is very strong," notes David Crist, the hotel's director of sales. The Hilton's executive team positioned the hotel to fit into this upscale niche, a strategy only enhanced by the Towers Class designation.

Some of the special services that the Hilton provides include valet parking; 24-hour fitness and business centers; room service; and large, deluxe guest rooms. Each of the property's rooms, including three presidential suites and 16 executive suites, boasts its own carpeted, furnished balcony with a beautiful view of the St. Johns River. The hotel also offers several outstanding dining options, including a Ruth's Chris Steak House, the elegant restaurant nationally known for its outstanding steaks. Guests also can dine at the hotel's own American Grill, a casual bistro open for breakfast, lunch, and dinner, or at Breezers Waterfront Bar & Grille, an open-air restaurant featuring live entertainment. Breezers is situated next to the Hilton's lovely outdoor pool and spa, which overlook the river.

The Jacksonville Hilton and Towers enjoys an ideal location on the city's Riverwalk—a 1.2-mile boardwalk lined with shops, res-

JACKSONVILLE'S BUSINESS ADDRESS: THE JACKSONVILLE HILTON AND TOWERS WAS DESIGNED TO MEET THE NEEDS OF BUSINESS TRAVELERS TO THE AREA.

THE HOTEL OFFERS SEVERAL OPTIONS FOR DINING EXPERIENCES, RANGING FROM A CASUAL BISTRO OR OPEN-AIR RESTAURANT TO ELEGANT CUISINE.

taurants, and museums. Easy access to Interstate 95 and the Jacksonville International Airport make it a convenient location for any traveler, while businesspeople benefit from its close proximity to the Prime Osborn Convention Center and the city's downtown business district. Other area attractions—including ALLTEL Stadium, home of the National Football League's Jacksonville Jaguars— are just a short drive or water-taxi ride away.

Business travelers appreciate the Hilton's 24-hour business center, which provides access to computer workstations, a copier, printers, a fax machine, and a full range of office supplies. Any guest, business or leisure, can take advantage of the 24-hour fitness center, which includes aerobic bicycles and treadmills, as well as a gym. Other convenient amenities include complimentary limousine transportation within the downtown area.

Jacksonville businesspeople and residents find that the Hilton is the perfect spot for their meeting and function needs. The waterfront views provide a lovely backdrop, and the hotel's experienced catering and meeting staff lend a professional, tasteful touch to any gathering. With more than 11,000 square feet of meeting space, the Hilton can accommodate groups both small and large in its elegant ballroom or flexible meeting rooms. In a unique approach, the hotel also offers use of a 103-foot, luxury yacht for receptions, meetings, or scenic river cruises.

A History in Jacksonville

While the hotel was recently reopened under the Hilton flag, the actual property has been a part of the Jacksonville riverfront for some time. In fact, the hotel is home to an interesting piece of Jacksonville trivia. Under the previous ownership, the hotel was the local favorite of the King

THE JACKSONVILLE HILTON AND TOWERS OFFERS AMENITIES RANGING FROM THE STANDARD SWIMMING POOL TO A 103-FOOT, LUXURY YACHT FOR RECEPTIONS, MEETINGS, OR SCENIC RIVER CRUISES (TOP).

EACH OF THE HOTEL'S ROOMS, INCLUDING THREE PRESIDENTIAL SUITES AND 16 EXECUTIVE SUITES, BOASTS A PRIVATE, FURNISHED BALCONY WITH A BEAUTIFUL VIEW OF THE ST. JOHNS RIVER (BOTTOM).

of Rock and Roll himself, Elvis Presley. Presley performed in Jacksonville four times over the years, and stayed in the Jacksonville Hilton, always using the same suite on the 10th floor. The hotel's management reserved this suite exclusively for his use over more than 10 years, until his death in 1977. As part of the recent renovations, the Hilton man-

agement licensed this suite with Graceland, and it is now available to guests as the Elvis Suite.

No matter what room they stay in, guests of the Jacksonville Hilton and Towers will all be made to feel like kings. That's what General Manager David Fincannon means when he says, "The only thing we overlook is the river."

Photographers

Sue Root Barker, a native of Flint, Michigan, graduated from the Media Institute in nearby Lansing, with a degree in photography. A resident of Jacksonville since 1988, Barker owns and operates Root Photography, where she specializes in architectural imaging and studio table-top photography. Her clients include IBM, Fujifilm, and Hertz, and her work can be seen in *Newsweek* and *Family Circle Magazine*.

Stephen Conrad, a lifelong resident of Jacksonville, studied fine art at Georgia State University. Currently employed at Fototechnika Incorporated, he specializes in landscape photography, and his work was exhibited in 1997 at Reddi-Arts Gallery and at Florida Community College at Jacksonville. For the past 10 years, Conrad has been making large-format images of the American landscape, including the coast of North Florida, the southern Appalachians, Maine, and Northern California.

Geoffrey A. Ellis is a native Californian who moved to Memphis in 1997 after spending a total of 11 years in Miami, Gainesville, and Jacksonville. A graduate of the University of North Florida with a degree in graphic design, he currently works for Towery Publishing as a production assistant. Ellis specializes in graphic design, freelance photography, and working with Super 8mm film. He also enjoys collecting 8mm and 16mm films, cameras, and LP records.

Paul Figura is a local, self-employed photographer who specializes in advertising, people, and lifestyle photography, as well as digital imaging. He works with various advertising agencies throughout North America, and his images have been featured in *Photo District News*. Born in Chicago, Figura grew up in Fort Lauderdale and attended the University of Florida, where he earned a bachelor's degree in computer and information sciences engineering.

Ann S. Fontaine works out of her Jacksonville studio, Ann S. Fontaine Photography, taking pictures of people and events. Her love of foreign travel and her interest in different cultures are reflected in her work on audiovisual/promotional and newsletter materials for a number of cities and international exchange organizations. Fontaine has produced newsletters for TPC Volunteer, Jacksonville Sister Cities Association, International Relations and Marketing Development Commission, and First Coast Women in International Trade.

Paula J. Griffin, originally from Pensacola, currently lives in Jacksonville Beach and works for Family Counseling Services as associate director of the Beach Office. She is the official photographer for the annual Springing the Blues Festival and the WaveMasters Society Surfing Contest. Griffin enjoys taking pictures of the nature and wildlife she encounters during her extensive travels, and her work has appeared in such major publications as *Birder's World*, *Popular Photography*, *Down Beat*, and *Petersen's Photographic Magazine*. Among the awards she has won for her work are the Photographic Society of America Gold Medal in the International Color Slide Competition and the Ollie Fife Award for photojournalism.

James H. Johnson, a native of Pennsylvania, moved to Florida at a young age. He began taking pictures during high school and continued his education at the University of North Florida. Currently employed by Bryn-Alan Studio, Johnson continues to build his personal client base, which includes Watson Realty, as well as *Intuition* and *Street Rodder* magazines. Taking pictures for *National Geographic* is his ultimate goal.

Van R. Jones Jr., a lifelong resident of the Jacksonville area, studied at Jacksonville University and the University of Miami, and served as a photographer with the Florida Air National Guard. In 1961, he began his long career at WJCT Channel 7 as a staff photographer, segment producer, and videographer/editor. Jones' clients include Vistakon, Kuhn Flowers, Blue Cross and Blue Shield of Florida, and Texaco.

Robert Kanner, a native of New York City, is a doctor at the Borland-Groover Clinic in Jacksonville. In addition to his work as a medical professional, Kanner enjoys capturing the Northeast Florida landscape on film and has a special interest in local waterway photography from the vantage point of a kayak.

Junko Kawajiri, originally from Tokyo, graduated from the Kunitachi College of Music. She moved to Atlantic Beach in 1994 and soon earned a degree in art from the University of North Florida. Kawajiri currently works at Fototechnika Incorporated where she specializes in photojournalism, as well as fine art, people, and landscape photography.

Kelly LaDuke, a native of Florida, moved to Jacksonville in 1984. A graduate of the University of South Florida, she owns and operates Kelly LaDuke Photography and specializes in photojournalism, portraiture, and annual report photography. Her work has been published in *Business Week*, *USA Today*, and *Florida Trend*. In spring 1996, LaDuke published her first book, a black-and-white photographic documentary on Little League Baseball titled *All Stars: One Team, One Season*.

Bud Lee studied at the Columbia University School of Fine Arts in New York and the National Academy of Fine Arts before moving to the Orlando area more than 20 years ago. A self-employed photojournalist, he was named *Life* magazine's News Photographer of the Year in 1967 and received the Military Photographer of the Year award in 1966. He also founded the photographers workshops in Florida and Iowa. Lee's work can be seen in *Esquire*, *Life*, *Travel & Leisure*, *Rolling Stone*, the *Washington Post*, and the *New York Times*, as well as in Towery Publishing's *Treasures on Tampa Bay: Tampa, St. Petersburg, Clearwater* and *Orlando: The City Beautiful*.

Bob Libby, a lifelong resident of Jacksonville, is a self-employed freelance photographer whose images have been published in *Golf Magazine*, *Inside Sports*, *Newsday*, *Sports Illustrated*, *Today's Woman*, and *Daily News Record*. His talents extend beyond photography to include camera work for movies, television shows, and news documentaries for major television networks. As an assistant cameraman, Libby worked on the sets of *Roots*, *East of Eden*, and *One-Trick Pony*.

Keith Reynolds served as a U.S. Navy photographer for 24 years before he began a career as a freelance photographer. He specializes in photojournalism, and enjoys taking nature and landscape pictures. His work has been published in a magazine for the American Automobile Association, the Jacksonville Zoological Gardens' quarterly magazine, and various newspapers.

Lans Stout, a graduate of the University of Florida with a degree in photojournalism and broadcasting, has received numerous awards for his work, including the Ozzie, Golden Image, Golden Peach, and various Addys at the state and regional level. Stout currently works in communications for PSS/World Medical Inc., in addition to doing magazine and editorial assignments. His photography has appeared in Time-Life books, *Travel & Leisure*, *Business Week*, and *Air Force Magazine*, and his clients include AT&T, Johnson & Johnson, and the Mayo Clinic.

Terry Taylor, born in Honolulu, moved to Jacksonville in 1983. Working full-time for the U.S. government, she still finds time for freelance endeavors, and specializes in landscape, cityscape, nature, and sports photography. An interest in stock-car racing has led Taylor to capture several NASCAR races on film, and she has had the opportunity to fly and photograph with the military. Taylor's images have been published in *Florida Wildlife*, a book titled *The Big Click*, and the Jacksonville Chamber of Commerce's relocation guide.

Christopher VanHouten, employed by Wolf Camera, also works as a freelance, retail, editorial, and corporate photographer. His specialties include taking pictures of lightning, fireworks, and weddings. VanHouten's clients include Pedestrian Contemporary Gallery and Conference Connections.

David Williams, originally from Connecticut, moved to Jacksonville in 1981 when he was enlisted in the U.S. Navy. A self-employed photographer, he specializes in commercial and entertainment photography, public relations, and stock images. Williams' work has been published in *Dollars & Sense* and *Word Up!* magazines, and his clients include Brooklyn College, Coca-Cola, ALLTEL Corporation, MCA Records, and the Radisson Hotel.

Gregory Williams, a lifelong resident of Savannah, graduated from the Savannah Technical Institute with a degree in photography and has studied under renowned nature photographer John Earl. In his freelance career, Williams specializes in landscape, unique architecture, and abstract photography, and many of his images are used in chamber of commerce guides across the nation. He is the winner of several regional Sierra Club photo contests and, in 1996, mounted an exhibit titled *Savannah and the Georgia Coast*. His images have also appeared in Towery Publishing's *Seattle: Pacific Gem*.

Other photographers and organizations that contributed to *Jacksonville: Reflections of Excellence* include John Cooper, the Florida State Archives, the Jacksonville Museum of Contemporary Art, Gordon Johnson, Ken Laffal, and Super Stock, Inc.

Index of Profiles